Author –
DON'T MAKE ME LAUGH!

*- The Life and Times of a
Spontaneous Scribbler -*

peter kerr

Published by Oasis-WERP 2024

ISBN: 978-1-0369-0273-5

Copyright © Peter Kerr 2024

All rights reserved

No part of this book may be reproduced, stored in a retrieval system, or transmitted in any form or by any means, without the written permission of the copyright owner. The right of Peter Kerr to be identified as the author of this work has been asserted in accordance with Sections 77 and 78 of the Copyright, designs and Patents Act1988.

A catalogue record of this book is available from the British Library

www.peter-kerr.co.uk

Cover design © Glen Kerr

Typeset by Glen Kerr

ALSO BY THIS AUTHOR

(Non-fiction)

Snowball Oranges
One Mallorcan Summer – (originally Mañana, Mañana)
Viva Mallorca!
A Basketful of Snowflakes
From Paella to Porridge
Thistle Soup
Don't Call Me Clyde!
JEN – A Border Collie's Tale

(Fiction)

The Mallorca Connection – Bob Burns Investigates
The Sporran Connection – Bob Burns Investigates
The Cruise Connection – Bob Burns Investigates
Fiddler on the Make – The Cuddyford Chronicles
The Gannet Has Landed
Song of the Eight Winds – Reconquista
The Other Monarch of the Glen
Goblin Hall

ABOUT THE AUTHOR

Best-selling Scottish author Peter Kerr is a former jazz musician, record producer and farmer. His award-winning *Snowball Oranges* series of humorous travelogues was inspired by his family's adventures while running a small orange farm on the Spanish island of Mallorca during the 1980s. Peter's books, written with warmth, gutsy style and spiky humour, are sold worldwide and have been translated into several languages. He is married, with two grown-up sons, and lives in East Lothian.

www.peter-kerr.co.uk

TABLE OF CONTENTS:

CHAPTER	PAGE
One	7
Two	20
Three	33
Four	45
Five	61
Six	78
Seven	96
Eight	106
Nine	116
Ten	128
Eleven	144
Twelve	162
Thirteen	178
Fourteen	196
Fifteen	211
Sixteen	223
Seventeen	241
Eighteen	256
Nineteen	271
Twenty	284
Twenty-One	311
Twenty-Two	325
Twenty-Three	336
Twenty-Four	354

"We haven't got a plan, so nothing can go wrong."
(Spike Milligan 1918 – 2002)

"Life is a lot like jazz – it's best when you improvise."
(George Gershwin 1898 – 1937)

* * * * *

AUTHOR'S NOTE

While the contents of this book are factual, the names of certain individuals and businesses have been changed to protect their privacy.

* * * * *

Chapter One
'PUFFING AGAINST THE WIND'

*

'Your writing is good,' said the literary agent after weighing up the publishing potential of my first novel. '*Very* good … at times.' He glanced down at the manuscript, nodding pensively. 'Yes, and the story's good too. Hmm…' He paused, looked up and shook his head. 'But I'm afraid no publisher will take it on. It's just that, well, to put it bluntly, the humour keeps getting in the way!'

I was tempted to ask him for examples of which bits of humour got in the way of what, but thought better of it. I'd lost count of how many agents and publishers I'd submitted the book to, only to elicit the same reaction from every one of them, though expressed in a dozen different ways. Humour was so subjective, they'd say. One man's meat and all that. Yes, and besides, humour was difficult to sell, unless of course the author happened to be a famous comedian – a TV 'celeb' of *some* sort at any rate – and then the books would fairly fly off the shelves, even if not particularly humorous or actually written by the notable name emblazoned on the cover. That was the way of the book business these days, and I'd either have to give up going for laughs or give up trying to be an author.

Fair enough, but the trouble was I *was*n't going for laughs. I wrote just what came into my head, transferring it straight onto the page as the story unfolded. Nothing was planned. There was no premeditated plot and no deliberate intention to inject humour into what, in this case, was a genuine whodunnit, complete with mandatory murder, good cops and bad cops, obvious suspects and unlikely culprits, convoluted twists and turns, cliff-hangers, blind alleys, red herrings, car chases and even a dead cat. Oh, and the expected spattering of swear words as well. With most of the action taking place between popular beauty spots in my native Scotland and spectacular locations on the Mediterranean island of Mallorca, *The Mallorca Connection* had seemed an apt and commercially attractive title to me. It was serious stuff, gripping too, I reckoned, but tempered here and there by those little shafts of humour that crept into proceedings of their own accord. As I say, nothing was planned. The way I saw it, if unravelling the mystery wasn't actually a mystery to me as I wrote it, there would be fat chance of it coming across as a mystery to the eventual reader.

Anyway, I suppose I'd have taken that agent's advice and spared myself the confidence-sapping punishment of more rejections by jacking in the writing caper there and then and redirecting my creative urges towards something less discriminatory, like knitting socks – *if*, that is, I hadn't already had another book accepted by a publisher a few days earlier. I'd called it *Snowball Oranges* and, would you believe, it was also set in Mallorca.

From my perspective, the only difference between the accepted book and the snubbed whodunnit was that one was a true story, the other a product of my imagination. I knew only one way of writing, the one that came naturally, so why, I wondered, were the results of my labours publishable when based on fact but not when made up as I went along?

Of course, there was a lot more to it than that: things like how strongly the subject matter would appeal to a large enough slice of the book-buying public, how easily they might identify with the characters, how much the settings appealed and so on. In short, publishers are in business to make a profit, and not all books have the same sales potential, no matter what their genre. I already knew that well enough, but such basic realities tend to get shoved to the back your mind when you're smarting from the sting of yet another rejection – and feeling just a wee bit sorry for yourself as well.

Fortunately, on this occasion I had the good news of a publishing deal for *Snowball Oranges* to console me, so I placed the whodunnit on the back burner, offered up my heartfelt thanks to Lady Luck, pinched myself and looked forward to relishing the joys that finally becoming a published author would bring.

I had a lot to learn…

* * *

It all started ten years earlier in 1990 when, at the tender age of fifty, I began jotting down brief notes about certain aspects of what my family and I had experienced after giving up farming barley and beef on a modest scale in our home county of East Lothian (known as 'The Garden of Scotland') to try our hands at growing oranges for a living on a little farm nestled in the lower folds of Mallorca's Tramuntana Mountains – a place, culture and type of agriculture we knew precious little about. There was nothing orderly about my notes: just bits and pieces scribbled on random scraps of paper as they came to mind. And I had absolutely no intention of developing them into a book. It was simply that friends used to ask about how we'd adjusted to the language, the heat, the food, the age-old ways of our Mallorcan farming neighbours and countless other details of what they regarded as our time spent 'living the dream' in the Spanish sun. The fact was, though, that we *had*n't been living the dream – not in the generally accepted sense at least – but had been working as hard as we could in pursuit of that elusive 'living' that is the pot at the end of every small farmer's rainbow. Consequently, I had already started to forget most of the details of the supposed *dolce vita* aspects of our experiences, so decided to jot some down for future reference before they escaped my memory completely.

I should probably mention at this point that our return to Scotland a couple of years earlier hadn't really been planned either, nor indeed had leaving family, friends and everything we were familiar with to go and live in Mallorca some three years before that. Yet it wasn't that we'd been acting impulsively on such life-changing issues, particularly as they also involved our two sons, Sandy (18) and Charlie (12), but rather that we were playing the cards fate dealt us in what seemed the best way at the time. And with no aces up our sleeves by way of a comfortable cushion of funds to fall back on should things go wrong, the consequences of those decisions couldn't have been more crucial – not to mention the cause of many a sleepless night as well.

Those aspects of our life didn't need the help of notes to remember. My wife Ellie and I had been chasing our own particular rainbow on several different roller coasters during almost twenty-three years of marriage, with each ride proving more variety-spiced than the last – and a bit more scary at times too. So, what had made us adopt a way of life that many would liken to following the flocks of wild geese that fly in from the north to graze the green fields of East Lothian every autumn, only to take off again for pastures new come spring? We have to go back even further to find an answer to that...

* * *

As I would relate years later in a book called *Thistle Soup,* I come from a farming background, and my ambition since childhood had always been to step one day into my maternal grandfather's straw-filled wellies, though it soon became clear that I was perched one branch too low on the family tree for that to happen. At school, an ability to draw and paint quite well conspired to steer me even farther off the muddy path to the farmyard and towards art college, then potentially – though the thought made me shudder – to teaching, or even worse, to being imprisoned forever in the design department of some dark, satanic ceramics or wallpaper factory.

A career in the administrative side of farming seemed a logical compromise – at least to my parents, though somewhat less to me. In due deference to them, however, I bit the bullet, applied for a post as an Executive Officer in the Ministry of Agriculture, was accepted, then promptly drafted into the Ministry of Labour instead. And you don't encounter too many Aberdeen Angus cattle waiting in line for welfare benefit at the local 'broo', the unemployment bureaux that existed in most Scottish towns of any size back in the '50s! Nevertheless, I was duly assigned to a department in the Ministry's Edinburgh HQ, where I was responsible for collating weekly employment/unemployment/industrial stats from all the 'broos' in Scotland and converting them into a narrative that would be easily understood by Edward Heath, the then Minister of Labour and future Prime Minister of the UK. Though it didn't occur to me at the time, I was actually sharpening my creative writing skills, albeit in the most uninspiring of ways and certainly without any chance of injecting the slightest modicum of humour into the text, intentionally or otherwise.

I stuck it for almost two years and escaped before the promise of a secure, generously-salaried, perquisite-sweetened and early-pensionable future lulled me into accepting a life that I feared would snuff out any spark of creativity that nature had kindled in me. To the astonishment of my superiors, and what I sensed was the tacit dismay of my parents, I resigned from the civil service, forsaking my feather-bedded future for one of the most insecure careers imaginable.

I became a professional jazz musician.

This could give the impression that I was behaving like a spoiled brat who had taken for granted an opportunity to progress in a career not open to many of my age at a time when the country was still recovering from the harsh years of post-war austerity. It was late 1960, I was not quite twenty, yet seemingly prepared to ignore any sacrifices my parents had made to set me on the road to a potentially more comfortable life than the one most hard working folk of their generation had endured. But the truth was that I deeply appreciated all my parents had done for me, and while I knew the risks involved in shifting to a career path pock-marked with pot holes big enough to swallow a horse, it was the only way ahead I could see. Years later, my mother confessed that she had been so worried at the time that she asked our family doctor if he thought I was right in the head. To which he replied that if I wasn't already nuts, I soon would be if I continued forcing myself to stay in a job I truly hated. Although outwardly the epitome of sanity, it was rumoured the doc had only studied medicine because he'd been coerced into following in his own father's footsteps. So, it's very possible that he knew exactly where I was coming from on the going-nuts front.

Maybe, like me, he should have mapped out an escape route by learning to play the bagpipes in his youth. Because, bizarre as it may seem, that's what started me out (albeit inadvertently) on the road to becoming a professional jazz musician. It's an episode I would one day write about at some length in a book called *Don't Call Me Clyde!*. But suffice to say for now that it was being introduced, by a fellow member of our local boys' pipe band, to a film featuring the clarinet artistry of Benny 'King of Swing' Goodman that prompted me to do any farm jobs I could scrounge at weekends and during school holidays until I had saved up enough to buy a beat-up old clarinet of my own. A like-minded chum did similarly for a trumpet, another for a trombone, yet another for a drum kit, until we had ourselves a six-piece jazz band.

Village hall engagements around the county eventually graduated into bookings at bigger venues farther afield, a radio spot on a network talent show, and eventually a recording date with a Scottish company that resulted in the release of two singles. By this time I was a reluctant Executive Officer in the Ministry of Labour, and when those records found their way into the hands of a German jazz club proprietor who was sufficiently impressed to offer the band a two-month contract, the escape hatch was opened and I was on my way to freedom.

Or so I thought.

* * *

Dame Fortune may well favour the brave, but she's also capable of kicking the foolhardy up the backside, and that's how it seemed she had decided to treat me at the end of what had been eight exhausting but exhilarating weeks as the leader of a full-time professional jazz band in Germany. Playing from 8pm till 2am seven nights a week with matinees on Saturdays and Sundays was hard going, but such things are taken in your stride when you're twenty and enjoying every minute of being paid for doing something you would gladly do for nothing. Then Dame Fortune paid me another visit, this time wearing her reality boots…

We returned to the UK with not one solitary offer of work. The so-called Trad Jazz Boom of the early '60s was rapidly gaining momentum, fuelled by the unprecedented pop chart success of jazz bands led by Chris Barber, Kenny Ball and Acker Bilk, with the result that there were more hopeful combos vying to emulate them than engagements to go round. While the boys in my band went back to their day jobs, I gulped down a slice of humble pie and braced myself to join the queue lining up for dole money at the local 'broo'. If you've resigned your position as an Executive Officer in the Ministry of Labour, there's no way back in – except as a 'customer'.

Then, just as quickly as my ride on the big dipper had hit rock bottom, I was on the way back up again, and in the most unexpected of ways. The Clyde Valley Stompers, Scotland's answer to Barber, Ball and Bilk, having already achieved the status of a 'super group' north of the border, were about to broaden their horizons (and earning potential!) by moving their base from Glasgow to London. Their clarinettist had opted not to go, and as they liked what they'd heard on those two records that opened the German door for me, I was asked if I would be interested in joining them. *Would* I? I clambered aboard their bandwagon before it had even stopped to pick me up.

And so began a period of hard but regular touring work that promised to provide the foundations of a rewarding career and, in so far as can be expected in the music business, a secure one as well. After just a year traversing the gold-paved highways and byways of England on a packed date sheet of one-night stands, the trombonist/leader of the Clyde Valley Stompers (who, crucially, was also the legal owner of the band's name) decided to retire, while continuing to control its financial affairs from the Channel Islands. He was still in his thirties. Although I was only twenty-one and pretty much the 'baby' of the group, he handed me the baton, ostensibly because I was the only member of the line-up with any experience of leading a band, but more likely because none of the other lads was naive enough to take the job on. The Clydes, to give them their abbreviated handle, had a history of friction between their decamping leader and a few of his erstwhile sidemen, with money being the root of all ill will, as I would find out to my cost in the fullness of time.

For the present, though, I grabbed with unbridled enthusiasm the dream-come-true opportunity to front a top-line jazz band. As might be expected, there were problems aplenty in trying to convince the public and promoters alike that a greenhorn wannabe could not only hold the band together but also maintain its high-flying status in the face of ever keener competition. London, like any big city, is no place to lose your grip when you're holding onto the survival ladder by the skin of your teeth.

But survive we did, thanks in no small measure to being signed by up-and-coming record producer George Martin, soon to become immortalised through his work with the Beatles. Our jauntily jazzed-up version of Prokofiev's *Peter and the Wolf*, recorded under George's supervision in EMI's iconic Abbey Road Studios, climbed swiftly into the UK's top-selling singles chart, propelling the Clydes for the first time into the razzle-dazzle world of mainstream pop music and all the lucrative dividends that come with it. Unfortunately, those dividends didn't materialise as quickly as expected in the wage packets we received from our agent. But fulfilling all the radio and TV engagements that rolled in on the back of our hit record kept us sufficiently sidetracked to allow any related misgivings to pass – at least for the present.

Film work involving top box office names of the day also came our way: playing the title music over the opening credits of a new Norman Wisdom movie called *On The Beat*, and actually appearing in *It's All Happening,* the latest big-screen production starring Tommy Steele. All these extra commitments had to be fitted into a hectic schedule of one-night-stands that differed from the previous norm in only the size of the venues and, presumably, the size of the fees. Yet the contents of our wage packets remained unchanged.

Though jazz musicians are generally regarded as fairly easygoing creatures who have a way of making light of life's bothersome intrusions through the buzz they get from playing, they are by no means a soft touch when it comes to money, which is notoriously hard to come by in their line of business. Accordingly, they are not inclined to easily submit, without appropriate recompense, to the nomadic lifestyle dictated by the Clyde Valley Stompers' management. This eventually manifested itself in an ominous sequence of defections from the Clydes' line-up, until the matter came to a head by my asking the absentee owner of the band's name (via our London agent) for all financial comings and goings to be made transparent. I was immediately fired.

Thus, after three years on the up-and-up, my seat on the big dipper of life bottomed out. Again.

* * *

It's said that everything happens for a reason, and looking back to the early '60s I can see that having my future as a jazz musician so abruptly nipped in the bud did actually kick me off on the path to becoming a published author a quarter of a century later. It turned out to be a long and twisting path, and not without its share of puddles either, but thanks to one positive aspect of my experience with the Clyde

Valley Stompers, at least I'd have good company and support along the way.

The future looked so rosy following the success of *Peter and the Wolf* that I took the plunge and married my schooldays sweetheart Ellie, who was immediately introduced to the loneliness that can often greet a new arrival in London, particularly one who has an itinerant jazz musician for a husband. But she took it all in her stride. She shared my optimistic outlook and was ready to take the rough with the smooth while laying the foundations of what we hoped would be a long and happy life together. And within a year, the arrival of our baby son Sandy added to the atmosphere of good cheer, only to be snuffed out by the sudden termination of my services as leader of what, financially at least, had never stopped being someone else's band. We duly made our way back home to Scotland, bruised, broke, but not beaten, and set about building a new future for our little family.

* * * * *

Chapter Two

'WHEN ONE DOOR CLOSES'

*

By 1990, when I started scribbling those notes about our time as rookie orange farmers in Mallorca, twenty-five years had passed since the end of my career as leader of a top-flight jazz band in London. On returning to Scotland, I had initially tried to earn a living as a freelance musician, but although a few local gigs and even some TV work did come my way, it soon became apparent that this precarious pursuit of my old trade was unlikely to generate enough money to feed three mouths for long. The roller coaster may have ceased to nosedive, but only because it seemed there was nowhere lower for it to go.

And that's when an aptitude for writing that had earned me a plaudit or two at school resurfaced to help things along. A journalist contact in Shetland, where I had toured with the band the previous year, invited me to contribute a weekly record-review column to the local newspaper. There was only a small fee involved, but I was glad of any addition to the family coffers, no matter how modest. Dame Fortune then took it upon herself to give me an extra boost by extending the uptake of the column to three other papers in different parts of Scotland. Of a sudden, I was 'syndicated' – not quite in the George Bernard Shaw league of music critics, admittedly, but very grateful to be afforded my first venture into print, even if only as a temporary source of extra income.

It was now 1966, and this change in my luck continued by being offered a chance to get involved in the technical side of record production by the Edinburgh studios responsible for those two singles that had provided me with an escape route from the civil service and subsequently the chance to join the Clyde Valley Stompers. Within a couple of years, I had progressed to being a record producer in my own right, using to good advantage the experience of having worked as a musician under George Martin, the producer who, through the massive success he'd gone on to achieve with the Beatles, had become one of the most highly regarded in the business.

It should probably go without saying that having an ability to empathise with the musicians involved is an essential for anyone entrusted with control of a recording session. A studio can be an unnerving place for any performer, no matter how experienced, and I'd learned that George Martin's maxim of creating a relaxed atmosphere at the start of proceedings should be the overriding priority of whoever is sitting in 'the booth'. The knobs and faders at his fingertips are inanimate objects to be tweaked and twisted at will, while the musicians on the studio floor are human beings, and frequently fairly sensitive ones at that, no matter how hard they try to appear otherwise. So, I made it my rule to adhere to the relax-'em-first policy, and it served me well over the coming years when, as a freelance producer, I had the privilege of working with a wide range of recording artistes whose talents were as diverse as those of Jimmy Shand, the legendary king of Scottish Dance Music at one end of the spectrum, and the Krankies, quirky stars of British TV comedy at the other.

* * *

In 1970, an unpredicted wind of change snapped a few twigs on the family tree and presented me with the longed-for chance to get a foot in the farming door, not as an office-bound administrator this time, but as a rain-or-shine, mud-on-my-boots, hands-on plougher of my own furrow.

Four or five hundred acres is considered an optimum size for an arable farm on the fertile expanses of East Lothian, so by those standards the fifty-acre holding we took the tenancy of was generally considered to be no more than a decent-sized field. To me, however, Cuddy Neuk represented not only a doorway to a long-coveted way of life but also a link to my childhood and all the cherished memories associated with it. For this was the little spread my grandfather had used as a stepping stone to a larger, more viable farm after coming south from his native Orkney shortly before the outbreak of the Second World War. It was where my own family lived until I was eight years old, and no matter how far away life eventually took me, Cuddy Neuk would always mean 'home'. I loved everything about the place.

But the reality that faced us when we took over could not be disguised by any amount of rose-tinted nostalgia. The farm was in a pretty run-down state, with only the most basic set of implements, and even those were on their last legs. But Ellie and I welcomed the challenge to return Cuddy Neuk to its former trim, productive state, and we put our shoulders resolutely to the wheel.

Our first concern was to get the land back in good heart, which hard work alone would not accomplish. We would need to invest in machinery that was fit for purpose, enough good seed and fertilizer to give our first crop of barley the best chance of producing a decent yield, and we would also have to buy livestock to contribute to the long-term fertility of the soil, as well as helping create a more diverse farming business for the future. All of this would take money – much more than the meagre funds we had at our disposal.

Any notion I may have entertained of instantly becoming a full-time farmer had to be quickly stifled. If I was ever to reach even a fraction of the way towards achieving that goal, I'd have to fund the effort by maximising my income from producing records. Inevitably, this would often involve spending more time away tending microphones and tape recorders than ploughing fields and scattering seeds, meaning

Ellie would be left to see to the day-to-day running of the farm. She also had to find time to look after our second son Muir, a boisterous wee lad who had been born three years earlier, although big brother Sandy, now seven, was always keen to lend a helping hand when he came home from school every evening. All in all, then, the cogs in our new-found wheel of fortune were clicking nicely into place, and even if there never seemed to be enough hours in the day, we couldn't have been more contented with our lot.

Just when we thought life couldn't get more hectic, along came the chance of even more recording work, which the hard facts of our financial situation dictated I was obliged to accept. America's mighty RCA Records had recently decided to set up their own production and distribution operations in the UK, having previously delegated those activities to British affiliates. RCA's policy was to quickly establish a 'stable' of British artistes embracing a broad range of musical output, whether classical, pop or what they classified as 'regionally typical', which included the music I was involved with in Scotland. I just happened to be the only freelance producer currently operating north of the border, so without any pushing on my part, the door to a significant source of additional revenue opened in front of me. All I had to do now was find performers of the right calibre to fit the bill: no easy task in a relatively small talent pool where the best-known names were already under contract.

While progress in netting suitable artistes was indeed slow when it came to the most popular types (singers of homespun songs, folk groups,

Scottish Country Dance Bands, etc.), I did manage to sign for RCA a military band of some repute which, having only recently returned home after several years abroad, had escaped the attention of British record labels. The Royal Scots Greys were one of Scotland's oldest regiments, with a long and illustrious history that included a legendary role in securing victory for Britain at the Battle of Waterloo. Yet 'The Greys' were about to fall victim to cuts in the government's defence budget by being amalgamated with another regiment and, though unthinkable to staunch upholders of military tradition, given a brand new name.

Amazing Grace by the Pipes and Drums and Military Band of what had become the Royal Scots Dragoon Guards was recorded as a last-minute filler for one side of an RCA album called *Farewell to the Greys*, a record the American company judged would have extremely limited sales potential. Who, after all, apart from people with sentimental ties to the old regiment, would be interested in buying an LP commemorating its change of name? In a nutshell, RCA's primary concern was to exploit the popularity of global superstars like Elvis Presley and Dolly Parton, not to finance a trip down memory lane for a handful of old soldiers in Scotland.

The album was recorded nonetheless, albeit on a budget commensurate with the company's lack of belief in its profitability. Despite all that, a fortuitous airing of one particular track on a late-night BBC radio programme in the spring of 1972 generated such an overwhelming public response that RCA were compelled to release it as a single. *Amazing Grace* shot promptly to the top of the UK pop charts, emulated that success internationally, and ultimately became the biggest-selling instrumental single of all time, with sales grossing some thirteen million.

Unfortunately, RCA's budgetary constraints were also reflected in the royalty rate stipulated in my producer's contract, but while I didn't earn anything resembling a fortune from the runaway success of *Amazing Grace*, it did provide us with enough capital over the next few years to add to our limited range of working tackle at Cuddy Neuk, create the foundation of a herd of breeding cattle, construct a spacious all-purpose building to augment the original pocket-sized steading, and generally invest in the little farm's prospects of becoming a viable business.

For all that we were grateful for this financial windfall, we would readily have forfeited every penny and much more besides to prevent the tragedy that followed in its wake. Wee Muir's death, at only five years of age, in a road accident that almost killed his elder brother too, put brutally into perspective the insignificance of material assets when set against the loss of a child. It took a long time to learn to live with that.

It's true, though, that keeping busy is the best way of coping with grief, and as crops and animals have to be tended through bad times as well as good, fulfilling those obligations did much to provide the incentive we needed to pick up the pieces and get on with the task of building a future for our family.

* * *

The Royal Scots Dragoon Guards' single of *Amazing Grace* had become a worldwide phenomenon, not because of any flash of inspiration on my part (as noted earlier, it was recorded as a last-minute album filler, and in only one 'take' at that), nor because of any high-powered marketing push by RCA, but solely because it struck an emotional chord with the many millions of people who heard it. Countering that reaction came a flurry of criticism from certain factions of the 'serious' bagpipe fraternity, who declared it a piece of blatant commercialism that showed a lack of respect for the glorious heritage of Scotland's national instrument. This didn't stop those same carpers from swiftly cashing in on this alleged irreverence by publishing a keenly-priced transcription of the melody for the edification of pipers at large. And although a hit featuring the Highland war pipes was widely seen by music industry 'experts' as a never-to-be-repeated fluke, there were still recording artistes astute enough to grab a slice of the action while it lasted – including one ex-Beatle with a holiday home on the Mull of Kintyre.

As was to be expected, the bagpipe bandwagon soon departed the fickle byways of mainstream pop music, and I was glad to have been distanced from much of the resultant hustle and bustle as it passed through. Yet, in its aftermath, my involvement in its creation did have a positive effect on the demand for my services as a freelance producer. Military bands had suddenly been added to the lists of must-haves by record companies previously indifferent to their existence, and as I now had a track record in that field, I got my fair share of calls to supply the goods – provided, as had become my stock-in-trade, I could deliver at a cost that kept risk to an absolute minimum.

These new commitments inevitably involved more travelling on my part, since it was cheaper to take mobile recording equipment to where the bands were based than to transport forty or fifty musicians to studios that were handier for the producer. As a result, military barracks in places as far afield as Catterick in Yorkshire, Tidworth in Wiltshire, Knightsbridge in London, 'Royal' Windsor, a string of British garrison towns across the north of Germany and even a slightly more exotic Beau Geste style fort in the Arabian Desert became familiar workplaces for me during the remainder of the '70s.

Meanwhile, long-suffering Ellie kept the home fires burning at Cuddy Neuk, prompting one of her chums to quip that she should be awarded a medal for stoicism – either that or a certificate of insanity! Joking aside, it can't be denied that trying to keep so many plates spinning at once was often tough for both of us. With the birth in 1973 of Charlie, a new wee brother for Sandy, Ellie had her hands full enough being mother to her own youngsters without having to bottle-feed batches of baby calves day and night. But that was just one necessity of many that were part and parcel of the development of the farm. By the same token, there wasn't a moment spent away on record production business when I wouldn't rather have been working at home, whether helping Ellie with her routine chores or keeping on top of essential field work, the timing of which is set by the passing of the seasons and the vagaries of the weather, not by deadlines imposed by any record company.

Even so, the occasions when one commitment clashed with the other were few, far-between and minor. The window of dates in nature's calendar for each and every operation in the farming year, be it ploughing, sowing, hay making or harvest, is ignored at your peril, and we paid due heed to that maxim at all times.

* * *

As the years passed and my record-review column had long since run its course, providing sleeve notes for some of the LP albums I produced became my only involvement in writing, which was still far removed from providing even the slightest hint that I might one day become an author. But who knows? Maybe fate was helping me keep my hand in, just in case.

And I suppose that even if I *had* harboured thoughts of dipping my pen in a 'proper' inkwell (which I hadn't), finding the time would have proved a major obstacle. As we approached the end of our first decade at Cuddy Neuk, maintaining a balance between farm work and record production hadn't become any easier, although the progress being made in both occupations gave us all the encouragement we needed to carry on regardless. What's more, we were enjoying ourselves!

The farm was now in tip-top trim, with the land

producing decent yields of malting barley and healthy swards of grass for our expanding herd of cattle. We had even started renting a couple of fields on nearby farms for extra summer grazing.

On the record front, demand for the supply of albums featuring military bands had returned to a more rational level since the passing of the boom times sparked by *Amazing Grace,* but as I'd kept my involvement with the 'civilian' side of the market intact throughout, I still had more than enough to do providing record companies with well-tried staples. Time-honoured favourites like Andy Stewart and Jimmy Shand may have stepped aside to make way for a new generation of Scottish entertainers, but I was on hand to help a fair few of those launch their recording careers as well.

So well were things going, in fact, that we made the momentous decision to buy the farm. This, of course, meant arranging a bank loan for more than we would have dared to even think about when taking on the tenancy just ten years earlier. But since then, a combination of hard work and good luck had helped improve and consolidate our financial position. And as there appeared to be no reason to suspect that our fortunes were likely to take a significant turn for the worse in the foreseeable future, we decided that, if we didn't make the ultimate commitment now, the chances were that we never would.

This buoyant outlook was given an additional lift in 1981 when I was asked to produce an album featuring the Krankies, Scotland's off-beat comedy duo currently amassing legions of new fans through weekly appearances on *Crackerjack*, the BBC's flagship TV programme for children. I solved the problem of their musical repertoire being a bit short on recordable material by composing several tailor-made songs. This was a new departure for me and I thoroughly enjoyed it, particularly writing lyrics aimed squarely at a young audience, which gave me an opportunity to play with words in a way I hadn't done before. The fun I had is exemplified in the lyrics I rustled up in an effort to capture the spirit of the Krankie's famous catchword, *Fan-dabi-dozi*. Very few nursery rhyme characters escaped the net!

When Little Jack Horner met Jack and Jill,
They boogied on up to the top of the hill:
To the Owl and the Pussy Cat's disco night,
And they Rock-a-Bye'd Baby in the pale moonlight.

Chorus:

It was Fan-dabi-dozi, Fan-dabi-dozi,
Fan-dabi-dozi and they danced all night.
Fan-dabi-dozi, Fan-dabi-dozi,
Fan-dabi-dozi, yeah, that's all right!

The Little Old Woman Who Lived In a Shoe
Rode a Cock Horse to the party too.
She saw Miss Muffet and the Crooked Man;
They were boppin' with Mary and her Little Lamb.

Chorus:

It was Fan-dabi-dozi, Fan-dabi-dozi etc...

*Wee Willie Winkie and the Three Blind Mice
Were jivin' with Pretty Maids and that was nice.
With a Hey Diddle-Diddle and a Ding-Dong-Dell
The Cat Played the Fiddle and he sang as well.*

Chorus:

He sang Fan-dabi-dozi, Fan-dabi-dozi, etc...

But not even the infectious sparkle of the Krankies could brighten the clouds of recession that were gathering over Britain in the early '80s. Record companies were not immune to the related downturn in demand for their products, and the result was a swift and sweeping reduction in output. Almost overnight, the market for my offerings fell from upwards of a dozen albums per year to zero. And with the resultant loss of income came the harsh realisation that we would no longer be able to meet our obligations to the bank.

Though heartbreaking, Cuddy Neuk and all the bittersweet memories it embodied would have to be sold.

* * * * *

Chapter Three

'FROM A PRUNING HOOK TO A HAMMER'

*

We arrived in Mallorca towards the end of 1984, having put our dashed hopes for Cuddy Neuk behind us, and determined to make a go of our new venture come what may. The prospect of growing oranges for a living in a sunny climate may seem like the stuff of dreams, but we knew the reality could well turn out to be the opposite. Basics like communicating in a strange language and getting to grips with a totally unfamiliar branch of farming presented even bigger challenges than those we'd faced when taking on the tenancy of Cuddy Neuk some fourteen years earlier.

We had made the decision to purchase the little orange farm of Ca's Mayoral after coming across it by chance while taking a short break in Mallorca following months of trying to buy a substitute for Cuddy Neuk in less fertile parts of Scotland, where land values were correspondingly lower. But with limited capital at our disposal and borrowing ruled out, asking prices for properties that might have suited our purpose were always tantalisingly beyond our reach. Once again, it seemed force of circumstances rather than a choice of alternatives was dictating the path we were set to follow.

No matter how much we tried to convince ourselves otherwise, making the move to Mallorca could justifiably be described as bordering on the foolhardy side of derring-do. Yet our determination to continue farming within the constraints of our budget remained undiminished, even if it meant migrating fifteen hundred miles to a foreign land to make it possible. It didn't take long for our resolve to be tested. Severely.

'Look!' beamed a well-meaning Mallorcan neighbour on our arrival at Ca's Mayoral. He was gazing with a mix of delight and amazement at the effect a freak snowstorm was having on the surrounding landscape. 'The weather has come from Scotland to welcome you!'

'So much for picking oranges in the Mallorcan sunshine!' I said to myself, smiling gamely while thanking him for his kind words. But although snow was the last thing I expected to see right then, I wasn't unduly concerned. I knew that even light falls, never mind mini blizzards like this one, were quite rare on the island, and mostly confined to the mountain tops anyway. The oranges on our trees down here in the valley would only resemble snowballs until the sun came out again; which it duly did, almost as quickly as it had disappeared. If this was the worst Mallorca had to throw at us, *no problema*!

Then we were informed that the removals van, which had been due to arrive ahead of us with all our goods and chattels from Scotland, was still making its way southward through France. Still, we thought, doing without a few familiar home comforts for a day or two wouldn't do us any harm. *No problema*!

Then the previous owners' two mongrel dogs and accompanying pack of semi-feral cats trooped into the house to give us the once-over, before exhibiting their opinions in cryptically-placed deposits of cat poop and selectively-aimed squirts of dog pee. But, hey! we thought, they were only innocent animals reacting to unwanted change in the only way they knew. They'd soon come round to accepting us. *No problema*!

Then the water boiler packed in. Still, we thought, it would be no great hardship to make do with boiling the kettle for essential needs until the local plumber came to our rescue. A couple of days at most without showering? *No problema*!

Then, a week later, the septic tank choked, causing the contents to back up and ooze out over the ground floor of the house. Another job for the plumber, who still hadn't come to fix the boiler. *Problema*!

But all of these setbacks paled compared to being informed by a neighbouring farmer that, although our orange trees might look fine to us, they had been neglected for so long that they'd become riddled with disease. Drastic measures would be required to return them to any kind of productivity – if indeed that proved to be possible at all. We had, he said, *un problema profundo,* which meant in any language that we had bought a complete lemon of an orange farm. We had been victims of our own naivety and, yes, foolhardiness too.

Then Christmas night arrived with a storm and a lightning strike that wiped out our electricity supply. Having no lights on the Christmas tree, although no great problem in itself, only added to a creeping sense of homesickness and a despondent feeling that our Mallorcan adventure seemed doomed to fail before it had even started.

And the removals van containing all the bits and pieces that make a house a home *still* hadn't arrived.

* * *

Ill-omened as those first few weeks at Ca's Mayoral may have been, we had crossed the Rubicon and there could be no going back. And thanks to the support and advice of our elderly neighbours in the valley, our luck soon changed and we settled into our new way of life with surprising ease. Even our practice of working as if there were no tomorrow gradually morphed into the *mañana* pace governed by the climate and observed by Spanish country folk since time immemorial.

Our two boys also adjusted to island life with a sense of expectancy that quelled any doubts they may have harboured before leaving 'home'. Our concerns about the culture shock that young Charlie might encounter when starting his new school also proved unfounded. He embraced with delight the informal dress code of jeans, T-shirt and sneakers that reflected the laid-back atmosphere of the classroom in general. And as his new school chums represented a diverse mix of nationalities, his outlook was broadened accordingly – even if his enthusiasm for certain educational aspects of schooling remained steadfastly limited!

His elder brother Sandy, on the other hand, couldn't have been keener to learn the ropes of farming Mallorca-style. He had already completed a course at agricultural college in Scotland, but the intricacies of pruning orange trees hadn't been on the curriculum, nor had the technique required to plough with a tiny, two-wheeled, walk-behind 'tractor' (or a diesel-powered donkey, as he wryly dubbed it) as opposed to the conventional 4-wheel-drive monsters he'd become accustomed to.

Ellie and I, meanwhile, breathed a sigh of relief that the unfortunate series of events blighting our introduction to our adopted home was now behind us. On the positive side, the experience had taught us that, in the face of adversity, laughter really is the best medicine, and although we didn't know it at the time, it would prove to be a remedy we'd find ourselves re-administering with remarkable regularity. For now, however, the future looked promising and, most importantly, we were enjoying ourselves again!

* * *

As details of our Mallorcan adventure are already well documented in the *Snowball Oranges* series of books, it's probably enough to briefly mention here that it developed into a thoroughly enjoyable three years: enlightening, fulfilling, occasionally nail-biting but predominantly happy. All things considered, it was an opportunity we feel privileged to have been granted. In fact, if it hadn't been for the detrimental effect that Spain's joining the EU had on small orange-growing businesses like ours, it's more than likely that we would have stayed there for the rest of our days. But, in a farming world with '*Big Is Beautiful*' as its byword, our abiding problem of having limited capital was bound to be even more to our disadvantage when attempting to compete in a location like Mallorca, where the value of land, even in out-of-the-way rural areas, is inexorably linked to tourism. We had been lucky to get a foot in the door once, the 'bargain' price we paid for Ca's Mayoral having reflected the poor condition of its orchards and the resultant absence of rival offers from in-the-know locals. But in the end, just as lightning never strikes the same tree twice, it eventually became clear that snow wasn't about to fall on our oranges for a second time either. Not even to bid us '*Adiós!*'

* * *

And so we revert to the start of this narrative and those notes I scribbled about what folks 'back home' imagined had been our time spent living the life of Riley in Mallorca...

On returning to the UK, our intention was to start a deer farm, which was something we had seriously considered before fate whisked us off to foreign climes. We eventually found a suitable block of land to buy on the lower slopes of the Lammermuir Hills in south-east Scotland. Again, the scale of the enterprise would be governed by the size of our budget, which had somehow survived the Ca's Mayoral venture, but was still precariously tight. Nevertheless, we had done enough number crunching to convince ourselves that, by following the Mallorcan *'poc a poc'* principle of treading carefully and proceeding little by little, we'd have a fair chance of making the gamble pay off.

After almost two years of preparation, which included divining for water then drilling a well, laying half a mile of underground electricity and telephone cables and actually building a house from scratch, we were finally ready to stock the property with the nucleus of a herd of fallow deer: a relatively small species well suited to our circumstances. It was November, 1989, and our roller coaster was on an upward trajectory once again.

Then the Berlin Wall came down. At a stroke, the British deer farming industry was shaken to its foundations. West Germany, a major market for this country's farmed venison, would now have access to unlimited supplies of the wild variety from the east, and at prices significantly below those required to show a profit for UK farmers.

We watched the TV news footage of elated Berliners setting about the hated concrete barrier with their picks and sledge hammers.

Ellie cast me a sidelong glance. 'Seems your timing has been just a *wee* bit off,' she said, observing a moment of pregnant silence before adding, 'Again.'

There was no answer to that, so I didn't offer one. I just sat there staring vacantly at the telly, stroking my chin and sensing the clouds of doom gathering above my head. 'Aye, right enough,' I ultimately muttered. 'As you say, it seems kinda like it.'

'And just when I was looking forward to putting my stamp on our new house too,' Ellie sighed, pointedly. 'You know … making a house a home?'

I waited for her to append the dreaded 'Again' word, but she didn't. It really went without saying. I knew she had shown the patience of a saint, putting up with everything from being an itinerant jazz musician's 'widow' in London, to shouldering the responsibilities of keeping a farm ticking over while I was away producing records, and even to lugging heavy crates of oranges about in the stifling heat of Mallorca. On top of all that, she'd wholeheartedly supported whatever venture I came up with, no matter how questionable its chances of success. She really did deserve a medal.

'You know, Ellie,' I said at length, 'I've come to the conclusion that it's high time I gave up this obsession with farming on a shoestring. We've given it our best shots, but let's face it, we're pissing against the wind.'

'I think you'll find the word is actually puffing.'

'Puff, piss, whatever. It still amounts to farting against thunder, and it isn't worth the effort.'

Ellie raised an eyebrow. 'So, what do you propose doing instead?'

I stroked my chin again, thinking hard but in no frame of mind to produce any worthwhile suggestions. 'I dunno,' I grumped. 'Maybe I'll write a book about it!'

Ellie raised both eyebrows. 'Maybe you should at that.'

'Me? A book?' I shook my head. 'Nah, no way.'

'Why not? I mean, think about it – you've got *plenty* of stuff to write about!'

'OK, OK, no need to come over all sarky. You've had a lot to put up with over the years, I admit, but –'

'I'm not being sarky. I'm being serious. I mean, you're pretty good at writing stuff … look at *Fan-dabi-dozi* for instance.'

I gave a little chuckle. 'Now I *know* you're having a go at me!'

'No, I'm not – honestly. What I'm trying to say is that you've got the material. You know, orange groves and tapas bars instead of Little Miss Muffet and Wee Willie Winkie – but it's still about juggling with words, so why not give it a go?'

I didn't share Ellie's enthusiasm, but I let the idea simmer for a while anyway. 'It definitely is *not* my bag,' I eventually told myself. 'No, but then again,' I wavered, 'there's no harm in having a look at those notes I've been jotting down. Hmm, maybe I'll get round to that tomorrow. Yeah, now that I think about it, why not indeed?'

But I still had no inclination to develop the hotchpotch of scribbled memory-joggers into a book. With our projected deer farm failing to materialise, I'd have enough on my plate trying to realise our assets by selling the land and house we'd just invested in, as well as attempting to find another source of family income. Again.

Whether it was a genuine, spur-of-the-moment brainwave or just a desperate attempt to head off any 'bright idea' I might put forward myself, I couldn't tell, but it was Ellie who got in first with a possible solution to our latest monetary conundrum…

'Why don't we buy an old property, do it up and flog it?'

'H-h-hold on a minute,' I spluttered. 'That'll take time. Yeah, and it'd tie up all our capital too.'

'So?'

'So, where are we gonna live in the meantime?'

'In the old house we're doing up, of course. Where else?'

I was dumbstruck. Here was a woman who had stoically endured being shunted around several cramped, charmless flats in London, had made the most of the damp, fungus-sprouting farm cottages we had rented on our return home, had turned the sadly neglected house at Cuddy Neuk into a bright, cheery and comfortable family home (all while having to adhere to a policy of make-do-and-mend), and now she was offering to rough it in what would inevitably turn out to be an indoor building site for months on end. I scratched my head. Perhaps she really did deserve that certificate of insanity her friend had teased her about. For a fleeting moment I was tempted to tell her that I reckoned the Mallorcan sun must have addled her brains, but opted for a more tactful response instead.

'Look, Ellie,' I said, 'I see where you're coming from and I appreciate the gesture, I really do, but –'

'But nothing! And it's not a gesture. It's facing the facts, that's all.'

'What facts?' I frowned.

'That it's time we made what money we've got work *for* us instead of using it to chase rainbows.'

This was the first time in all the years I'd known her that Ellie had dug her heels in like this. Not that she wasn't adept at getting her own way when the fancy took her, but she'd always employed more subtle ways of going about it. Suitably admonished, I took a deep breath, braced myself and motioned her to continue.

She had been thinking about it for some time, she revealed, and had come to the conclusion that now was an ideal time to get a toehold in the local property market. The East Lothian countryside had always been a great place to live, but despite its proximity to Edinburgh had been relatively undiscovered by city dwellers until the recent building of a connecting motorway. House prices were on the rise, so why not try to get in on the act while the going was good? And before I could offer any objections, she pointed out that she'd become a dab hand at papering and painting over the years, and she couldn't remember a day at Cuddy Neuk and Ca's Mayoral when I hadn't toted a hammer or spanner or saw or suchlike either. Necessity had been the mother of making do and mending, she concluded, and what better qualification was there for tackling the transformation of a house in need of some TLC? We'd already done it often enough for our own comfort, so why not do it now for profit?

I could have stated the obvious by arguing that making a profit was liable to be more an aspiration than an inevitability, but decided against it. Ellie had the bit firmly between her teeth, and it seemed only fair to let her have her head. Besides, I couldn't think of an alternative proposition, far less a safer one. All I could do was shrug my assent.

It was only then that Ellie divulged that she had already identified our first project: a lovely old stone-built house in our home town of Haddington, centrally located, with an open outlook to the front, a walled-in garden at the back and even its own private garage.

'Sounds interesting,' I said, guardedly. 'Maybe we should arrange to see round it sometime – depending on the asking price, of course.'

'I've already been to see it,' Ellie piped up with a self-assured smile. 'It's just what we're looking for!'

'Depending on the asking price, of course,' I reiterated, a tad apprehensively this time.

'*And* I've spoken to the owner,' Ellie continued. 'Recently widowed – nice old man – very attached to the house – doesn't want it to go to just anybody – likes the idea of us doing a sensitive refurb. Needs younger people to breathe new life into it, he said.'

'Depending on the price, of course,' I persisted, despairingly.

'All taken care of,' Ellie breezed. 'Quick sale for the old boy, good deal for us.' She tweaked my cheek and winked. 'And don't you worry, Mr Tightwad, it's well within our budget too!'

* * * * *

Chapter Four

'AN AMERICAN PRESIDENT & TWO CUSTARD PIES'

*

The 1990s had only just begun, and by the end of the decade we'd have 'done up' ten houses, having lived in each one while enduring whatever inconvenience and discomfort the work in progress presented. What we hadn't known about the required DIY skills at the outset we very quickly learned, thus limiting the expense of hiring help to matters that safety regulations demanded should be left to experts. A disruptive lifestyle it certainly was, but we soon became accustomed to it and actually looked forward to the satisfaction that came with the completion of each project.

Yet, as Ellie commented after we'd put the finishing touches to the third property, 'I think it can be safely said that we're developing a knack of turning houses into homes. Trouble is we never get to keep one for ourselves!'

Although she'd said that with a twinkle in her eye, it was obvious we couldn't continue in this way indefinitely. Sooner or later we'd have to find the wherewithal to buy ourselves a permanent abode that was independent of what had already become an ongoing business. But that would require either a considerable increase in the size of the profits we'd managed to turn so far, or taking out a bank loan which, after our experience at Cuddy Neuk, was a path we were reluctant to go down again.

We were sitting on a couple of packing cases with a takeaway of fish and chips one evening, surrounded by a typical clutter of kitchen cupboard flat-packs, shelving, a stainless steel sink, a twin-flush lavatory cistern, tins of paint and miscellaneous other items awaiting incorporation into our current undertaking, when Ellie happened to hark back to the circumstances that had precipitated our departure from Cuddy Neuk.

'It's funny,' she said, 'how the end of one creative period in your life has eventually resulted in the start of another – I mean, after all that time in Mallorca and everything.'

'Sorry, Ellie, but you've lost me.' I took a slug from a can of beer. 'You're not suggesting that stripping wallpaper and sanding floor boards is in any way creative, are you?'

'No, no, not that,' she assured me while nibbling on a scrap of batter. 'Although I'm prepared to admit my painting technique is now approaching a standard Michelangelo would have been proud of.'

'Yeah, well, slapping white emulsion on the ceilings in this old joint will be *right* up your street.'

Ellie let that wisecrack pass without comment. 'No, what I meant,' she mumbled through a mouthful of chips, 'was now that you've finished writing your book, maybe it'll lead to a whole new career as an author. You know, maybe even earn us a fortune – movie rights and all that.'

I almost choked on a pickled onion. 'You're counting chickens before the hen's even laid an egg, Ellie. OK, I've finished writing *a* book, but it took two long years and a lot of double-ended candles, and the chances of getting the thing published are slim. *That* much I've already sussed.'

I had even surprised myself by finding the time and concentration to get this far. But Ellie's persistent hint-dropping had eventually worn me down and I'd flicked through those sketchy notes of mine one day in the old Haddington house, having retreated upstairs while a team of damp-proofers sloshed buckets of boiling tar over the ground floor.

For some odd reason, reading those notes reminded me of my time in the Ministry of Labour when I'd gathered up weekly stats and related reports from all over Scotland and converted them into a narrative that would be easily assimilated by Ted Heath, the future Prime Minister, not the bandleader! I thought it might be fun to do the same with the Mallorcan memos, so started scribbling away on the back pages of an old exercise jotter. A page became two, two became three, and so on until, almost without noticing, I had written the makings of a chapter. One chapter became two, two became three, three became four, and then I went out and bought a bigger jotter. I was having a ball, the free-and-easy writing process proving a welcome relief from the daily grind of sawing, hammering, climbing ladders and hauling out old lavatory pans.

Ironically, one of the first things I noticed about committing past events to paper was how quickly I abandoned the very notes that had set the whole thing in motion. Word pictures of us basking in some sort of 'good life' paradise were never going to be anything but phoney, so trying to shoe-horn them into a warts-and-all memoir of our experiences would only serve to alienate *all* potential readers. I had learned from my years in the music business that you can't cater for every taste in one bag of sweeties, and it's counter-productive to even try.

I also noticed that some happenings we had found to be trying or even disheartening at the time, like the series of mishaps that tainted our first few weeks on the island, very often had a comical side when looked at through the prism of hindsight. And so elements of humour crept into my account, and became an essential ingredient that would either amuse or irritate, depending on the individual reader's sense of humour. As touched on at the start of these recollections, humour, and my natural inclination towards it, was to become a bone of contention I'd have to grapple with in the fullness of time, but for the moment I was happy to welcome amusing aspects of events whenever they paid a visit to the page being written.

I suppose it must have been about eighteen months into my nightly therapeutic scribbling that it dawned on me that, no matter how unintentionally, I was well on the way to completing a book. Not just an essay or even a short story, but a full-length actual book. I had already written upwards of two hundred pages, the end was in sight, and I hadn't even dipped into details of our story beyond the first winter on the island. The only person to have read my efforts so far had been Ellie, who had always shown encouragement, while also being quick to target anything she thought inappropriate. She had grown accustomed to expecting the latter when hearing whoops of mirthful self-acclaim emanating from whichever bolthole in our current indoor building site I happened to be using as a writing den. Those situations invariably coincided with when I attempted (very occasionally!) to oil the wheels of creativity with a liberal intake of wine: a method advocated by Laurie Lee, one of my favourite observational authors and a master of descriptive prose.

'I thought as much,' Ellie would remark on casting a critical eye over my work next morning. 'You've been doing a Bruce Lee again, haven't you?'

'His name's Laurie. Bruce is a karate expert.'

'Very apt, because this rubbish needs to be given the chop as well.'

And so I would be spared the embarrassment of being offered the same advice, though minus the leg-pulling element, if ever I plucked up the courage to present my literary efforts to book business professionals. Which I duly did, some two years after I'd scrawled the first sentence in that old school jotter. And, perhaps not too surprisingly, it was Ellie who'd goaded me into it.

'What was the point in spending all that time snuggled up writing when you could have been getting on with bread-winning stuff like tiling a bathroom or wallpapering a bedroom or something?'

'Everybody needs a break of an evening, Ellie.'

'Maybe so, but for all you know, what you've been doing in your rest time over the past two years may have produced a bestseller – or at least a decent earner – so don't hide your candlestick under a bush, or whatever the expression is. Finding a publisher for your book will be no different from finding a record company for any of the albums you produced, so don't dilly-dally. Get stuck in!'

What Ellie neglected to mention, however, was that while I'd had many valuable connections in the record business, I had none at all within the literary community. All I had was the current copy of *The Writers' and Artists' Yearbook,* containing brief details of what appeared to be every publisher and agent in the English-speaking world, each one of whom would be inundated daily by submissions from one-book, have-a-go merchants like myself. Still, never ventured...

The first approach I made was to an 'old school' Scottish publisher known for the editorial quality of its output, with commercial considerations low on the list of priorities. Perhaps unsurprisingly, the company was finding times difficult in the face of increasing competition from publishing houses focused primarily on the bottom line of the balance sheet. Even in what had traditionally been regarded as a staunchly art-for-art's-sake world, accountants and hard-nosed sales executives were having ever more say about which books should be taken on. This being the case, I thought that maybe this doggedly dyed-in-the-wool publisher might lay more store by the content of my book – which had been created with all the care and attention I could lavish on it – than by its potential as a bestseller, which I had no reason to be confident about myself.

'Your book is eminently publishable,' they told me, 'but not one that would fit our current lists.'

Even at that early stage of trying to find an outlet for *Spanish Farm,* which was the working title of what would eventually become *Snowball Oranges*, I had a feeling that this was a pretty standard rebuttal, soothed with a dab of encouragement. And I did indeed take some encouragement from being advised that the book was 'eminently publishable', though oblivious to the fact that the publisher may not have read any of it beyond the first couple of pages. With a new batch of manuscripts landing on their desks every single day, it followed that commissioning editors were bound to use first impressions as a yardstick. Anyhow, my initial hunch was soon proved correct when submission after submission prompted essentially the same response, but with one additional piece of advice: 'Get an agent if you want your work to have the best chance of being looked at by a publisher.' In other words, snowed-under publishers were using trusted literary agencies as sieves to separate the wheat from the chaff, which was understandable enough, but from a wannabe author's point of view meant that an equally daunting barrier still had to be breached. As in the record business, if you didn't have an 'in', whatever you were pitching would very likely be destined for limbo land, or at best consigned to what the book business refers to as the 'slush pile', there to await being stumbled upon by a passing intern who just happens to have the boss's ear. Some lottery.

Nevertheless, adhering stoically to the dictum that 'You gotta be in it to win it', I switched my attention to the index of literary agents included in my well-thumbed copy of *The Writers' and Artists' Yearbook*. But it wasn't much of a surprise that similarly negative responses became the norm, with the watchword 'Your book doesn't fit our lists' replaced by 'Our agency's roster of clients is already full.'

Déjà vu! Remember the end of my jazz band's return from two months in Germany some thirty years previously? Luckily, on this occasion the door was only being closed on a pastime, but one I had grown to enjoy *and* develop a paternal attitude towards. I was also sprouting the first green shoots of what can fairly be described as a persecution complex: why were the keepers of the gate so glibly shutting out the progeny of an ex-jazz musician's dalliance with the hallowed muse of writers? Lowborn the baby may have been in their eyes, but it was *my* baby and I wasn't about to abandon it on *any*one's doorstep – at least before I'd given it a really good scrub. And so I undertook a meticulous revision of the text (especially the first few pages!) followed by what I resolved would be my last big push towards making a breakthrough as an author.

I could do worse, I reckoned, than draw some hope from a famous 1920s quote by US President Calvin Coolidge:

'Nothing in this world can take the place of persistence. Talent will not; nothing is more common than unsuccessful men with talent. "Press on!" has solved and always will solve the problems of the human race.'

Mind you, it was shortly after he made this claim that the human race was hurled into the gaping chasm of the Great Depression. But hey ho! According to Ellie's evaluation of my leisure hours, any failure on my part now would actually be *rewarded*, if only with the option of being gainfully employed tiling bathrooms and wallpapering bedrooms – or something.

*

Back in the early '90s, the standard method of approaching an agent was, as now, to send a short introductory letter accompanied by a one-page synopsis of your book, and if those landed on the right desk at the right time, you might be asked to send the first fifty or so pages for evaluation. The difference between then and now, however, was that communication by email was still a rarity, as was the ownership of home printers. Consequently, every submission involved the expense of postage and the inconvenience of paying a visit to the nearest Xerox shop – not so handy if you lived in the sticks. Also, if your pitch was unsuccessful and you wanted your print-out back, you were required to include the cost of p&p up front. But that was how the system worked, and you either went along with it or opted out.

Back then, it was becoming a generally recognised stipulation that authors should not submit their proposal to more than one agency at a time. Agents were extremely busy people after all, and couldn't be expected to invest their time reading and appraising a book to discover at the end of the exercise that a competitor had snatched a possible source of commission from under their noses. All of this was perfectly reasonable from an agent's perspective, but from an aspiring author's it added yet another course of bricks to the wall he was desperately trying to scale. And to add spikes along the top, some agents were even advising hopefuls that if they hadn't received an acknowledgement of their pitch after six months, they should assume that it hadn't passed muster. Oh, and no phone calls in the interim, please! A less obstructive option presented by others was the opening of brief 'windows' in the calendar when unsolicited submissions would be accepted. But even those, well-intentioned as they may have been, offered cold comfort to aspirants whose patience was already exhausted.

Such frustrations spawned a rash of vanity publishers, promising new authors an instant realisation of their dreams (at a price!) but delivering only disappointment – or satisfaction, if receiving a few paperback copies to impress friends and family was all they'd *really* been aiming for in the first place. An opening for straightforward, efficient and affordable self-publishing would eventually be born out of a reaction to such scams, but that was all for the future and I was faced with the harsh realities of the present. If I didn't find an agent soon, it would be 'goodbye' to evenings devoted to becoming a writer and 'hello' to more constructive rest-time pursuits like sawing, hammering, climbing ladders and hauling out old lavatory pans.

But just before capitulating to a situation that now had '*Flogging a Dead Horse*' written all over it, I did manage to find a sympathetic agent. How did I do it? Well, by employing the scientific principle of throwing a dart at a dart board with my eyes closed, or to be more specific, by the use of a pin on a randomly opened page of the good old *Writers' and Artists' Yearbook*.

*

Libby was a member of a rapidly dwindling fraternity of 'traditional' publishing folk: proudly autonomous, unashamedly idiosyncratic, and happy to leave the ascendant breed of whizz kids dancing to the tune of their bean-counting, profit-obsessed masters. She had a lifetime of experience in books, first as an editor, then as the head of her own independent publishing company, and since its takeover by one of the larger presses, the one-woman work force of her personal 'bijou' literary agency. If ever I needed proof that a guardian angel of struggling scribblers existed, the letter I received from Libby provided it.

She liked my style, she said, the three chapters of *Spanish Farm* I'd sent her showing a nice spark of individuality; a bit rough round the edges, certainly, but refreshingly unaffected and patently honest. If I'd be good enough to send her the rest of the text, she'd make a point of reading it as soon as possible and get back to me with her frank opinion of its potential – or lack of it.

I liked *her* style too: straight down to business, no clichéd excuses about the length of time she might need, and no attempt to appear in any way 'superior'. She was obviously aware of my position at the bottom of the literary heap, yet appreciated my keenness to progress. And, true to her word, she got back in touch a week or so after receiving the complete manuscript. Novice though I was (and at fifty-two considerably longer in the tooth than most), she respected what I was attempting to do, and came across as genuinely interested in trying to help. Here, at last, was a person favourably disposed towards someone with a creative bent who required the refining influence of not just an expert, but one with an open mind as well.

'Two custard pies aren't funnier than one,' was just one of many pieces of advice Libby gave me, but it's the one that comes most often to mind, even after all those years. And she wasn't casting aspersions at the humorous aspect of my writing, which she'd sometimes found a tad earthy for her own taste, but conceded was well suited to the 'rustic' character of *Spanish Farm*. No, what she'd meant by the custard pie adage was that I should avoid the common pitfalls of repetition and using more words than were absolutely necessary to describe a scene or situation. 'Always leave something for readers to work out or imagine for themselves.' And Libby demonstrated exactly what she meant through the use of her blue editing pencil on the pages of my manuscript, which she posted back for amendment every few days. She was unstinting in her attention to detail, using that pencil with the precision of a surgeon's scalpel, and although she could come across as a mite dogmatic at times, she knew what she was talking about and her input was invaluable. In just a matter of weeks, she had honed and polished the narrative meticulously, and had even changed the name of the book to *Finca in Mallorca*, her line of thought being that using a Spanish term for 'Farm' lent a greater sense of place to the title. Who was I to argue?

Over the ensuing few months, Libby took full advantage of her contacts in the most respected 'old school' publishing houses in London – influential people that an outsider like me could never have accessed directly – and they duly demonstrated their regard for her by reading my book and giving comprehensive and fair appraisals. But time after time the familiar old reaction was repeated. The mood may have been more convivial, but the message was just as blunt: 'Your client's book has much to commend it, but we regret it isn't one for us.'

I couldn't blame Libby for eventually throwing in the towel. She had shown that her belief in my book was genuine and had done all she could to place it. But her time was as valuable as any other agent's, and if the prospect of earning even a modest return for her efforts failed to live up to expectations, then it was inevitable that she would have to direct her energies elsewhere. Ten percent of nothing won't pay the rent.

Custard pie metaphors aside, I was given many pieces of advice from Libby that have also stood the test of time. One of the most beneficial (and ultimately prophetic) came in a phone call at the start her campaign to find a taker for *Finca*. While she got on with that, I wasn't to sit back and idly wait for it to be published. If I was really serious about making the grade as an author, I had to keep writing, to utilise everything I had learned to date and build on it. In short, I must start writing another book – now!

Caught completely off guard, I resisted the immediate temptation to tell her that doing up houses, currently our sole source of income, wasn't ideally suited to finding the time and conditions required for even writing letters, never mind another book. Aware that Libby would have told me in no uncertain terms that even the most legendary of scribes had been obliged to make personal sacrifices in pursuit of success, I responded to her advice with a positive mien and the first idea that came into my head.

'So, you reckon I should start work on a follow-up to *Finca in Mallorca*, is that right? OK, that would make sense, because there's still loads of stuff I could write about. I mean, so far I've only covered the first few months of the three years we spent in Mallorca and –'

'No, I'm absolutely *not* suggesting that,' Libby cut in, 'because it would be taking for granted that this book is going to be published, and there's every chance that it won't. And that's no reflection on your writing – just the reality of the book business.'

This came as no great surprise, but took the wind

out of my sails nonetheless. Writing one book hadn't been something I'd planned, and I really hadn't allowed the thought of following it up to take root. Being a probationer property developer was a risky enough way of earning a crust, without taking my eye off the ball to concentrate on something even more speculative. At the same time, here was a consummate publishing professional encouraging me to give writing a serious go. How many accidental scribblers were on the receiving end of *that* kind of luck? Yet I was at a loss as how best to move on. If it was premature to consider writing some more about our Mallorcan adventures, what the hell *was* I to write about? Tricky question, but who better to answer it than my esteemed agent?

'Well, you've made a good stab at non-fiction,' she said matter-of-factly, 'so why not try your hand at fiction next?'

'Fine, but what kind?'

'Detective stories are always popular.'

'Yeah, but I don't read detective stories.'

'So?'

'What I mean is my mind doesn't work that way – you know, all that convoluted mystery stuff with complicated plots and everything. I don't know anything about that sort of book.'

Libby gave a little laugh. 'Perfect! A detective story it is then.'

I allowed myself a few moments to think about that, then said, 'Sorry, but I don't understand.'

'Easy! Look at it this way – even if your detective story turns out to be duff, at least it'll be original!'

'And commissioning editors are always looking for originality, right?'

'Absolutely. But don't bank on it. You'll find in the publishing game that originality is like humour.'

'Subjective?'

'Correct. One man's meat and all that.' She gave another little laugh. 'You know, like a kilted Scotsman wading through a swamp while hoping to avoid any alligators with a taste for haggis?'

I knew what she meant.

*

As I say, I liked Libby's style, and I would have been delighted if our author-agent association had survived, but fate decreed otherwise and I was left ploughing my own furrow once again; except, of course, in the business of doing up houses, where stalwart Ellie was both an inspiration and becoming a dab hand at more refurbishing skills with every project we took on. But how many more properties with potential would we be able to find … and at the right price? That was a question always at the back of our minds, aware as we were that the more popular rural East Lothian became with big city commuters, the more competition there would be for buying old houses ripe for improvement. All the more reason, then, to persevere with my efforts to some day pocket a bob or two from writing books.

I'd come this far, so, as my old farming grandfather would have said, 'Why start eatin' a coo if ye're only goin' to choke on its tail? Press on, boy! Press on!'

* * * * *

Chapter Five

'WALKING ON EGGS'

*

Keeping your cash flow fluid is the obvious benefit of a quick sale after doing up a house, given, of course, that the next project materialises without too much delay. And that depends on two factors: one, the availability of another property that suits your purpose, and two, a purchase price that promises to leave you a fair chance of making a profit. But as already mentioned, as the '90s wore on and more people from outside the area were attracted to the quality of East Lothian country life, so the competition for such properties increased. And so did the prices being paid, which resulted in a reduction of the potential profit margin for anyone aiming for a quick turnover. Like us.

Over the years, we had become conditioned to looking on the bright side when clouds appeared on the horizon, so were inclined to view the changing conditions in the local property market with an assumption that they would level out in time, and we'd trim our sails accordingly. That's the attitude we *tried* to maintain, though the ghost of experiences past kept whispering in our ears that a pessimist is actually an optimist who has discovered the facts. But we'd also become prone to selective deafness when that particular spook was sitting on our shoulders, so we would crack on regardless, while resigning ourselves to the fact that we had no alternative anyway.

We were now in the process of trying to turn over our sixth property in as many years, and it was taking more time than usual. But the market was buoyant and there had been plenty of viewers, all of whom had liked what they'd seen, or tended to give that impression. However, we were now wise to the fact that not everyone who comes to view a house is actually a potential buyer. Many are just spending an hour or two having a leisurely drive through the countryside, and there's nothing like a 'For Sale' sign to prompt a pit stop for nosey time-killers. In fact, our initial inspection of Ca's Mayoral had been a perfect example, albeit that back then Ellie's curiosity had resulted in an immediate sale. But *to* us rather than *for*.

The upside of the delay in securing a buyer on this occasion was that it gave us an opportunity to actually enjoy the fruits of our labours for longer than had normally been the case: a treat that was well overdue, for Ellie in particular. True to form, she had never once complained about having to close the door on the results of months of hard graft without having a chance to enjoy the up-to-date features of a kitchen she had designed herself, or to luxuriate nightly in the bubbles of a newly fitted bathroom. But I knew it rankled. To make matters worse, there had been situations when time lags between projects made it necessary to put all our furniture and personal belongings into storage until conditions allowed us to install them in our latest new 'home', but only until the sale of *that* one made it necessary to put them back into storage again. So, the sluggish nature of this particular selling exercise didn't meet with any complaints from her – or from me for that matter. We would reset our sails when the wind changed.

Since parting company with agent Libby some five years earlier, I had followed her advice by continuing to write whenever time and place allowed, which had meant sticking to the old routine of spending evenings hunched over a makeshift writing table in the corner of a box room full of … well, boxes. The main difference now was that I was hunched over a computer keyboard instead of a ballpoint pen, but my modus operandi remained the same: sit down, engage imagination and see what transpires. And in this particular house I was afforded the luxury, for the time being at least, of having my own comparatively spacious and well appointed 'study' in which to make the most of visits from the muse.

At first I'd thought Libby had been a mite frivolous in suggesting I should write a detective story, bearing in mind that I wasn't in the habit of reading mysteries and therefore knew nothing of what their devotees expected. But when I thought about it some more, I could see what she'd been driving at: the best way to develop my writing muscles would be to give them something challenging to lift – but first having to find that 'something' in a dark room without tripping over it. This was more or less how I set about writing anyway, so I picked a location I was familiar with, a central character I could identify with, a situation that was completely alien to me, and then wrote the first thing that popped into my head. Which turned out to be the inscription on a headstone in an East Lothian village churchyard…

*

Here lies
"BERTIE" McGREGOR *Died 13 July, 1990.*
Aged 77 Years
"DIXIE" McGREGOR Died 13 July, 1990
Aged 5 Years
TOGETHER FOREVER

*

Next, Bob Burns, a farmer's boy turned detective (who happens to have a droll sense of humour) explains to the attendant gravedigger that he has been placing a rose on the grave of someone who, despite being called Bertie, was actually a little old lady. And the five-year-old buried beside her wasn't a grandchild, but her cat. Both Bertie and the cat had been bumped off suddenly, simultaneously and without apparent motive in the flower bed of a local cottage hospital. Whodunnit? It'll be up to Bob Burns to find out.

And that was it. I was up and running on my first

foray into fiction, with no road map to follow, except the markers and milestones which would be revealed by Bob Burns and his fellow protagonists as the story unfolded. I had noticed this same phenomenon when writing about our Mallorcan adventures, but had assumed it was only an illusion created by my familiarity with those *real* characters and the factual situations that they – and I – had been involved in. But now it was happening in a fictional context too, and I couldn't have been more surprised *or* pleased.

Weird and far-fetched though all of this may sound, it does happen, and I found it particularly helpful when making my first attempt at constructing a mystery without a pre-conceived plot. It was a bit like doing a complicated jigsaw puzzle with no picture to refer to. As each piece clicks with another, so the overall image becomes clearer. Naturally, mistakes are made and each mistake begets another, so that going back to 'piece one' to try another match is a regular occurrence. The puzzle, consequently, is a mystery for the puzzle solver until the complete picture is finally revealed: the dénouement of the whodunnit … or the end of *any* brain-teasing yarn, I suppose.

But how does a fictional character help develop the story for you? Well, firstly you have to create someone with an identifiable personality – age, background, looks, moods and quirks – then place your friendly (or unfriendly) Frankenstein's monster into a particular set of circumstances, and chances are that he or she will react in a way that comes naturally to the type of person you've cobbled together. And the fascinating thing is that every character you create starts to interact with the others, either positively or negatively, like jigsaw pieces that genuinely fit or merely seem to at first. Is this only a weird and far-fetched product of an over-active sense of imagination? Maybe, but it works for me. In any event, here's a word of caution for fellow spontaneous scribblers who may be tempted to give it a try for themselves: keep a tight rein on the input of those invented characters of yours, because they're mischievous little devils who, given half a chance, will take over the entire operation. And not necessarily for the better!

*

The bonus months we spent in house number six allowed me time to take stock at last of everything I had attempted to do on the writing front since jotting down that gravestone inscription some five years earlier. Twelve months later the inscription had become the introduction to a full-length detective story which I'd called *The Mallorca Connection*, as a deliberate though somewhat tenuous tie-in with *Finca In Mallorca*, and had appended the subtitle *Bob Burns Investigates*. I had enjoyed the exercise so much that I spent my 'leisure' evenings during the following year writing another *Bob Burns* mystery, this one called *The Sporran Connection*. Both were, to my mind, bona fide whodunnits, with a common denominator of starting in rural Scotland before moving on to more 'exotic' foreign locations: an ingredient which, together with a light peppering of humour, I hoped might help set the stories apart from those in the darker 'Tartan Noir' vein proliferating at the time.

Much midnight oil had been burned and even more grey matter exhausted. Yet, despite my persistent submission of synopses, sample chapters and even the occasional full manuscript, there were no takers for the books. On the plus side, there had been no dismissive comments either, and some feedback was actually of a really positive nature. The *originality* of the storylines was what attracted most agents and publishers who had given them at least a cursory look, but this was often qualified with a remark along the lines of: 'Your book has been rejected because it is difficult to place in any bracket of crime writing currently in vogue.' So, they wanted something original, but only if it slotted neatly into an existing pigeonhole. As contradictory as this seemed at first, reading between the lines I detected a common feeling of uneasiness about those little injections of humour that were a feature of everything I wrote. This uneasiness was actually taking precedence over the alleged value of originality, which reminded me of a piece of advice agent Libby had given me on that very subject: 'Originality, like humour, is subjective, and nobody likes their favourite genre to be parodied – particularly fans of detective stories.'

Talk about walking on eggs! Anyway, I still had a lot to learn, so in deference to those professionals who had taken the time to read my submissions and offer constructive criticism, I thought it only right to give the matter careful consideration. My intention had never been to poke fun at hard-boiled detective stories or, even worse, to make light of serious crimes. Where the humour crept in was always in relation to slip-ups made and clangers dropped by characters whose personalities I had deliberately devised to make such occurrences seem perfectly natural. In any case, the essential component of suspense remained unsullied throughout, and I genuinely felt that timely interludes of light relief actually added to the tension of the ongoing action as well.

Even so, on reading the stories again, I could see how a staunch crime fiction buff might have thought the mickey *was* being taken. Fair enough, I appreciated that such sensitivities exist in all branches of creativity (and none more so than in jazz, as it happens), but from a creator's point of view, the old axiom of 'You can't please everybody' eventually holds sway. So, if some mystery purists were offended by an occasional touch of drollery, that was something I'd just have to take in my stride – broken eggs notwithstanding.

*

In the fullness of time we did find a buyer for house number six, but it took several more months to come by number seven. During the intervening period we had to rent somewhere to live, and this, together with the extended stay in the previous house, meant that our reserve of 'housekeeping' money had been correspondingly depleted. On top of that, the demand for the type of property suitable for our purpose had increased to such an extent that, just to stay in contention, we were having to pay considerably more than we knew was prudent. People from parts of the south-east of England, for example, had more than enough ready cash from selling a fairly modest flat in their own area to enable them to buy a large farmhouse in East Lothian, and at considerably more than the upset price at that. The Scottish system of property sales is based on an 'offers over' procedure: in essence a blind auction whereby sealed offers are submitted by a closing date, with the highest bid prevailing. It was a tricky game for us to be competing in, and one to which we could no longer afford to turn a blind eye.

In the meantime, Ellie would drop hints, subtly but pointedly, about making more constructive use of my spare time. But giving credit where it's due, no matter how late the hour or how aching the limbs, if time was of the essence for the completion of a doing-up project, tiling bathrooms and wallpapering bedrooms always took priority over writing a book or trying to find an outlet for it. At the end of any working day, rejection letters from agents and publishers don't pay the bills. Plus, more often than not, Ellie was already working overtime in those bathrooms and bedrooms anyway, and there's nothing like setting an example to make the dropping of a subtle hint sound surprisingly like a starting pistol!

*

With no doors opening for my fiction efforts, I started to devote more of whatever time I had to finding a home for my original 'baby', *Spanish Farm* alias

Finca In Mallorca. Not that I'd neglected it after Libby bowed out: in fact, I'd probably sent out more submissions for that book than for both of the *Bob Burns* books put together. My hopes of getting it published had never waned, but I always kept in the back of my mind Libby's warning that this might never happen, so tempered my outlook accordingly.

One of the first things I had done was to change the title yet again, only because I thought *Spanish Farm* a bit bland, and I had a suspicion that '*Finca*' could be confused with 'Fink', which in American slang means an untrustworthy or reprehensible person ('asshole' in common parlance). And though conceding that a touch of self-deprecation can have its advantages, I couldn't see any benefit in putting myself down *quite* so harshly as that!

To find a new title I started skim-reading the first page to see what might catch my eye. What did the trick were the final two words in a sentence describing the freak fall of snow that had welcomed us to Mallorca: '*A cold mantle of white was rapidly transforming our sunny paradise into a bizarre winterscape of citrus Christmas trees, cotton wool palms and ... snowball oranges*'.

Perfect! The coupling of those words instantly struck me as snappy, appropriate and quirky enough to attract the casual bookshop browser. And my liking for the new title was shared by many of the book business folk I subsequently approached. Unfortunately, though, they still thought the book itself 'would not fit our current lists'.

More often than not no reason was given, but some

I did receive had me wondering if the senders had been reading the same book. Their comments ranged from 'Too coarse' (I had made passing references to a dog peeing all over me, the egg-laying advantages of a hen with a clean arse, and a claim that sheep can't fart), through 'Too *chichi*' (meaning pretentious and affectedly pretty), to 'Too commercial to qualify for an Arts Council grant'. I thought the last one was a cracker. Did this mean a book could be published about, say, *'The renaissance of naked Highland dancing during the Big Freeze of 1947'*, with the publisher being paid a financial inducement by a culture-promoting government agency just because they deemed the book to be 'intellectual in concept' and, crucially, untainted by the likelihood of selling more than half-a-dozen copies? Another beauty, coming from a self-styled educational publisher this time, stated that they'd like to discuss publishing my book, but on the understanding that, no matter how well it might eventually sell, no royalties would be paid 'because too many aspiring authors these days are only interested in making money.'

But the most frequent observation of all was that the demand for this type of 'travel-related' memoir had been killed off a few years earlier by the phenomenal success of Peter Mayle's *A Year In Provence*. I couldn't get my head round this. Surely the success of that particular book suggested that there *was* a demand for factual stories of the travel-related kind, especially if embracing different circumstances, if set in different countries and told by different voices. Well, many people of influence in the publishing business didn't see it that way, which could be taken, as agent Libby might have said, as a prime example of the subjectivity of originality. To which I'll add a coda of my own:

'It's a wonder more wannabe authors aren't driven to drink!'

* * *

It had never occurred to me that moving house for the umpteenth time might provide the inspiration for writing a comedy novel, but that's what arriving at our next 'project' actually did. And it had nothing to do with slapstick scenes featuring me falling off the back of a removal van carrying a box of fragile dinner dishes, or getting a close-up view of our new kitchen floor after tripping over a doormat with '*Welcome*' on it. Although both of these custard-pie mishaps did happen, it was only when looking back after an adequate cooling-off period (Ellie really *had* loved those dishes!) that their funny side became apparent. But anyway, the inspiration didn't come from such knockabout situations but from meeting our nearest neighbour who, paradoxically, was the absolute opposite of the character who would become the leading man in my first fictional caper...

Old Wullie across the lane was the epitome of an honest, friendly, straightforward and unassuming small farmer. He supplemented the income from his few acres by delivering sundry items of equipment and animal feed for a local agricultural supplier in his trusty old pickup truck, and always accompanied by his wee dog Syd. I was immediately struck by the picture of simple, down-to-earth contentment they portrayed when exiting their farm gate that afternoon. Wullie drew up beside me to introduce himself through his driver's window, chuckling proudly as Syd jumped across from his customary perch on the passenger's seat to offer a welcoming bark and an accompanying few licks of my hand.

It would have been difficult to imagine anyone happier with his lot than old Wullie, a perfect example of a man who didn't have all that much materially, but craved no more than that. I couldn't help but wonder if he would have swapped an hour of my rainbow-chasing experiences in the bright lights of London, the orange groves of sunny Mallorca or even the thousand-and-one-nights setting of a recording session in the Arabian Desert for one minute in this sleepy backwater of East Lothian. I knew he wouldn't and, deep down, I couldn't blame him. But I had to resist any pangs of envy. I had ploughed my own furrow for better or for worse, and it had started to look increasingly likely that turning to my pen might be one way of avoiding the latter – even if 'clutching at straws' did seem an obvious addition to the metaphorical mix.

It was as I was waving goodbye to old Wullie that the inspiration for my next book struck me: I'd write a story about a farmer who, accompanied by his wee dog, tootles cheerfully around the countryside in his pickup truck. The big difference, though, would be that Wullie would be replaced by the fictional Jigger McCloud, a waggish, Jack-the-lad farmer half Wullie's age, with a talent for playing the fiddle, an eye for the ladies and a flair for making a quick buck at the expense of the well-heeled retirees and big-city commuters who were colonising his local village of Cuddyford.

On Syd's seat in the pickup I placed Bert, a randy little wire-haired mutt with an eye for lapdog ladies and a craving for hamburgers. I then allowed the rest of the oddball-but-loveable McCloud family to introduce themselves one-by-one. First appeared Nessie, Jigger's beautiful tomboy of a wife, who sidelined in speedway racing and motocross. Next came his delinquent, moped-mounted Granny; his stunning, keep-it-all-under-wraps-until-you-bag-a-rich-guy daughter Maggie; and finally his less promiscuously-fussy son Davie. Once these leading players had made their entrances, the story almost wrote itself, with a procession of supporting characters materialising in the shape of chinless-wonder aristocrats, bent local politicians, a sinister eastern millionaire, a bunch of toffee-nosed 'townies', a WW2-displaced Ukrainian who ran Jigger's illicit whisky distillery, and a bibulous double bass player who had converted his instrument into a cocktail cabinet. My hardest task was keeping them all under control!

As much as I had fun chronicling the shenanigans of the McClouds and their cast of larger-than-life cronies, I did worry that I may have created a book with an even smaller chance of finding a publishing niche than the *Bob Burns* mysteries. On the one hand, this book wasn't short on originality, and on the other it was brimming with offbeat humour. Both qualities had a high 'subjective' rating, so the difficulty would be finding one prospective taker with a sympathetic attitude towards both. It didn't happen. As one publisher put it, 'While I like your individualistic treatment of the subject matter, which swings joyfully between farce and satire, the overall effect is too off-the-wall for a British public conditioned to comfy-cosy images of country life as depicted in *The Darling Buds of May* and *The Archers*.'

Hence, *The Cuddyford Chronicles*, which had become the book's working title, joined the two *Bob Burns* stories filed under 'Pending' in my computer. I had given fiction writing a good go and, as agent Libby predicted, I'd learned a lot in the process. One side issue I'd also learned a bit about was the practical aspect of script writing. It wasn't a subject I'd ever given any thought to, as I wasn't an avid fan of drama on either film or television. However, Libby had perceived what she referred to as a distinct 'visual' element in all of my literary efforts, and was sufficiently convinced of its potential, particularly as evidenced in *The Cuddyford Chronicles,* to recommend the book to a long-time associate of hers called Celia, who ran a small but highly-regarded script writers agency in London.

It came as a complete surprise to me when Celia, clearly without any thought of short-term advantage to herself, took a real interest in my work and encouraged me to learn as much as I could about the lay-out and working essentials of film/television scripts from tutorial books she suggested, and also from actual scripts of current TV drama series that had been written by some of her clients. I found the subject fascinating, and did indeed take Celia's advice by eventually converting the early chapters of *Cuddyford* into a one-hour pilot script for television. Again, Celia was sufficiently impressed to suggest some alterations I should make before she could finally begin submitting the script to TV networks.

Her eventual pitch attracted some very promising responses, but unfortunately, health issues resulted in Celia's retirement and sad passing before any of them could be developed. However, I had become so taken with the subject and what could be learned from it regarding economy of description and realism of dialogue that I continued to follow her advice. Somehow, I managed to grab enough time between book writing and house doing-up duties to do similar TV-script adaptations of the two *Bob Burns* mysteries and also to write a couple of feature-length film scripts featuring brand new stories that hadn't had a previous life as books. One was *Goblin Hall*, a fantasy adventure for a family audience, inspired by the eponymous ruined castle near the village of Gifford in East Lothian; the other an offbeat comedy set in the Scottish Highlands entitled *The *Other* Monarch of the Glen*.

I told myself that some day I'd get round to finding another Celia to look at them and advise me about the best way to proceed. But for the present at least, all of my writing-related energies would be devoted to finding a publisher for *Snowball Oranges*. There had been a fair few detractors in the seven years since I finished writing it, but at least none had considered the content 'too off-the-wall' for the book-buying public. So, there was still hope … although the list of agents and publishers remaining untapped in *The Writers' and Artists' Year Book* was now looking ominously short.

* * * * *

Chapter Six

'CATCH-22 ... SNOWBALL ORANGES'

*

As the '90s drew to a close, our latest two doing-up projects had hardly yielded any profit at all, and we hadn't seen another property within our price bracket to buy either. It was no longer just a case of affluent 'incomers' paying more for an old house than doer-uppers like ourselves could prudently afford; the problem now was that some buyers were prepared to fork out as much as, or even *more* than, the improved value of a property before any improvement work had even been started.

We had finally been priced out of the market, and if we wanted to continue living in what international estate agents now referred to as '*This beautiful and much sought-after corner of Lowland Scotland*', the only way would be to buy a small house to treat as our home until the wind changed in our favour ... forlorn a hope as that might be. The alternative would be to up sticks and start afresh in an area where property values were lower. But it only took an exchange of glances for Ellie and me to knock that idea on the head. Chasing farming rainbows fifteen years ago had been one thing, but leaving again to look for pots of gold behind old lavatory pans somewhere we might not particularly want to live was quite another.

The upshot of all this was that, after ten years and twelve 'flits', we finally achieved our aim of buying ourselves a house that would be separate from those we planned to sell on. Maintaining a semblance of family life during this period hadn't been easy, but we'd managed it, and our two sons would now have somewhere they could finally regard as a proper parental home. In the interim, they had established independent careers for themselves: Sandy as a freelance agricultural contractor, and Charlie as a graphics designer. Both lived within easy travelling distance, so there would be no problem keeping in touch and getting together whenever the fancy took us. But, with the door closed indefinitely on more selling-on projects, Ellie and I were now faced with the task of finding a way to generate an income. Catch-22.

But, cometh the dilemma, cometh Dame Fortune. Again.

* * *

One of the biggest headaches of moving into a 'permanent' home after living like gypsies for so long was finding a place for everything that had been perpetually shunted in and out of storage, some items having never left the packing cases in which they'd been shipped back from Mallorca twelve years earlier. The problem was further exacerbated by the house we'd bought on the outskirts of Haddington being considerably smaller than Ca's Mayoral, our previous 'permanent' abode. But Ellie had become expert at separating essentials from items which, if not immediately qualifying as clutter, were bound to be before long. I could never quite fathom how she arrived at some of her decisions, particularly when it came to differentiating between potential clutter of mine and essential items of her own.

'You'll have to go through all that old paperwork of yours,' she told me on the first evaluation session in the kitchen. 'I mean, look at all the bundles – bits and pieces of notes and scribbles that go back as far as that record column you did for the *Whajamacallit Weekly* or whatever.'

'It was the *Shetland Times*, and there's historical value in those scribbles – hand written and everything. You know, some day when I'm a famous author dead and gone, that's the sort of stuff that could make a right few quid at auction.'

If Ellie hadn't been in such a hurry, I'm sure she would have stood with her hands on her hips and laughed herself silly. She elected instead to plonk the various bundles in a heap in front of me, with a curt suggestion that I sift swiftly through the contents, salvage any of the *historical* pages, pop them into an A4 envelope for posterity and chuck the rest in the fire. While I did the sifting, Ellie busied herself going through a case full of frocks that hadn't seen the light of day since our last summer in Mallorca.

'You'll be getting rid of that lot too?' I ventured, then nodded towards the kitchen window on which a shower of hailstones was drumming a tattoo. 'A bit on the flimsy side for the Scottish climate, no?'

'Global Warming,' Ellie replied, grinning like a kid on Christmas morning as she re-folded the frocks and arranged them into a neat pile. 'Once they've had a wee freshen up, I'll get plenty more wear out of them yet, never fear.'

As committed as she sounded, I knew from similar situations in the past that most of the frocks would be flogged to second-hand clothes shops when the time was right. But for the moment, they would be kept in readiness for … well, for whatever Ellie might suddenly decide. It would have been futile to comment, so I didn't.

The first papers I sentenced to burning were the rejection letters I had received over the previous eight years. There was quite a stack, and I had initially intended keeping them as some sort of memento. But Ellie was right: they'd never be of interest to anybody else, and it was hardly likely I'd ever want to be reminded of the feeling of disappointment each one represented. I'd make a list of them instead, just to avoid the risk of aiming future pitches at the same target twice.

That's when Dame Fortune smiled on me again, or on one particular rejection letter to be exact. It had fluttered to the floor when I emptied the folder containing it onto the kitchen table, so I gave it a quick read – just for *auld lang syne*, so to speak. Out of all the letters I'd received, I had special reason for remembering this one. It was in reply to the first submission I'd made following the end of agent Libby's involvement, when I was left with no option but to concentrate on the smaller publishing houses she had bypassed.

Chestervale Publishers had only recently been established by two enterprising young English writers who, I was told, had set the company up to publish their own travel books after deciding, presumably, that they'd rather be masters of their own destiny than be dictated to by one of the major presses. Their commissioning editor had asked me to send him the full manuscript of *Snowball Oranges*, had read it and liked it – immensely! The writing actually seemed to 'lilt', was what he said, and the story of our family adventure in Mallorca was consistent with the company's policy of specialising in travel-related memoirs. I'd almost reached for the champagne glasses when something told me I'd better read the rest of his letter first...

'Unfortunately,' he went on, 'as a small and fairly new publisher, we don't yet have what we consider would be sufficient marketing strength to fully exploit the potential of your book, so I very much regret we must pass.'

To be turned down after such a promising build-up was actually a bigger disappointment than all the blunt rejections I'd had up to then. But I'd taken consolation and encouragement from his positive attitude towards the book, and I hadn't forgotten that. Now, seven years later, his letter had 'presented itself' to me again, and it got me wondering if good old Dame Fortune had decided to give me another kick – but with a beneficent boot this time. 'Well,' I thought, 'there's only one way to find out, and it'll only cost the price of a postage stamp.'

A few days later, I received a reply from Chestervale's new commissioning editor to inform me that, coincidentally, they had been in the process of giving further consideration to *Snowball Oranges*, as they were now better equipped to sell it in what had become a more receptive market for this type of narrative travelogue. If I was still interested in having the book published by them, a draft contract would be sent for my perusal.

Bingo! Ten years after scribbling that first sentence on the back page of an old exercise jotter, I was finally about to become a published author. But instead of the anticipated feeling of euphoria, what I experienced was an overwhelming sense of relief, mixed, it has to be said, with a sizeable measure of surprise. No champagne glasses were called for, only a silent offering of thanks to Dame Fortune ... and, of course, to US President Calvin 'Press On!' Coolidge for promoting the power of persistence.

It transpired that, since my first contact with them, Chestervale had developed a reputation for being what some described as 'the reverse highwaymen' of the publishing business, in that they had a way of watching and waiting until they spotted an upcoming trend, before emerging to make what they considered to be a worthy contribution, thereby adding momentum to the trend as well as gaining from being part of it. It was a trick that called for a sharp eye *and* the agility to grab the main chance when it came their way.

Another advantage of being comparatively small was that they were nimble enough to have a book ready for release in less time than it normally took the more cumbersome 'big boys'. But that didn't mean cutting corners, particularly when it came to editorial matters. Although agent Libby had left the *Snowball Oranges* manuscript in ready-to-publish order, Chestervale's young editor Izzie had her own way of looking at things. She worked on a full revision of the text with me (initially by post but latterly via email, which speeded up the process and saved a fortune on stamps!) and while only relatively minor changes were ultimately made, I found the exercise both instructive and highly rewarding. It taught me never to underestimate the value of having your work looked at by a fresh pair of eyes, no matter how fine-toothed the comb you've already used to groom it. I was fortunate to have had the attention of two professional editors who, although of different generations, saw possibilities in my writing and were happy to encourage any 'unrefined' aspects they believed had some value. It seemed that the subjectivity of originality was working in my favour at last.

While the book's final proofreading was being undertaken by Chestervale's typo-spotters, Izzie phoned me to say she had received some feedback from a certain book critic who, as was normal 'lead time' procedure, had been sent an uncorrected proof copy in advance of the magazine he wrote for going to press. 'Would you believe,' she gasped, 'he actually said that "with prose as elegant as this, *Snowball Oranges* is one travel book that requires no illustrations." Honestly, I couldn't disagree more!'

This hit me like a slap on the face. I knew I was no Laurie Lee, but to put down an unexpectedly glowing compliment like that seemed a bit brutal. Suitably crestfallen, I was stuck for an apt reply, so just mumbled something about agreeing with her that the praise was well over-the-top. But even so, I hadn't thought my writing was all *that* bad.

I heard Izzie having a little chortle to herself. 'No, don't worry, it's not the bit about the prose being elegant. What I disagree with is the bit about the book not needing illustrations, that's all.'

I covered the phone to muffle a whistle of relief.

'Hello! Peter – are you still there?'

'Yeah, yeah, just ehm…' I faked a cough. 'Just a frog in my throat. So, illustrations you say? Hmm, 'fraid we've only got snaps taken by visitors on their hols. Standing with cheesy grins under an orange tree – that sort of thing. Wouldn't be any good for the book.'

'That's not what I'm thinking about anyway. No, what caught my eye was a line in your publicity bio that says you were something of an artist at school. So, what I'm thinking about is black-and-white drawings to put at the start of each chapter. Think you can handle that?'

'Depends what you've got in mind. I mean – schooldays – that's over forty years ago, and I haven't really –'

'Look, it doesn't matter how naive the drawings are. Fact is I quite like naive drawings.'

'Well, actually, naive was never my thing – not when it came to drawing anyway – so anything I could come up with now would probably still be … well, not naive.'

'Doesn't matter. Just do what comes naturally – like your writing – and we'll see how it works out. OK?'

I really wasn't too comfortable about this, but while I was mulling over how I could talk her out of it, Izzie was already giving me details of what she was after: ten individual illustrations – one per chapter – each one depicting a scene, thing or person relevant to its chapter – and all to be delivered by the book's ready-for-the-printers deadline in two weeks time.

I covered the phone to muffle another whistle, this one panic-generated.

'OK then, Peter, I'll leave that with you,' Izzie chipped in. 'Just send the illos down one-at-a-time as you do them. Talk soon. Cheers!'

Izzie was certainly of a much younger generation than agent Libby, but she had the same get-right-down-to-business attitude, and I liked it – or decided I did after I'd caught my breath. I was now an integral part of the book-publishing process, and the publisher, having taken the risk of investing in an unknown author, was entitled to call the shots regarding how and when the various links in the chain should come together.

I counted myself lucky to be involved, so swept the cobwebs off my old drawing pad and started work on those chapter headings without further ado. However, if I'd thought that this, following the two years I'd spent writing the book and a further eight trying to get it published, would be my final contribution to the process, I had another think coming.

* * *

With a plethora of new books coming onto the market every week, it's inevitable that some get lost in the crush. Big publishers can ensure their new releases are noticed by allotting budgets to promotional campaigns that are beyond the means of their smaller competitors, and as Chestervale were in the latter category, every marketing penny in their purse had to be put to best use. High-priced hype was out. So, instead of throwing money at banner ads on the sides of buses, they had to make do with their PR lady using her persuasive powers to get as many media mentions as possible – for free. Not easy, when so many publishers are vying for coverage in the limited amount of column inches devoted to books in the mainstream press. In any case, there's no chance of being considered for a review in one of the serious broadsheets unless you're a well established literary 'name', or the one-in-a-million rookie who's been shortlisted for the Booker Prize. Accordingly, Chestervale concentrated on wooing key regional papers and a few carefully selected magazines, and I chipped in with a list of old media contacts in the areas of music, farming and even property development that wouldn't normally be promotional targets for a travel-related book.

But once again, it was the highwayman approach that did as much as anything to help get *Snowball Oranges* noticed initially, particularly when the natural pairing of citrus fruits was deftly brought into play. Chestervale's lookouts had espied a book in the current bestseller charts with *Lemons* in the title, so they slipped *Snowball Oranges* into the trade lists of forthcoming releases while the citrus connection was ripe for the picking. The ploy got the book over the notorious 'discoverability' hurdle with booksellers, after which, like any new book, it would depend on the public to determine whether it kept running or fell flat on its face. For it's an inescapable fact that there is no better promotional tool than word-of-mouth – and, ironically, it's the very one that no amount of money can buy.

* * *

The London Book Fair, one of the industry's biggest and most prestigious showcases, was scheduled to take place in late March, a couple of months before the official release of *Snowball Oranges,* now sporting *One Mallorcan Winter* as a subtitle. As we knew Chestervale would have a stand featuring the latest additions to their catalogue, it seemed an ideal time to say hello in person and also to sample the atmosphere of this annual gathering of the movers and shakers of the publishing world.

Situated in fashionable West Kensington, Olympia is a vast indoor arena that hosts major events as diverse as horse shows, rock concerts, boxing matches and even a beer festival. The Book Fair is more than just a shop window in which publishers show off their latest releases to UK trade buyers. It's also a global marketplace for translation rights between British companies and their foreign counterparts, with specialist literary agents very much to the fore in negotiating deals that can involve extremely large sums of money. To say there was a buzz about Olympia would be an understatement.

Chestervale's stand, though not the biggest in the hall, had an attractive, welcoming look, and I was pleasantly surprised to see that pride of place had been given to a blow-up of the *Snowball Oranges* front cover. Three young members of staff were busy offering Tunnock's marshmallow *Snowballs* and Terry's *Chocolate Orange* segments to a group of clients, while also regaling them with details of the other titles on display.

Naturally, I was delighted by the attention being paid to my book, but equally impressed by the company's inventiveness in their choice of promotional handouts which, for a modest outlay, probably did more to fix the name of the book in people's minds than some flashy, bells-and-whistles presentation ever would. The members of the Chestervale team were a cheerfully energetic group of young people who were obviously keen to make the most of every minute to promote all of their company's wares. Even so, they took time out to introduce themselves and tell us they were 'very excited' by all the interest being shown in *Snowball Oranges*.

They seemed to be sincere in what they were saying, but even if they were merely being polite, it was considerate of them and greatly appreciated. I immediately thought it a pity that Chestervale didn't publish fiction, because on this showing they would have done my *Bob Burns* and *Jigger McCloud* yarns proud. But the owners of the company knew their own business best, doubtless considering it better to be with the front runners in one race than down among the also-rans in two.

There was no doubting it had been worthwhile coming all the way from Scotland to meet Izzie and a few of her colleagues and to thank them for the good work they had done on my behalf. Even so, while under the same roof as most of the publishers who had sent me rejection letters over the years, I thought it might be a good idea to put out a few feelers. You never know. Face-to-face contact can make all the difference. Sometimes.

It soon became apparent, however, that the book fair was a place where marketing people congregated to propagate the sales potential of the 'product' for which authors provided the basic ingredient. But back in the year 2000 – twenty-four years before the establishment of an exclusive Authors' Lounge – it was not, by and large, an occasion that required their presence. And that's fair enough. Why, for instance, would a convention of bacon manufacturers want to have pigs running about the place? Not that I was treated with anything less than courtesy by the people manning the stands I popped into. But it was pointed out to me that most of their time at the fair was taken up with appointments made well in advance, and few if any were made with authors. Book *festivals* were where the spotlight shone on authors, whereas book *fairs* were where the people behind the spotlight did their best to make money for all concerned – including authors. Point taken. I was, when all was said and done, only a tiny fish in a vast pond, and if I wanted to hawk my literary efforts around publishers, this was not the best place to do it. To which was added the inevitable: 'Get yourself a good agent.'

Talk of the devil – or an angel, maybe?

As we were heading for the exit, I heard my name being called, and turned round to see a petite, conservatively-dressed woman in her mid-forties whom I'd noticed talking to another member of staff on the last stand I visited.

'I hope I'm not being rude,' she smiled, 'but I couldn't help overhearing snatches of your conversation back there, and when the chap called you by name as you were leaving, it dawned on me that I'd been exchanging letters with you not that long ago.' Noticing my blank expression, she canted her head inquisitively. 'Your Mallorcan memoir and the *Bob Burns* mysteries? Remember me now?'

I had exchanged so many letters on the same subjects with so many people that she might as well have given me a telephone directory and asked me to pick a name at random. 'Sorry, I can't quite place...'

'Please, no need to apologise. It's just that if I'd known you were going to be here I'd have arranged to meet you. I'm Bette. Bette Tanner of the Eltan Literary Agency. I said I liked your writing, remember?'

I did indeed remember, because she was one of the few people who had actually replied with anything other than a stock rejection letter, which suggested that she'd given the manuscripts more than a cursory flick through before turning them down. I had thanked her for that in a letter at the time, and I thanked her again in person now.

'But it was the humour, wasn't it?' I said. 'You thought the humour didn't help – at least in the mysteries.'

'Just my opinion, of course, and there will be many who disagree. Anyway, I do like your writing, particularly the non-fiction, so it's a shame I couldn't place your Mallorcan book for you.'

'Not to worry, it eventually found a publisher anyway.'

'Yes, I noticed the display on Chestervale's stand. Very impressive.'

'Well, they're giving it every chance, and I'll be eternally grateful to them for that.'

'So, uhm, can I ask you which agency negotiated that contract for you?' She smiled again. 'Sorry – just being nosey.'

'No problem. But there wasn't *any* agent involved. I did it all by myself.'

'Great! Good for you, and I'm sure you covered all bases. But contracts…' I noticed the hint of a squirm. 'Well, you can't be too careful – royalty rates, translation rights, options on subsequent books and so on. That's when having an agent is so imp–'

'Forgive me for interrupting. I understand what you're saying and I appreciate your concern, but the reason I didn't have an agent to guide me through the contractual maze was that none of the many agents I approached about the book offered to take me on as a client.'

Grimacing slightly, she nodded her head. 'Touché! I asked for that, didn't I? But honestly, I didn't mean to be patronising. It's just that, when it comes to contracts…'

'Yes, I know – the devil's in the detail. But don't worry. After half a lifetime in the music business, I know a bit about record contracts, and you'd be surprised how similar they are to the book publishing variety, so I don't think I've dropped any major clangers. Anyway, I'm in the process of joining the Society of Authors, and their legal eagles vet contracts carefully for members – for free.'

'Yes, I always advise new clients to join the Society – great upholders of authors' rights, so you're doing the wisest thing.'

'I think so, although I realise they don't pretend to take the place of an author's agent when it comes to actually *getting* a publishing contract. But I'm just taking one thing at a time right now, and I'll cross the bridge of negotiating translation rights and so on if and when I come to it.'

'You've got the right approach,' she said, 'and although I've never dealt with Chestervale personally, I'm sure you'll do well with them. But anyhow, I hope I haven't delayed you too much.' She offered Ellie her hand. 'It's been nice meeting you, and I did enjoy reading about your orange-growing escapades in Mallorca. I envy you – seems you had lots of fun.'

'Well,' said Ellie with a little sigh, 'fun's a bit like humour, I suppose.'

'Like humour?'

'Yes, subjective. You know – one person's laugh is another person's groan. But yes, thanks, it was a great experience and we did have our fair share of fun.'

When all our goodbyes had been said, I told Ellie she'd surprised me with her slightly acerbic use of the 'subjective' word.

'You're a fine one to talk,' she retorted, 'putting in those digs about getting no support from agents and everything.'

'No offence was intended and I'm sure none was taken.'

'Snap! Anyway, all that aside, I'm not a bad judge of character, and I actually got pretty good vibes from that lady. I mean, she went out of her way to introduce herself, and it's not as if she had any kind of axe to grind.'

'Yeah, she came across as all right to me too. And she said to keep in touch – to let her see anything I write in the future.'

'Only non-fiction, though.'

'Hmm, no further forward for *Bob Burns* and *Jigger McCloud*, I'm afraid'

'Yep, everything still depends on *Snowball Oranges*, but that's a light at the end of the tunnel we didn't have when we sold that last house.'

'Good point, Ellie! Onwards and upwards it is!' Suitably heartened, I took Ellie by the elbow and shepherded her out. 'Come on, there's a pub along the street there. We'll celebrate with a pie and a pint.'

'Charmed, I'm sure, considering I don't drink and never eat pub pies!' Ellie cast me an admonishing glance. 'And in case you didn't notice, we passed a nice wee Italian restaurant on the way here in the taxi.'

'So?'

'So, you can either have a pie and a pint on your tod, or join me for a nice creamy Spags Carbonara ... which *you* can wash down with a glass of plonk, of course.'

'You drive a hard bargain, Ellie, but if we can up the ante to two glasses of plonk and a nip of *Strega,* you've got a deal!'

* * * * *

Chapter Seven
'WHEN THE BEST WAY FORWARD IS BACK'

*

No matter how many newly-released records I'd received copies of in the past, I always got a kick out of seeing the end result of something I'd been involved with. But I had never experienced quite as big a buzz as when I opened the box of complimentary copies of *Snowball Oranges* I'd been sent shortly before its publication in early June 2000. And it wasn't just the jacket design that grabbed me, eye-catching though it was, or the reproduction of my drawings at the head of each chapter, or indeed seeing all those scribbled notes of mine finally transformed into upwards of three hundred perfectly printed pages. It was more a sense of relief that the project had actually materialised at all, for even after seeing the promotion the book had been given at the London Book Fair, I had harboured a dread that it all amounted to some sort of fanciful bubble that was bound to burst at any moment. Ten years from writing the first tentative sentence to finally holding the paperback edition in your hand is a long time to wait without getting just a tad neurotic.

But I also allowed myself a wry smile at the quote from a magazine review that had been placed prominently on the book's front cover: '*This should do for Spain what "A Year in Provence" did for France.*' Although I genuinely doubted that my book would emulate anything like the massive popularity enjoyed by Peter Mayle's trail blazer, I couldn't help but see the irony in the comparison, after being told so often that the demand for my type of travel-related memoir had been killed stone dead by the success of that very Peter Mayle book. But Chestervale's Dick Turpin-inspired instincts had come to the fore again, and I could only hope that their brandishing of that review would deliver the desired message to book sellers and buyers alike.

The initial test was due to take place a couple of days later, when I'd been invited to do my first ever book signing, and at no less eminent a venue than one of Edinburgh's foremost bookshops, Waterstones at the west end of Princes Street. Quite how Chestervale's sales folk had managed to set this up baffled me, because I was still completely unknown and there had been no formal 'launch' of the book, other than a press release and review copies being sent to selected media targets. I approached Waterstones with some trepidation, which was far from quelled by a handwritten notice taped to the door, stating simply that: '*Peter Kerr will be signing "Snowball Oranges" here today at 6pm.*' It struck me that the immediate reaction of anyone who read this would be: 'Who's

Peter Kerr and what the hell is a snowball orange?' Still, maybe some sort of enlightenment would be provided inside the shop.

A table had been placed in a prominent position at one side of the entrance, and on it were two dozen copies of the book and a ballpoint pen. But no enlightenment, anywhere. I was staring vacantly at the table when a sales assistant, her face wreathed in smiles, appeared from the inner sanctum of the shop.

'Peter, I presume! Hi! I hope you like the wee display we've put on for you.' She picked up one of the books and gave it the quick once-over. 'Nice cover, eh?'

'Yes, it's eh … yes.'

'Anyway, I'll get one of the boys to bring you a chair and that'll be you all set.'

'Yes … thanks. But, ehm, no offence, but how will anyone know who I am? I mean, there's just the notice on the door, and that doesn't really –'

'Ach, don't worry about that,' she breezed. 'People are nosey, and when they see you here with all your nice books, they'll ask you soon enough.'

'Right, OK,' I nodded, trying not to appear too much like a fish out of water, but feeling very much like one nonetheless. 'So, you think quite a few … I mean, do you normally expect quite a few, ehm…?'

'Punters to turn up?'

'Uh-huh.'

'Never can tell. Just depends if they like the author.'

'Or even know who he is?' I suggested, meekly.

'Aye, dead right!' she agreed, straight-faced. 'For instance, last week we had a kids' author here – big name – comedian bloke, always on the telly – and you could hardly get in the door for mothers and their sprogs.' She raised a nonchalant shoulder. 'Other times it's only a few ... maybe twenty or so, coming and going, like. Not all at once.'

I cast my eyes round the empty foyer. 'I hope nobody gets hurt in the stampede tonight, then.'

'Aye, very good – very droll,' she chuckled, then glanced at the books on the table. 'So, eh ... your book there. Comedy as well, is it?'

I nodded my head, stoically. 'It's got a bit of humour, yes. But that's subjective, isn't it?'

Thankfully, she showed no interest in contributing to that pointless debate.

'OK, I'll leave you to it,' she said, still smiling. She looked at her watch. 'Give it about an hour. Awkward time of day, this. Folk hurrying home from their work and that.'

'So, all those copies of the book here ... what happens if nobody buys any?'

'Not a problem. All on sale-or-return. We just send them back to the publisher. No loss for us. Oh, which reminds me – the manager apologises for not coming to see you. He's off to a meeting at one of the other branches.'

With that, she was gone, leaving me to stand gazing optimistically towards the door, like one of those stone statues on Easter Island. However, any customers who did pass through paid no attention to me, my books or the ballpoint pen, but scurried past into the main body of the shop to make their purchases and retreat from the premises with equal haste. As the sales assistant had said, it was an awkward time of day, this: 'Folk hurrying home from their work and that.'

Just as it was nearing the sixtieth and last minute of my lonely vigil, one member of the public did approach the table, but slowly. She was staring around and upwards with an air of detachment, as if trying to give the impression that she wasn't heading for my table at all. She was of oriental appearance and gave me a stiff little bow before picking up a copy of *Snowball Oranges* and opening it. She nodded approvingly while reading. My hopes of a sale rose, but were abruptly dashed when I noticed she was holding the book upside-down. She gave me another stiff little bow before replacing the book and heading for the door, purposefully.

I told Ellie all about the so-called book signing when I got home that evening. 'Talk about a non-event!' I grumped.

Ellie adopted a consoling mien. 'Well, I'm sure they were only breaking you in gently. I mean, you'd probably have freaked if there had been a queue the length of Princes Street.'

'Yeah, but Chestervale would've been delighted if even half a dozen had turned up. Instead of that, they're gonna get all those books back on sale-or-return.' I raised my eyes to the cloud of doom hovering above my head. 'Bloody writing career's buggered before it's even started.'

I pretended not to hear Ellie's stifled snigger, preferring to continue wallowing in my puddle of self-pity. 'Telling you – I had a feeling something negative was about to happen when we came out of Olympia that day.'

'Be fair, the Spags Carbonara wasn't as bad as *all* that. OK, it wasn't great, but it was better than a pub pie.'

I could tell Ellie was trying to make light of the situation, but I wasn't about to let that get in the way of what was developing into a good-going whine. 'What I'm saying,' I went on, 'is that coming away from the London Book Fair I noticed a sign pointing to Earl's Court.'

'Who's he?'

'It's not a *he*, it's an *it* – another big arena like Olympia – just a stone's throw away.'

'OK, but what's Earl thingy in London a few weeks ago got to do with a book-signing in Edinburgh today?'

'It wasn't a few weeks ago, it was 1961 … or maybe '62.'

Ellie was getting exasperated now. 'You're not making any sense. What *are* you talking about, for heaven's sake?'

'It's just that I got thinking about the early '60s, when I was with the Clyde Valley Stompers and we were actually featured in a colour TV demonstration in Earl's Court. It was the National Radio Show – a big deal, and colour TV was still a novelty, so a band had to be a pretty big deal as well to be picked for a big-time demo like that.'

'I still don't get the connection with Waterstones bookshop in Edinburgh.'

'Well, a few days after the Earl's Court gig we

were playing in the Royal Albert Hall to something like five thousand people.'

Ellie pouted sagely and nodded her head. 'Oh, *now* I get it. And a few days after being part of the book-business razzamatazz at Olympia you were appearing before absolutely nobody in a bookshop.'

'Yeah, and even appearing at the Albert Hall didn't save me from getting the bum's rush from the band – eventually.'

Ellie was shaking her head now. She gave me a reproving look. 'Trying to make a connection between these two things is complete balderdash, and you know it!'

She was right, of course. I was allowing self-doubt to get the better of the 'Press on!' attitude that had seen us through life's ups and downs so far. I hunched my shoulders, feeling duly chastened, but unable to shake off the worry that I hadn't come up to Chestervale's *or* Waterstones' expectations.

Ellie must have read my thoughts. 'Come on, cheer up! One book-signing flop isn't the end of the world. If nothing else, it's another experience to add to many others – and not *all* of them got off to a good start either, don't forget.'

'Which could be the understatement of the century,' I acknowledged, dryly.

'You said it! Anyway, put the book signing behind you and try to take something positive from it.'

I dipped into my breast pocket and pulled out a ballpoint pen. 'This positive enough for you? I nicked it off the signing table at Waterstones.'

Ellie took the pen and rolled it between forefinger

and thumb. 'Says here it was made in Japan.' She looked me in the eye and winked. 'Which draws a fitting line under the entire episode, no?'

I gave her a stiff little bow, and we left it at that.

*

The next morning, I got a call from Chestervale, not to give me the bum's rush, but to apologise on behalf of Waterstones for the 'slight administrative hiccup' that had adversely affected my book-signing session. Apparently, someone had got a couple of dates mixed up and they hadn't twigged until the afternoon that I was booked to appear that actual evening. Hence the hurriedly-prepared A4 notice taped on the shop door. But I wasn't to worry: no harm had been done.

This, of course, was assuming my self-confidence had come through unscathed, which it ultimately had – if only because of Ellie's pep talk the previous evening. What this experience had served to remind me about was that recognition has to be earned. There are no shortcuts, as even the TV comedian who had packed them in at Waterstones the previous week would have had to earn his stripes in his 'day job' before becoming a draw as an author. I was starting from scratch.

It had been thirty-five years since I last achieved any measure of recognition as a performer, and none of the jazz fans from that era would have had any reason to associate me with a person of the same name who was flagged up to be autographing pieces of frozen fruit in a bookshop. What I couldn't afford to forget was that I was almost sixty years of age, and being given a chance to re-invent myself in a way I hadn't thought remotely likely a few months before. So, to balance things up, I also had to expect a few kicks in the pants, which I could either regard as a means of gaining forward impetus or use as an excuse to sit on my backside and feel sorry for myself.

Chestervale explained that though it may have seemed premature to thrust me in at the deep end with a signing date at a major book store in the heart of Scotland's capital, they had been presented with an opportunity that was both unexpected and too good pass up. Waterstones was the UK's biggest book-selling chain, with dozens of branches throughout the country, and as a result of *Snowball Oranges* being ordered for the Edinburgh event, the book was now listed in the company's central-buying database. Gold dust.

Nor was I to concern myself about the risk of unsold books being sent back. Sale-or-return was an accepted method of trading in the industry – all factored into a publisher's financial commitment – and while its implementation would indicate a book's failure to attract buyers, *Snowball Oranges* was emitting no such signals. On the contrary, the feedback from retailers since the London Book Fair was pointing to the likelihood of re-orders rather than returns. And there could be no better base from which to build a promotional campaign – with me, it was stressed, doing my bit to further the cause. There may not have been enough money for advertising on the side of a bus, but it didn't take much to buy a ticket. I'd better get ready to hit the road!

But paradoxically, the best way forward initially would be to take a few retrograde steps in order to foster connections in my own back yard. An interview was featured in the local *East Lothian Courier*, which triggered an enquiry to do a meet-the-author event at my local library, which in turn resulted in the promise of a signing session at my local bookshop. All of these were relatively modest affairs, but taken together could create the possibility of each feeding off the other in terms of positive reaction to the book.

It was tempting to hope that a word-of-mouth endorsement for *Snowball Oranges* might just have been set in motion. As I already knew, not only was this the most effective marketing tool of all, but also one that no amount of money could buy. Yet I recognised that such good fortune was far from being a foregone conclusion in this case. There had been initial curiosity in my home area simply because I was a local guy who'd had a book published. Which was all well and good, but would that interest sustain, never mind spread?

Helping develop the momentum would be my priority now. This was early June 2000 and internet retailers such as Amazon were still regarded in the book trade as embryonic seven-day wonders, while social media platforms like Facebook and Twitter weren't even twinkles in the most imaginative of publicists' eyes. Consequently, while travelling on a metaphorical bus might not immediately feature in the process, I *would* have to hit the road, and the sooner the better at that.

* * * * *

Chapter Eight
'A LATE HARVEST WORTH WAITING FOR'

*

Chestervale had sent me some posters featuring the front cover of *Snowball Oranges,* so, with those stowed safely in the boot of the car, Ellie and I set off on a whistle-stop tour of south-central Scotland. I felt a bit like a door-to-door hawker paying cold calls at bookshops, especially since most of the proprietors hadn't yet noticed the book's release listed in the trade press. All the same, every one of them took time to listen to my spiel, before explaining that space for displaying posters was limited, but that they'd do their best to find a place for mine. Bookshop folk in general seemed a friendly lot, and although I was probably just one of many wannabes who routinely 'dropped by' to plug a new book, they had a way of making you feel they were pleased that you'd taken the trouble. They reminded me of people I'd met working in record shops back in the day: in their element surrounded by stock in which they had a genuine interest, and believing that making a living by selling it was actually a privilege.

And as it happened, the subject of making a living was seldom far from our own thoughts just then either. The £500 advance on royalties I had received may well have been slight compared to the sums major publishers would routinely dole out to, say, a sports personality credited with being the author of a new autobiography. But I realised that Chestervale were operating on a much more canny basis, and just as when I became a professional jazz musician in Germany almost forty years earlier, I would gladly have signed their contract for nothing. When opportunity knocks, why expect a tip from the postman?

I was totally committed to doing all I could to help get sales of *Snowball Oranges* rolling, no matter how long it might take. And while I was aware that delivering posters to a scattering of bookshops in one area of the country would have a correspondingly limited effect, it was a start. But the cold reality of attempting to make a living as a full-time author was already beginning to kick in. As is the norm in publishing agreements, I would receive sales statements and associated royalty payments biannually. However, even if the book sold in sufficient numbers during the initial accounting period to cover the advance royalty, earning £500 in six months would hardly amount to a realistic 'living'.

To put it in round figures, a first-time author who doesn't happen to be a 'celeb' might expect to be paid a royalty of ten percent of the fifty percent of the book's retail price received by the publisher. So, for a book retailing at £7 (a typical price for an average length paperback in 2000), the author would receive 35p per copy – more or less.

It was clear that, no matter how frugal our lifestyle, reaching the stage of being able to live off royalties alone could take a very long time, if ever. Meanwhile, we would have to keep dipping into the 'housekeeping' fund we had used to live off while doing up properties. The big difference now, of course, was that speculative book sales, as opposed to even a tumble-down heap of bricks and mortar, had no value as collateral, so although we had become accustomed to walking a financial tightrope over the years, we were now doing it without a safety net.

You might say that the obvious solution would have been for me to get an honest, down-to-earth job for a change. But there were two problems attached to that way of thinking. Firstly, there aren't too many career openings for a sixty-year-old, one-time cattle-rearing, barley-growing, orange-picking, record-producing jazz musician; and secondly, even if there were, it'd be difficult to hold down even a casual job and still have time to go all out promoting a book. Which gets you thinking about how, in days of yore, almost everyone who aspired to be an author had to be of independent financial means. For instance, if Robert Louis Stevenson hadn't had the financial rock of a prosperous lighthouse-building family for support, would he have found the time to write *Kidnapped, Treasure Island* and the rest while obliged to double as a night watchman on a building site? Unfortunately, the same conditions do occasionally persist to this day, one way or another.

I had fully expected sales of *Snowball Oranges* to start off slowly, then build up gradually – if luck was on our side. What I couldn't envisage, though, was how luck would manifest itself. It was obvious that my fleeting visits to a handful of bookshops wouldn't do the trick. At best, a measure of goodwill may have been established with a few outlets in a relatively small part of the country, but even that would quickly evaporate if it wasn't followed by members of the public actually turning up to buy the book. I willed myself to keep thinking positively about Chestervale's assertion that indications were promising in that respect, but the old roller coaster trope kept nagging away at me, as did visions of sitting huddled in front of a night watchman's brazier at the foot of a half-built block of flats. But why was I giving myself all this strife? I had always prided myself on having at least *one* virtue, and that was patience, which necessity had long since turned into a stock-in-trade. Predictably, Ellie wasn't slow to remind me of the fact...

'Will you *stop* pacing up and down! *Hon*estly! That carpet was only laid a month ago, and the way you're going it'll be worn through in half and hour!'

'Yeah, yeah ... just, you know, thinking...'

'Look, the publishers have said they'll keep you posted about any developments, so relax! The book's only been out for a week or so, don't forget.'

'Yes, but I like to keep busy, and this hanging about waiting for news... I mean, it was OK when we were going round those bookshops – at least I was doing *some*thing, but this waiting is driving me bloody nuts.'

Ellie made swift capital out of that. '*Don*'t go nuts, then. Be busy. There's still all that turf to lift in the garden – for the patio area you promised to make, remember?'

'Ah, well, yeah, but maybe I'll get a call to do another book signing or something, so…'

'OK,' Ellie shrugged, '*go* nuts, then, but take your shoes off while you're doing it.'

I opted to start work on the patio preparations, which would have to be done eventually anyway, like a multitude of other tasks that were needed to make this house a home. Since our return from Mallorca, Ellie had endured twelve years of living like a nomad, so it wasn't expecting too much for me to control my restiveness for even a few more weeks. I readily accepted that, but it was the thought of nothing happening at all on the book front that was making me fidgety. Putting it in farming terms, it had been a decade since the seed was sown, and although green shoots had finally appeared, there was still the very real possibility of a failed harvest. What's more, our 'housekeeping' cache wouldn't last forever.

It seemed that fears about the consequences of abandoning the security I'd been guaranteed as a civil servant were finally emerging from the back of my mind, where I'd kept them locked away for so long. But allowing such negative thoughts to challenge the spirit that had sustained us through thick and thin would achieve nothing, so, borrowing from another farming analogy, I put my trust in the arrival of some sunshine to ripen the crop. And it didn't take long.

The very next morning, while I was busy heaving barrow loads of divots away from the planned patio area, Ellie came skipping out of the house, all smiles and waving a piece of notepaper...

'That was Chestervale's press lady on the phone. She was really excited – jabbering away nineteen to the dozen, but I managed to write down the gist of it.'

I scanned Ellie's scrawled notes. 'What's this?' I said, frowning. 'She's got the...' I peered more closely. '...the *Farmers*?'

Ellie nodded, enthusiastically.

I checked the note again, then squinted at Ellie. 'The *Farmers*? But ... but that's rhyming slang for ... haemorrhoids!'

'Eh?'

'Piles.'

'What!'

'You know ... the Farmer Giles ... the *Farmers*, for short.'

'Oh, for goodness sake!' Ellie tutted, snatching back the piece of paper. 'You can't read the Queen's English, that's your trouble. 'Look!' she stabbed at the paper with her index finger. 'It's quite clear, if you'd open your eyes. They're all newspaper names – and magazines too, some of them.'

I responded with a compliant shrug. 'OK, you have the floor. Tell me all about it.'

'This one – your rhyming slang thingy – that's the *Scottish Farmer* magazine. Then there's the *Caledonia,* and that one beside it there is the...' She paused to allow closer inspection. 'That's the … ehm…' After a few silent moments, she looked at me for assistance, reluctantly.

'Well,' I sighed, 'at first glance, it reads *Wooden Popery*, but I've a hunch it's an attempt at writing – in Queen's English – *World of Property,* which, if I'm not mistaken, is also a magazine, right?'

'Yes, which is exactly what I've written. And also…' Ellie took a deep breath and proceeded to decipher the rest of her hieroglyphics for me.

The sum and substance of it all was that Chestervale's distribution of advance information sheets and review copies had paid dividends, and more generously than they might have expected. Not just reviews, but comprehensive features were being published in key 'provincial' newspapers such as *The Scotsman* and *Glasgow Evening Times,* as well as in nationals like *The Independent* and *Sunday Express*. What's more, the prudence of cultivating specialist magazines had resulted in full-page spreads in those publications whose names I had misread in Ellie's notes. And there was more to come, including radio interviews, both local and national, plus a spot on Scottish Television's *Room At The Top* current affairs programme.

After just a fortnight, the book's first print run of 1,500 copies had sold out, having hit No 2 in Amazon's Travel Writing chart and snapping at the heels of the pace-setting Bill Bryson's *Down Under*. Copies of the *Snowball Oranges* paperback were literally flying off the shelves. Editor Izzie was quickly on the phone…

'Good news, Peter! We're taking up our option on a sequel. And – wait for it – we'll need you to have it written by next March, which gives you almost nine months. That OK?' Izzie was buzzing. My head was spinning. Things had been moving so fast it was all I could do to organise the commitments I'd already made to help promote the existing book, never mind write another at the same time.

'Nine months, you say, Iz?'

'Yup, gotta hit while the iron's hot.'

'Wow! It's just that ... well, it took me two years to –'

Izzie cut me short with one of her little chortles. 'Don't you go worrying about that. Nothing like a tight deadline to get the creative juices flowing.'

I knew those wouldn't be the only juices flowing if nine months passed and I'd only written half a book. In fact, I was already on the verge of wetting myself at the very thought.

Then Izzie hit me with another continence tester. 'Oh, and we'll need some more drawings too.'

'Drawings *too*?' I warbled.

'Oh, absolutely. They really added that certain touch of originality to *Snowball Oranges*. Our customers love them, so doing the same for the follow-up is a no-brainer.'

'A ... no ... brainer,' I parroted, vacantly.

'Absolutely. One for each chapter, as before.'

'As ... before,' I droned.

Izzie chortled again. 'That's right. Oh, and I know what you're thinking. You'll need another contract, right? Don't worry – already in hand – improved advance royalty and everything. *Much* improved, actually.'

That snapped me out of it. Advance royalty. Damn! I'd been forgetting about that side of things. Writing and illustrating a new book while going around plugging the old one was one kind of problem, but earning enough to live on in the meantime was quite another. Still, this was what I'd been working towards for a very long time, so it was now a matter of stepping up to the plate, both creatively *and* commercially.

'OK, Izzie,' I breezed. 'A sequel it is – to be finished by next March, drawings and all.'

'Excellent!'

'Meanwhile, just send the contract up and we'll take it from there.'

'Splendid! I knew we could count on you. Oh, and just one little thing – the book will have to be about the same length as the first. About ninety thousand words, give or take a sentence or two. That OK?'

The sound of 'ninety thousand' being articulated so definitively had me almost wetting myself again, but I crossed my legs, shuffled over to my computer, sat down and awaited the arrival of the first word. Phew! Only eighty-nine thousand, nine hundred and ninety-nine to go – give or take a panic or two.

At least the new contractual terms offered some comfort. The advance royalty had been increased fourfold – £1,000 on signature of the agreement, with a matching sum payable on delivery of the finished manuscript. As much I was grateful for this welcome input to our coffers, I also had to acknowledge the business acumen behind its calculation. In essence, I was being paid from the publishers' income already being generated by the sales of my existing book. However, I took no issue with that. It reminded me of a saying that had long been taken as gospel in the music industry: *'Your future is only as good as the success of your last record'* – or words to that effect.

In any event, simply putting my signature to the contract had provided us with a slightly better financial cushion than before. All I had to do now was earn the second tranche by coming up with the goods by next March.

'Nine months – shouldn't be a problem,' Ellie remarked in a matter-of-fact way. 'Just the normal gestation period.'

'Yeah, well, putting it that way,' I replied deadpan, 'at least I now know how it feels to be told you're up the duff!'

Ellie responded with a slow, sagacious shake of her head. 'I don't think you do,' she said. 'No ... I *really* don't think you do!'

* * * * *

Chapter Nine

'OLÉ?' ... NO WAY!'

*

True to their word, the good folks at the public library in my home town of Haddington wasted no time in hosting a meet-the-author event. It turned out to be a fairly informal affair, well attended by people I knew, and more like a communal chinwag than a bona fide book reading. Tackling the latter wouldn't have come easily to me in any case, although I was aware that it was the accepted form on such occasions. Standing with a copy of my book held aloft while I recited carefully chosen passages from notes wasn't for me. Apart from anything else, I was no Sir Laurence Olivier when it came to the eloquent delivery of a prepared script. Actually, as well as having a jazz musician's instinct for improvisation, I also regarded myself as more akin to a mumbling Marlon Brando in terms of diction.

This was an image that dated back to my last year at school, when I had to take my turn at standing on stage during morning assembly to read excerpts from the scriptures in front of the entire complement of pupils and staff. It resulted in the headmaster taping one of my performances and playing it back to me in the hope that I'd be shocked into improving my 'vocal projection'. The revelation certainly made me more conscious of my muttered delivery, but as none of my fellow pupils ever complained (probably because they weren't listening anyway!) I wasn't about to be bulldozed into taking elocution lessons. I regarded the way I spoke as a mark of workaday Scottishness, a distinction to be afforded the respect it deserved. In fact, if Sean Connery had been around in his stellar glory back then, I would probably have adopted his *shelebrated lishp* as well.

Simon Kesley, the owner of Haddington's small but bustling bookshop, was also as good as his word in arranging a signing session, which was prominently advertised in the previous week's edition of the local paper and consequently well patronised by a steady stream of customers. It's only fair to say that many of them were friends and acquaintances from as long ago as my schooldays, a few of them greeting me with wisecracks like: 'I hope your book-writing's better than the way you sign your name. Looks like a fly with diarrhoea just staggered across the page!' It was all good-natured banter and worked wonders as an antidote to the feeling of failure that still lingered after my wipe-out event at Waterstones in Edinburgh. Simon Kesley had taken what I saw as a big gamble by ordering five dozen copies of the book, but assured me that any stock remaining after the signing session would be snapped up within a few days. I admired his optimism and appreciated his support, which would prove to be unwavering as time went by. Chestervale's PR people had been right: build your promotional campaign from familiar foundations up.

I regarded those two home-town events as experience-building exercises in advance of my first *proper* reading engagement, which was scheduled to take place in no less daunting a venue than James Thin's Bookshop in Edinburgh. Thin's (now Blackwell's) was one of the city's oldest and most venerated book retailers, its proximity to the university having long established its first-floor events room as a platform for serious readings by equally serious authors – and primarily those with an academic dimension to their books. Why they had asked me to do a 'turn' was beyond my comprehension, but while acknowledging that the occasion could well turn out to be a bloodbath, I gritted my teeth and prepared to step into the arena, armed only with the intention of persevering with the more-of-a-chat-than-a-recital formula that had seen me emerge unscathed from my debut at Haddington Library.

As I approached the shop, I caught a glimpse of a familiar building just round the corner. The Royal Oak pub in Infirmary Street is a popular haunt of Edinburgh's folk music fraternity, and I recalled having visited it to check on a couple of singers in my capacity as a record producer some twenty years earlier. I remembered it as being a cheery and welcoming old establishment, just the place for a chap to down a quick glass of pre-performance Dutch courage. I stepped inside and duly downed one.

All the same, I can't deny that it still felt as if flocks of fruit bats were doing aerobatic displays in my stomach as I climbed the stairs in Thin's and heard the babble of voices coming from above. A hush descended as I entered the room, and what seemed like a vast sea of faces (probably only twenty at the most) followed my progress to the lectern that had been provided for this evening's 'speaker'.

Suddenly, I felt alone, exposed and threatened in a way I'd never felt before, even when addressing audiences of hundreds or even thousands in jazz clubs, ballrooms and concert halls all over the country. But on those occasions I'd only been announcing the next number, with maybe the odd quip thrown in about whichever of the boys was being featured. Back then, it was a frequent source of amusement at the start of a gig for us to exchange whispered hopes that the doormen had frisked the customers for concealed blowpipes and poison darts before letting them in. The thought struck me again now, but without the same degree of frivolity. As a member of a band, I'd been only one of seven potential targets for would-be assassins, and if I'd split a clarinet reed or taken a coughing fit in the middle of a chorus, there had always been at least one of the other musicians ready to step in and cover for me. Not any more.

Anyway, there was nothing else for it: I'd either have to make a start as a solo 'act' there and then or make a dash for the nearest window and throw myself out. Perhaps, if we'd been on the ground floor, I'd have settled for the latter, but I didn't fancy my chances against thirty feet of gravity, so took a beep breath, smiled bravely and said, 'Good evening.'

To be honest, I don't remember much of what transpired after that. I was on auto-pilot, winging it for dear life, but actually starting to enjoy the experience when the shop's manageress appeared at the back of the room and gave me the 'wind-it-up' sign. I'd always been regarded by those who knew me as a fairly talkative sort of bloke, finding it difficult, when conditions favoured, to stop gabbing once I'd warmed to a theme. And that had apparently been the case this evening, to the extent that I'd over-run my forty-five minutes 'spot' by almost a quarter of an hour. Some people had buses to catch, as the manageress said by way of apology to the audience at the start of her brief but hearty vote of thanks for my 'entertaining and refreshingly a*d-lib* approach to the talk', which she was sure everyone had enjoyed as much as she had.

And it seemed to me that they had too, judging at any rate by the reaction of a trio of elderly couples who came over to speak to me at the end. They had spent frequent holidays in Mallorca over the years and were fascinated to hear first-hand about what it was like to live there, particularly in a location so far off the beaten tourist track. But was it true, they wanted to know, that our old Mallorcan neighbour actually cleaned our chimney by climbing onto the roof and stuffing a live hen down the chimney pot? I assured them it was indeed true, but their concerned expressions turned to smiles of relief when I added that the hen was more put out by Ellie's well-meaning attempts to give it a bath after the event. Anyway, flapping chimney sweeps aside, they assured me they'd be buying copies of *Snowball Oranges* at the front desk on their way out of the shop and visiting some of the places I'd mentioned on their next trip to the island.

All positive, confidence-bolstering stuff for me.

Then two dark-haired young ladies, who already had copies of the book in their hands, emerged from a corner of the room, where I'd noticed them hanging back until all the other members of the audience had left. Their books had page markers protruding from the edges. The girls were smiling, but in a slightly admonishing way – a bit like teachers in an infant school doing their best to make one of their charges feel less mortified about having pooped his pants in class.

'*Qué tal?*' they said in unison.

'*Muy bien, gracias,*' I replied, slipping into Spanish without even thinking, which would not have been the case if I'd been asked anything more complicated than 'How are you?' It had been thirteen years since we lived in Mallorca, and even a limited vocabulary becomes rusty if not regularly exercised.

'We are from Mallorca – exchange students here in Edinburgh,' said one of the girls. 'I am Setta and this is my friend Cati.'

'To a Louse,' said Cati.

'*Perdón?*' I queried, instantly wondering if she was proposing some kind of toast – and if so, to whom?

'*O wad some power the giftie gie us,*' they chorused in a fair attempt at a Scottish accent, '*To see oursels as others see us.'*

Now I got it! They were quoting from Robert Burns' famous ode to a flea he had seen clinging to the bonnet of a stylish young lady sitting in front of him in church one day. Presumably, this was the girls' way of saying that they'd found my foreigner's depiction of their homeland revealing. 'Ah, so you appreciate the work of our national bard?' I beamed. 'Yes, what he says in that poem is very true – very observant.' I gave a nervous laugh. 'For a moment, though, I thought I might have offended you somehow.'

'But you *have* offended us,' Setta said, looking suitably stern, but clearly still in school-teacherly mode. She held up her copy of *Snowball Oranges* and opened it at one of the marked pages. 'You see, as Mallorcans we do not approve of *la corrida de toros*, the bullfighting.'

For the life of me, I couldn't recall making even passing reference to bullfighting in the book, never mind associating it specifically with Mallorca. In any case, although I was aware that there was a robust anti-bullfighting lobby on the island, with which – after witnessing the opening stages of just one *corrida* – I wholeheartedly concurred, it didn't alter the fact that there was a large, long-established and (at that time) well-patronised *Plaça de Toros* in the capital city of Palma, with other bullrings in the provincial towns of Alcudia, Muro, Felanitx and Inca.

'Sorry,' I said, 'but you've lost me.'

At that, Cati pointed to the offending entry on Page 23, which described the conclusion of my first meeting with the two dogs that belonged to the previous owners of the orange farm we had just bought. The mutts clearly resented our presence on their patch, and expressed their desire to see the last of us by peeing on a front wheel of our car, then back-heeling sprays of gravel over the bonnet, as if to say, '*Olé*, and *adiós, amigos*!'

'You see,' the girl now explained, 'it is the *Olé* word that we find offensive, because it is the crowd's exclamation of praise for the matador when he is tormenting the bull in the arena.'

'Yes,' her friend confirmed, 'and you have also used it in the title of the last chapter of your book.' She showed me the relevant entry in her copy. 'Look! *Olé Hogmanay* you call it, and there are no bulls in Mallorcan New Year celebrations.'

'*Correcto*!' her chum concurred. 'And we have been to your famous Old Year's Night party here in the Princes Street of Edinburgh, and we never saw no bulls there neither!'

I couldn't help smiling at that last remark (Spanish-style double-negatives and all), and the girls soon saw the funny side of it too, giggling tellingly when I said that while there may not have been bulls in the Edinburgh streets at midnight on Hogmanay, plenty two-legged animals would have emerged from the pubs when they finally closed in the wee, small hours. Although the connection was tenuous, I tried to point out that my use of the offending word in that particular example had only been an attempt to give a Hispano-Scottish flavour to the Mallorcan New Year party about to be described in the book. There had been a bare-bummed Scots bagpipe player involved, as they might recall? So, all I could do was apologise for the inappropriate use of the '*Olé*' word on both occasions and assure them that I would be more cautious if alluding to the well-crafted thoughts of Robert Burns in future.

I treated the girls to a bottle of wine in the Royal Oak round the corner and reminisced about Mallorca for a while, then left them singing along with a folk group belting out *Flower of Scotland*, while a TV set on the wall showed highlights of our national rugby team being thumped by England.

Aye, to see oursels as others see us, right enough…

*

The event at Thin's Bookshop taught me two more lessons. The first was that, if the audience there had been anything to go by, the type of people who attend book readings aren't there to pick faults in the author's presentation, or to make him feel in any way on trial. On the contrary, they are willing him to do well, while welcoming the opportunity to engage with the person whose latest book they have read – or in my case, whose *only* book they *may* read, if they like the cut of his jib. They know most authors aren't likely to double as stand-up comedians, Shakespearean play-actors or indeed street-market sales-pitchers. They see them as more likely to be fairly introverted individuals who spend most of their lives cooped up alone in a proverbial garret, hunched over the present-day equivalent of a quill, an inkwell and a scatter of stubbornly-empty sheets of paper. They want the poor sod to enjoy this rare opportunity to bond with fellow humans, and they do their best to make it happen. In essence, book-loving people are by nature affable sorts, whether selling an author's work in a shop or listening to him talk about it.

The other thing I learned was that, despite my avowed intention not to, *reading* from your book is actually not such a bad idea, even if it's only a snatch or two here and there. And my reason for saying this is that one lasting memory I do have of my off-the-cuff address is that there were a couple of occasions when, as they say in thespian circles, I 'dried'. I suddenly ran out of something to say – just momentarily, but even those fleeting seconds seemed like forever, made all the more awkward by the sound of members of the audience clearing their throats and the sight of others exchanging whispered comments. This embarrassing turn of events could have been avoided if I'd had a straw to clutch at in the form of a list of pages in the book that contained suitably snappy anecdotes to quote. I got away with it on this occasion because I was talking to a room full of seasoned literary-event patrons who recognised that I was new to the job – a sort of 'mature apprentice', as it were – and they accepted my little drop-outs as understandable shortcomings. That they gave me a hearty round of applause at the end of my stint was, I hoped, a sign that at least they had liked the cut of my jib. But I realised I'd have to work at doing better next time. Which didn't take long to come round…

*

Thanks to the folks at Haddington Library, my details had been added to the Scottish Book Trust's directory of authors available for speaking engagements under the auspices of their Live Literature Scotland scheme. This is a Scottish Arts Council facility set up to help fund and support approved author events organised by libraries, local book festivals, schools, colleges and community organisations like writers' clubs, book groups and even Women's Institute meetings. To encourage authors to participate, a fee of £100 per session plus basic travelling, accommodation and subsistence expenses was payable in those days (duly increased over the years), with a sizeable proportion of the total cost covered by the Trust. Not only is the scheme a highly commendable way of boosting literacy within all age groups and at every social level, it also provides an extremely valuable platform for the promotion of new books – and generously subsidised at that. This is manna to small publishers with limited budgets, so Chestervale were delighted that my name had been added to the Live Literature list. Being on the list would count for little, however, unless I was invited to take part, and that privilege could never be taken for granted. I'd have to establish myself as a good enough 'draw' first, which gave me another Catch-22 situation to grapple with.

Then, at the behest of an inspired local librarian, along came Dame Fortune, this time aided and abetted by Bacchus, Ceres and Apollo, those merrymaking old gods of booze, food and music. How, the librarian asked me, would I feel about fronting a book-reading session that took the form of a Spanish-themed soirée? The plan would be to have a CD of Flamenco music playing in the background as the audience arrived and seated themselves at tables, where a tasty selection of tapas and a glass or two of vino awaited them in preparation for being regaled with my tales of sunny Mallorca.

I didn't have to be asked twice. I knew from past experience how helpful the availability of liquor and grub can be in attracting customers to gigs involving even the most obscure of bands, so why shouldn't the same formula work in a literary context? Consequently, on a chilly autumn evening in the charming (though distinctly un-Spanish) town of North Berwick on the East Lothian coast, I undertook the first of what would prove to be many similarly fortified and, on most occasions, well supported 'reading' engagements throughout the UK and far beyond. Serendipity! Dame Fortune and her trio of good-time deities had done me a timely favour.

* * * * *

Chapter Ten

'DOWN TO EARTH WITH A DRAM'

*

It was now August 2000, less than two months since the publication of *Snowball Oranges*, and John Gibson, the legendary diarist at the *Edinburgh Evening News,* had quoted Chestervale Publishers as confirming that this was their biggest and fastest seller to date. The initial print run of 1,500 copies had been repeated many times over, and sales continued to climb. Although the elusive word-of-mouth phenomenon appeared to have provided the impetus, it was impossible to attributed this to any one factor. In some ways, it reminded me of the unlikely success of *Amazing Grace* all of twenty-eight years earlier, insomuch as it had been a low-budget project, its likelihood of attaining 'hit' status depending on an unforeseen stroke of good luck. But unlike the single blast-off on national radio that launched *Amazing Grace*, it could be that a *series* of comparatively small occurrences – perhaps even those early mentions in relatively modest-circulation magazines – had been responsible for creating the spark that ignited public interest in *Snowball Oranges*. We would never know, but all that really mattered was that enough people had shared their enjoyment of the book to have started the snowball rolling.

It's worth mentioning, though, that the greatest difference between the *Amazing Grace* record and the *Snowball Oranges* book was that the latter wasn't selling by the million. Not by a long chalk. But it was doing a helluva lot better than expected, and I couldn't have asked for more. Every night, in fact, I would go to sleep counting my lucky stars – and occasionally just a few Mallorcan snowflakes too.

It was also towards Mallorca that promotional attention would be directed next, albeit speculatively. While what seemed like spontaneous combustion was now driving demand in the UK, one potentially valuable overseas market had still to be tapped, namely the English-speaking expat community in Spain. I'd always been told that native Spaniards weren't all that keen on books by foreigners giving their impressions of what it was like to live among them, but since no translation into Spanish had yet been mooted, that particular bridge would be crossed when or if we came to it. Meanwhile, Ellie and I hopped aboard a Mallorca-bound plane at Edinburgh Airport and took off on a mission to promote the original English-language edition.

One thing I'd already found out since undertaking 'reading' engagements which involved travelling was that I wasn't much good at writing 'on the hoof'. My natural inquisitiveness about things going on around me may have been an advantage when it came to the observational aspects of writing, but it didn't lend itself to blanking my senses off from the outside world when work was in progress. And since I had made a contractual commitment to deliver in short order the completed manuscript of the book that was now going under the jocular working title of *Son of Snowball Oranges,* one day was all that could be allotted to this trip.

Editor Izzie knew full well that the March deadline we had agreed would be a tough one for me to meet, so had suggested an arrangement whereby, whenever I'd completed a chapter, I would send it to her for editorial comment. This was a tricky one to comply with from an author's standpoint, as concentration was continually having to be switched between working on the next chapter while simultaneously re-working the last. And on top of that, I had the chapter-heading illustrations to draw. I was being kept on my toes all right, but we were on schedule (just!) and a certain operating rhythm had developed – something like the rock-breaking chants of a chain gang being replaced by the steady 'ping' of emails. And as if all that weren't enough, bookings for Spanish-themed 'reading' engagements had started to come in from farther and farther afield, so this flying visit to Mallorca had to be just that.

*

Straight off the plane, we paid courtesy calls to two specialist bookshops in Palma city which catered for the island's international community and stocked books in many languages, including English. Perhaps not surprisingly, my introductory spiel was met with polite but slightly blasé reactions in both places, giving the impression that an English-language book about Brits growing oranges in Mallorca was no more remarkable in their view than, for example, a book in Danish about Danes exporting early Mallorcan potatoes to Iceland. I could see what they meant, sort of, but left them with a poster apiece anyway. At least they'd know what their local sales rep was on about if he mentioned *Snowball Oranges* next time he called.

Which took us to our next port of call: the headquarters of a company called Distribuidora Rotger, principal wholesalers of books in Mallorca and the neighbouring Balearic Islands of Ibiza and Menorca. Rotger had links with Comercial Atheneum, their counterparts on the mainland, so making *Snowball Oranges* known to the management at Rotger might open up a potentially lucrative channel to English-language retail outlets throughout Spain; in particular the burgeoning expat enclaves on the Costa del Sol, Costa Brava and Costa Blanca. This was the link Chestervales' sales people had asked me to sound out on a personal level, their theory being that a handshake and a smile from the actual author could be worth several cold phone calls from the UK, especially if having to converse in Spanish!

Cue Jock Burns, my old Jack-the-lad chum from Haddington, who had lived for many years in Mallorca and had helped us enormously when we first moved to the island. His contacts had proved invaluable in many respects, as had his well-earned reputation as a stop-at-nothing Mr Fixit whose exploits would ultimately provide the material for many an amusing anecdote in my books. Jock was also a fluent Spanish speaker and could conduct a conversation with a high-level civic dignitary as comfortably as with a half-cut holidaymaker in the bar where he played piano to supplement his income as a school teacher.

Thanks in no small measure to Jock's skills as an interpreter (as well as his customary injections of disarming small talk and blatant baloney), trading lines were established with Rotger that would give Chestervale access to a potentially fruitful export market, not just for *Snowball Oranges* but also for any of the other books in their catalogue that might appeal to émigré Brits in Spain. Jock had come up with the goods again, but not without grabbing a piece of the action for himself by sweet-talking Chestervale into taking him on as their personal PR man in Spain – for an appropriate remuneration, *naturalmente*. Jock was a great believer in the maxim that there is no such thing as a free lunch, unless of course he happened to be on the receiving end, which he invariably was. Like many of Jock's money-making ploys, his deal with Chestervale would die a natural death after a few months, but both parties benefited to some extent while it lasted and parted company with no hard feelings.

Qué será será. Or, as Jock would say, 'Stuff it! *Mañana*'s another day!'

First thing next morning, I headed for the offices of the *Majorca Daily Bulletin,* the island's legendary

English-language newspaper, while Ellie took a well-earned break from book-related business to revisit some of her favourite clothes shops in the trendy and conveniently placed Avenida Jaume III. I'd known Luis, the *Bulletin*'s features writer, for many years and had made an appointment to see him when arranging this trip. Ever the sharp-eyed news hawk, he cut straight to the chase by asking me if it was true that Michael Douglas, the Hollywood superstar who owned a large estate on the island, had been in touch with me to make an offer for the film rights to *Snowball Oranges*.

'Yes and no, Luis,' I replied. 'Yes, he's been in touch, and no, he hasn't enquired about film rights.'

Luis squinted quizzically. 'So, OK, when you say he's been in touch…'

'Just that he sent a letter via the publishers saying that he'd read the book when he was last here and enjoyed it.'

'And that was *it*?'

''Fraid so,' I shrugged, 'but it was a nice touch, coming right out of the blue like it did.'

'Hmm,' Luis pouted, 'but you don't get letters from the likes of Michael Douglas if there isn't an angle. He must have *some*thing in mind.'

'Well, that's as may be, but a polite letter is all there is to it right now, and I won't be counting any chickens.'

I could tell Luis was disappointed that I hadn't been able to give him the scoop he'd been hoping for, but he got down to the job immediately in hand without further ado and took some notes about my book-related visit before summoning a photographer to snap me plucking an orange from the nearest tree, which happened to be an ornamental fig plant standing in the corner of the office. Well, they say it's first impressions that count in newspaper pics, and an orange is an orange. In any event, I could depend on the good old *Daily 'B'* giving my book a generous plug in their upcoming weekend edition: always a must-read for seasoned expat residents and in-the-know visitors alike.

At that time, there were two British-owned bookshops close to the west of Palma: the Universal Bookshop in the international resort of Portals Nous, not far beyond the outskirts of the city, and the Bookworm, a tiny establishment situated just off the main drag a bit farther out in the bustling holiday Mecca of Palma Nova. To date, both had been having *Snowball Oranges* shipped out from England in dribs and drabs as required, so I had arranged in advance to call by to thank them for going to so much trouble and to sign any copies presently in stock. It was a small gesture, but one I hoped would be appreciated by the owners, as would my news that they might soon be able to source the books locally.

What the Bookworm shop lacked in size was more than compensated for by the enthusiasm of Mo, its ebullient and equally diminutive Scottish owner, who had invited me to do a meet-the-author session the moment she learned of my impending visit. I'd been in the shop a couple of times before, so was keen to find out how she planned to fit the presentation into a space that was hardly big enough to swing a mouse in, never mind a cat. Located in the corner of a small plaza facing the local branch of McDonald's, the Bookworm was overlooked by apartment blocks rising above a hotchpotch of souvenir and beach-wear shops, tapas bars, liquor stores, cafés and pizza parlours: not the most obvious of settings for a 'literary' event, perhaps, but with an unpretentious, happy-go-lucky atmosphere, which Mo herself epitomised.

She was standing in the doorway of her shop to greet me, the smile on her face as warm as the midday sun.

'I'm expecting a really good turn-out,' she beamed, indicating a large blackboard on an easel at one side of the door. 'I've been advertising the event all week, and everybody's talking about it.'

Sure enough, the multi-coloured chalk announcement stated all that needed to be said and even featured a drawing of snow-bedecked oranges in one corner. Wee Mo had made a big effort and I told her so. Then, getting down to practicalities, I peeked over her shoulder into the shop. There still wasn't enough floor space to accommodate more than half a dozen people, and they'd need to have been standing shoulder-to-shoulder at that.

'But, just wondering, Mo ... I mean, unless you can turn the place into a sort of Dr Who's elastic-sided Tardis, how can we...?'

Mo released a peal of giggles. 'No, no, no! Don't be daft!' With a nod, she drew my attention to the blackboard again. 'See, at the bottom there ... the big arrow ... where it says *"HERE AT 12.30pm TODAY"*.'

I took a close look. 'But – but,' I faltered, frowning, 'it's pointing to the bar next door.'

'Aye, that's right!' Mo cheerfully chimed. 'Brilliant, eh? I mean to say, you surely didn't think I'd – you know…'

'Well, I did wonder,' I admitted with a sheepish smile. 'So, ehm, yeah … in the pub, you say.' I looked towards the bar, with customers sitting at outside tables under sun shades, and the clatter and clink of glasses and the sounds of uninhibited carousing coming from within. There was also the sound of a jukebox competing with the drone of a TV newsreader and the 'ping-pong-clatter' of a fruit machine. All typical features of a Spanish boozer and all perfectly acceptable as such. But for a *book-reading* event? What, I wondered, had I let myself in for?

'Anyway, you'll be fine,' Mo breezed. 'Tolo the barman's a real good *amigo* of mine and he'll look after you, so don't you worry about anything.' She nodded towards the dim interior of the bar. 'We've set things up for you at the back corner in there. Should be nice and quiet for your talk. And besides, I'll be just next door.' She glanced in the direction of the entrance to her shop, through which two potential customers were passing, then patted me on the arm, raised a shrewd eyebrow and smiled, 'Gotta look after the business, eh?'

In a swirl of ankle-length cotton she was gone, and I was left to acquaint myself with my new *amigo* behind the bar: a grey-haired, wiry chap, with a twinkle in his eye and a cheerful but worldly expression that suggested a long career at the sharp end of the Mallorcan hospitality trade.

'Ah, Señor Pedro!' Tolo grinned, his manly handshake followed by a slap on the shoulder that almost knocked me sideways. '*El autor famoso*, eh?'

I did my best to explain in my rusty Spanish that I wasn't actually famous, and not even a proper author: just an ordinary *hombre* who scribbled some stories in his spare time.

But Tolo would have none of it. He insisted that, as he had already told all his regulars that a famous author from England was making a personal appearance in his bar today, a famous author I was. And that was that.

I hunched my shoulders in grateful resignation, thanked him for the compliment, then leaned over the counter and whispered, 'Only one thing, Tolo...'

'*Sí, señor?*'

'...I'm from Scotland, *not* from England, OK?'

'Ay-y-y-y! *Lo típico!*' he guffawed, slapping my shoulder again. *Sí,* the Señora Mo had told him many times about this: how telling a Scotchman he is English is almost as bad as telling a Mallorcan he is Spanish. He cupped a hand to his mouth, checked that nobody was within earshot, then said with a conspiratorial wink, '*Viva la independencia, no?*'

I returned his wink, then squinted into the shadows at the back of the room. 'Looks as if there are a few people waiting for me. I'd better go and get started.'

Tolo grabbed me by the wrist. '*Un momento,* Señor Pedro.' He turned round, selected a bottle from the gantry, then plonked it on the counter in front of me.

'The *Chivas Regal*! The *numero uno* Scotch whisky for the *numero uno* Scotch *autor*!' He then proceeded to gurgle a goodly gargle into a tumbler and handed it to me with a flourish. 'Get that doon ye, pal,' he demanded in a commendable stab at a Glasgow drawl. 'Ye cannae whack a guid fuckin' swally!' Clearly, he had been well tutored in the social niceties of Scotland by the kilt-clad lads with rolled-down socks and Doc Martens who invaded the adjoining resort of Magaluf every July. But he was none the worse for that, as their inherent bonhomie was reflected in his presenting me with an accompanying glass of beer. 'A hauf an' a hauf, son,' he grinned, referring to the time-honoured routine of Glasgow bar flies ordering half a 'dram' of whisky (a robust measure, the exact size of which would traditionally have been determined by the pourer!) chased with half a pint of heavy ale. 'Nae bother, eh!'

I didn't have the heart – or common sense – to tell him I wasn't a whisky-drinker, far less a connoisseur, so said I would just take his kind offering with me to sip while I talked my talk. But Tolo wasn't buying that. There was nothing better for the voice, he assured me, than lubricating it with a decent dose of whisky. *Dios mío*! he had seen it often enough in his time: the more whisky the Scotchmans drank, the more they talked. 'So, Señor Pedro, get it doon ye!'

With another flourish, he took a glass from under the bar and clinked it against mine, though I noticed he had prudently charged his with straight water. Still, I couldn't let my country down, particularly as a group of local guys at the other end of the bar were now watching us intently. I inhaled deeply, closed my eyes and downed the whisky in one.

'*Estupendo*!' Tolo enthused while I suppressed a puke and the guys at the other end of the bar sniggered. Tolo then indicated my tumbler of beer. 'Now the other hauf, China. Get that doon ye as well, eh!'

I'd been nicely suckered, but only in a jokey, playful kind of way: doubtless a variation of situations Tolo had witnessed countless times during bravado contests between young bucks on the first night of the annual Glasgow Fair holidays in Magaluf. At least I had only been competing against myself and was free to admit defeat before I suffered any real damage. On reflection, I'm actually tempted to believe that the 'get it doon ye' ploy had been planned by Mo and Tolo to reduce the risk of my being spooked by the prospect of 'performing' in a boozer. Safer, in other words, to sedate the horse in advance than have him bolt the course when the tapes go up.

But they needn't have worried, for I had already assumed that the members of the audience seated in the murky far corner of the bar were unlikely to be expecting too much in the way of cultural edification from me anyway. Judging by the suitcases parked beside their tables, they were regarding this as a time-killing interlude between vacating their holiday accommodation and the arrival of the bus to the airport. And despite what I'm sure had been Mo and Tolo's best efforts to publicise the event, only six people had turned up.

I introduced myself and chirpily asked if I could

join the group, eliciting nods and mutterings of assent all round. I suppose it could have been all too easy to take umbrage at Mo's offhand way of presenting this 'event', but I saw it from another perspective – even if partly brought on by the mollifying effect of Tolo's generous 'swally'. To me, Mo was a commendably hard-working though easy-going type of person who minded her own business (literally) and expected others to do likewise. She ran a tiny bookshop, and I happened to have written a book which she had generously volunteered to help promote, no matter how limited and unconventional the means at her disposal. The ball was now firmly in my court and I prepared to give it my best shots.

It transpired that the members of my audience were actually three married couples – in their forties, I guessed – and although from different parts of the UK were on first-name terms, having spent the past fortnight rubbing shoulders in the confines of the same hotel. As it was obvious from their demeanour that the end-of-holiday blues had already started to kick in, they were cheered slightly when I told them that what was about to ensue was nothing more formal than a go-as-you-please chinwag. And the husbands at least were even more elated when I told them to feel free to order themselves more drinks whenever the notion took them. This, I assured them, would not detract from proceedings in any way.

What actually ensued could be described – with a slight stretch of the imagination – as an authentic version of the simulated Spanish-themed events that were to become a regular feature of my meet-the-author dates back home, even if this one did lack the sedate atmosphere that would be regarded as a prerequisite of, say, distinguished literary pageants like the Edinburgh International Book Festival. Nevertheless, it's only fair to give Tolo credit where it's due, in that he *had* shown admirable consideration by unplugging the jukebox and fruit machine and turning off the TV sound as soon as I took my seat. I greatly appreciated this selfless gesture, acknowledging that, like Mo, he had a business to run and it seemed unlikely that my transient sideshow would contribute much to its immediate profits. So, while his everyday entertainments were temporarily silenced, the sounds of his everyday sources of earning a living continued unabated...

The coffee machine hissed, spat and bubbled, cups and saucers rattled, trays clattered, glasses clinked and bottles clunked, waiters shouted orders into the kitchen and the group of local lads at the end of the bar yelled obscenities at a football match being played minus commentary on the telly. While this merry mayhem may not have proved an ideal background for 'normal' bookish gatherings, compared to being faced with the task of holding the attention of a group of jaded package tourists in the tranquillity of more conventional surroundings, it actually served my current purpose surprisingly well. It reminded me of a saying reputed to have been much quoted by downtrodden farm workers when giving their wives a reality check in times gone by: *'Blessed are they who expect nothing, for they shall not be disappointed.'*

Yet it would have been unfair to apply this dictum

without reservation in this instance, because during the criss-cross of conversation I learned a fair amount about how to convey aspects of the 'real' Mallorca to people who might not become aware of them during a typical sun-seeking fortnight by the beach. And if that resulted in Mo selling a few more copies of *Snowball Oranges*, then mission accomplished. But the prospects of that happening were tempered by one of the husbands in the group admitting to me at the end of my chat that the choice they'd been faced with on leaving their hotel that morning was between spending an hour with me in the bar or paying a visit to Palma Nova's famous Marineland zoo park just along the road.

'Wow!' I grinned. 'Some compliment! I mean, I've seen the shows at Marineland myself – terrific! – and I never dreamed I'd ever be pitted against their dancing dolphins and performing parrots, far less beating them into second place.'

'You weren't, mate! It costs a bloody arm and a leg to get into that place, and coming here was free – apart, of course, from the price of a drink, which me and the lads were gagging for anyway.' He tapped the side of his nose. 'Bit of a farewell piss-up last night, know what I mean?'

I sat pondering whether I'd been praised or insulted as he lifted his suitcase and turned to leave. 'Oh, nearly forgot!' he said. 'I noticed you enjoying a belt of the *Chivas Regal* earlier.' He hooked a thumb towards the bar. 'So, I've stood you another dram. Bottoms up!' While I offered my thanks through a strained smile, he slouched off, trailing his suitcase behind him, then paused in the doorway and shouted back, 'And good luck with your *Snowball Orgies*, mate. Great title for a dirty book, by the way! Got pictures as well, has it?'

* * * * *

Chapter Eleven

'CAVEAT SCRIPTOR!'

*

If ever I'd needed reminding that it's best not to take yourself too seriously if you venture to 'go public' with anything that's even remotely creative, my experience at the little bookshop in Mallorca would have done just that. Fortunately, I'd learned the value of that maxim as an eleven-year-old when, on my first parade through the streets as a member of the Haddington Boys' Pipe Band, there seemed to be more interest from certain quarters in what, if anything, I wore under my kilt than how well I'd learned to play the bagpipes. It was a lesson I never forgot, and it served me well, when combined with a parallel resolve to take *very* seriously anything I decided to devote time and energy to. If a job's worth doing, it's worth doing right – even if, as most of us find out at some stage, the eventual dividend doesn't always justify the investment.

That fleeting Mallorcan trip also proved that our

roller coaster ride through life was far from over, for although *Snowball Oranges'* star appeared to be in the ascendancy in the UK, it was still barely a glimmer on the horizon beyond these shores. Yet, only a few weeks later, it became evident that certain foreign observers had been watching it's trajectory and were poised to hitch their wagons accordingly...

The Frankfurt Book Fair is arguably an even bigger event on the book-business calendar than its London counterpart, and in any case is generally accepted as being the principal global marketplace for the sale and purchase of translation rights. Publishers and literary agents from all over the world gather in the German city every October to pitch their wares and clinch deals that can vary in value from prudently circumspect to eye-wateringly extravagant. *Snowball Oranges* may have been at the lower end of the range, but some buyers *were* prepared to bid for its translation rights, and Chestervale's representatives were ready to listen to their offers.

Terms were agreed during the fair for publication in the German, Swedish, Dutch and Chinese languages, while negotiations were initiated with publishing houses in Poland, Finland, Hungary, the Czech Republic, Russia, Korea, Estonia and Thailand. Also, export deals for the English-language edition were concluded for Australasia, Canada and South Africa, all combining to provide the book with the makings of worldwide exposure, as well as creating a windfall in the form of advance royalties. As these moneys would be shared between Chestervale and myself, I'm sure the prospect was as welcome to a relatively small young publisher like them as it was to a relatively old rookie author like me.

But those advances were routinely set to arrive piecemeal: half when the individual contracts were finally signed and half on publication of each foreign edition, which, depending on the corresponding company's publishing schedule, could be as much as a year or more down the line. So, although an unexpected boost in income had been duly welcomed, I had to stay focused on the more immediate task of completing the half-finished sequel to *Snowball Oranges,* particularly as its March deadline was now less than five months away. In the meantime, it was also vital that I remained committed doing whatever I could to promote the existing book, since, to paraphrase yet another farming proverb, the sun might never shine so kindly on my hay field again.

For all that working in the record business had disciplined me to the 'catch-up' system of royalty earnings – in other words, producing the goods, receiving a down payment as an advance and then waiting for the goods to sell over an indefinite period of time before realising their optimal monetary value – one aspect of its equivalent in the book business was new to me, so please bear with me as I try to explain…

As a record producer, I had always dealt directly with the 'buyers' – that's to say the record companies who manufactured and sold the goods – whereas my dealings with book publishers were now complicated by the universally accepted involvement of middlemen, specifically literary agents, and in particular those who specialised in the administration of 'subsidiary' rights. Those might include dramatic rights (most notably adaptation for film and TV), audiobook rights, press serialisation rights and licences to publish in foreign languages. Following the Frankfurt Book Fair, the main emphasis in my case was on the latter. Although my direct point of contact in these matters would still be Chestervale, to whom I had assigned the worldwide administration of *all* my subsidiary rights, they might elect to follow the common industry practice of employing specialist UK agents to conduct the actual contractual negotiations with individual foreign publishing houses. Occasionally, though, more ingredients would be added to an already complex broth by those primary UK agents engaging foreign *sub*-agents to do the required spade work in their own respective territories. In such cases, both agents would work on a split-commission basis of sharing, typically, twenty percent of revenues derived from the book involved. All such sums would be deducted from the royalties eventually paid to the original UK publishers, who in turn would deduct these commissions before paying the author his 'nett' royalty, which they would be obliged to remit – in accordance with pan-industry principles – 'promptly on receipt' from the primary UK agents.

Still with me? Well, stay focused, because this slice of the subsidiary rights pie might routinely be retained and administered by the author's *own* literary agent, in return for that agent's statutory ten or fifteen percent of his client's share. Phew! At least I could take comfort in the knowledge that languishing in the ranks of the un-agented meant I didn't have *that* additional subtraction to factor in, which did seem like a blessing ... at the time!

Anyway, I hope the foregoing illustrates that it's essential for an author who aspires to make a living from his writing to regard himself as a *business* whenever his work becomes integrated with and dependent upon established commercial practices. Business, after all, is business, and it brooks scant room for sentiment. It should nevertheless be remembered that an author is allowing others to trade in a commodity that is uniquely the progeny of his own creative input: in legal terms, his personal 'intellectual property'. It follows, then, that one facet that is more essential in *his* business than in those of a more material nature is ... trust.

So, '*Caveat scriptor*!' Author beware! A warning I would have reason to heed soon enough myself, and with potentially painful consequences to boot.

*

By January 2001, six months after its release, *Snowball Oranges* had hit the No 2 spot in Amazon's Travel Books chart and No 4 in the *Sunday Times* equivalent. It had sold more than 30,000 copies in the UK alone, the volume of retail orders necessitating the continuation of additional print runs well in excess of original estimates. Also, contracts had recently been exchanged for the first eight translation agreements struck at Frankfurt three months earlier, with the added fillip of North American rights in the English language now being taken up by a prominent US publisher.

Yet, apart from signing on the various dotted lines (which I did with an overwhelming sense of gratitude), my energies were still firmly focused on writing the next book. This was now bearing the official title of *Mañana, Mañana*, for no more studied a reason than it repeated a word in the penultimate sentence of *Snowball Oranges* which just happened to fit the mood of its sequel perfectly. Everything else, I told myself, was in the safe hands of people who knew their side of the business best, leaving me to get on with minding my own.

By now, this included the fulfilment of those 'reading' engagements that had been coming in since *Snowball Oranges* broke surface and which, although still mainly in locations I could go to and return from on the same day, did entail travelling costs, not all of which came under the benevolent auspices of the Scottish Book Trust's Live Literature Scheme. But when you're fortunate enough to be asked to set out your stall in places where, to be absolutely frank, you're still just one name in a lengthy list of little-known authors, you put such pragmatic matters to the back of your mind and grasp the opportunity without a second thought. Businesslike bean-counting can be left for a 'less creative' day.

*

It turned out that being so busy was at odds with the narrative of the new book which, in keeping with the humorous character of its predecessor, dealt with our ongoing efforts to adapt to the laid-back, *mañana* approach to life habitually attributed (justifiably or not) to Spanish people in general, and in our case to Mallorcan country folk in particular. After the no-time-to-spare, up-and-at-'em work ethic we'd adhered to in Scotland, slowing down had become an increasingly pleasurable 'chore'. Now, I was not just back in the hurly-burly I'd been used to in our pre-Mallorcan days, but actually trying to keep more plates spinning simultaneously than I'd ever done before. And I was enjoying it – in the main.

But what about Ellie meanwhile? She had never shown any inclination to get involved in the actual book-writing process, but was always happy to cast an eye over my ongoing efforts and offer her honest – if not always complimentary – opinion. For instance, you may recall how she never hesitated to bluntly dismiss as dustbin fodder any corny repartee I'd regarded as the epitome of wit when writing with the (rare) assistance of an immoderate intake of wine! Now, however, she was gradually becoming exposed to the realities of sharing the world of a would-be full-time author: an unpredictable way of life that owed less to her past experiences as the mature, ever-responsible wife of an itinerant jazz musician turned record producer, turned beef-and-barley farmer, turned orange grower, turned tyro property developer, and more to the attitude of a teenage dropout who runs away to join the circus.

Despite the fact that her chosen circus was only a one-man show, she was destined to pitch up with it in places as far-flung and far apart as the edge of the Arctic Circle in the north and the fringes of the Tropic of Cancer in the south. There was no doubting she really was walking a tightrope without a safety net now, and never did her friend's quip of many years ago ring more true: '*She either deserved a medal for stoicism or a certificate of insanity.*' Fortunately for me, however, unbridled impetuosity had never been part of Ellie's makeup, even though she *had* always been a staunch supporter of anything I set out to achieve. In any event, her support was what I needed more than ever now, for we were finally approaching the road to Damascus, and it probably goes without saying that I didn't have a route map.

I had thought, indeed hoped, that I'd put my 'on-the-road' days behind me forever when I parted company with the music business. Mind you, that doesn't mean I hadn't enjoyed touring with a group of like-minded musicians in my youth, because the camaraderie generated was part and parcel of the whole jazz experience. But it had been a different story when it came to going away on record production duties. Apart from the occasions when it had been possible to tag along with a mobile recording unit, my journeys to studios in distant places were undertaken on my own. And I confess to being less than enthusiastic about solo travelling. Unlike Sir Francis Chichester and his stalwart ilk, who clearly relished traversing the globe for months on end in a floating camper van for one, I got lonely when left on my tod for even a night or two in some comfy hotel just down the road – relatively speaking. Crunching cornflakes at an individual table in the corner of the breakfast room had never been one of my favourite experiences.

*

There had been many occasions during the nine months I spent writing the ninety-thousand words required to complete the next book when I doubted the wisdom of my commitment, yet the larger the dreaded delivery date loomed, the easier the words seemed to flow. Maybe editor Izzie had been right: *'There's nothing like a tight deadline to get the creative juices flowing.'* Whatever, by the end of March 2001 I had dispatched the finished manuscript to Chestervale, along with the twelve black-and-white drawings needed to head each chapter.

It had been a dash against time, a whirlwind combo of marathon and sprint, with the occasional medley of three-legged, egg-and-spoon and sack races chucked in for good measure. So what now? A well-earned rest, maybe? Not a bit of it! My pulse rate was up and the adrenaline pumping, so thoughts of taking my foot off the gas didn't enter my head. The first thing that came to mind, in fact, was agent Libby's advice from way back at the start of this journey: *'Don't rest on your laurels. Keep writing, for there's no guarantee your present project won't bite the dust.'*

Something along those lines anyway. And it tied in with my nagging fear that whatever success *Snowball Oranges* had enjoyed to date might prove to be a flash in the pan; that I would turn out to be nothing but a one-trick pony, soon to fade permanently into the sunset as the sole performer in my own one-man, one-book circus. And worse, as depicted in a regularly recurring nightmare, with Ellie finally at the end of her tether and cracking her ringmaster's whip at my hind quarters to goad me on my way.

Thus spurred on, I galloped into a burst of activity that centred, not on any notion of conceiving a second *Son of Snowballs* before the first had been delivered by midwife Izzie, but on filling the three months between now and the date of the 'happy event' with renewed attempts to generate interest in my fiction and script-writing efforts dating back to those eight fallow years between completing *Snowball Oranges* and finding an obliging publisher. Accordingly, into the 'Pending' files of my computer I delved and dug out the manuscripts of the two humour-laced *Bob Burns Investigates* mysteries and *The Cuddyford Chronicles* country comedy, together with first-episode TV adaptations of each. I also retrieved the straight-to-screenplay scripts of my *Goblin Hall* fantasy adventure and the set-in-the-Highlands caper I'd called *The *Other* Monarch of the Glen*.

The majority of book publishers were now insisting that authors should only submit 'unsolicited' material to one publisher at a time (the same qualification was also being applied by literary agents), with more of them than ever advising hopefuls that, if they hadn't received an acknowledgement after six months, they should assume that their proposal was of no interest. It's what had become known to legions of stoical aspirants as *The Long 'No'*. But I had already spent too many years waiting in vain for this policy to be administered in a more lenient way, so, while still targetting publishers and agents singly, I'd give it a couple of weeks and if I hadn't received at least a simple confirmation of my approach by then, I'd move on to the next most likely names listed in the good old *Writers' and Artists' Yearbook*. This didn't change my luck for the better, but with all correspondence now being conducted by email, there was some consolation in being able to make my approaches for free, with the added satisfaction of knowing that no trees had been felled in the process.

I should add that my adoption of this attitude reflected no disrespect for the recipients of my submissions, but at almost sixty-one years of age and time flying, I felt I could be excused for not playing strictly by rules compiled by those farther out of reach of the grim reaper's scythe than myself.

But book publishing issues aside, it was actually easier then than it is now for a newcomer to make contact with and get feedback from film production companies when pitching screenplays for movies and scripts for potential TV series. I suppose the risk of being accused of plagiarism is the reason for the door being closed so firmly these days, since there must have been many instances along the way when producers had read a script, turned it down, but inadvertently developed another with a vaguely similar concept some years later, only to be sued for infringement of copyright by the creator of the long-forgotten reject.

Luckily for me, such restrictions were not so prevalent in 2001, so I made the most of the relative ease of access by preparing to fire my material off to as many likely-looking production companies as possible. However, as with bar-stool football pundits, it seems there are those in every walk of life who purport to know enough about the downside of everything to put you off trying your hand at anything. Which sums up the reaction I got from a casual acquaintance who claimed to have a friend who knew someone who was a second cousin of a guy who had once sent the scriptwriters of the *Braveheart* movie some snippets of 'authentic' Scottish dialogue for consideration.

This fellow was credited (allegedly) with having come up with the inspiration for Mel Gibson's immortal line, *'They'll never take our freedom!'*, by offering: *'See Scotland? See England? Nae danger they're ever gonny take wur fuckin' freedom, by the way!'* Although the expletive – together with certain subtleties of the vernacular which were deemed likely to be lost in translation – had ended up on the cutting room floor, my casual acquaintance felt eminently qualified to warn me that most of the so-called production companies I placed so much hope in were nothing more than one bloke sitting in his bedroom editing souvenir wedding-day footage he'd shot with a hand-held video camera while patiently awaiting his dream commission to produce a TV commercial for toilet rolls. Maybe so, but we all have to start somewhere, I reasoned, and I wished such wannabe producers well. For in all honesty, I would personally have welcomed the opportunity to write a script trumpeting the super-kind-to-your-bahookie virtues of the Thunderclap Toilet Roll Company's product over those of the competition. To which my casual acquaintance remarked that he was sure I was eminently qualified to perform that very task.

I took from this that he had read *Snowball Oranges* – or bits of it – and hadn't been too impressed. His demeanour suggested he was of the opinion that anyone of no particular note (such as myself) who saw fit to write a memoir of his humdrum life must be a raging egotist with a grossly inflated idea of who might be interested – if anyone. This reminded me of a comment an eavesdropping expat made when I was leaving Tolo's bar in Palma Nova at the end on my confab with the group of homecoming holidaymakers I mentioned earlier:

'See yerself as some kinda expert on Majorca, do yer? Yeah, well, all of us Brits wot lives 'ere could've wrote a bleedin' book an' all, Jock, *if* we was bovvered!'

He may well have been right, but the inferred inevitability of exaggerated self-regard on the part of anyone who *could* be 'bovvered' was way off the mark – at least in my case and, I fancied, in that of many others who had tiptoed timorously down a similar path. As to having seen myself as 'some kinda expert on Majorca', the opposite had been the case when we embarked on our orange-growing adventure, and a degree of blissful ignorance about the island, its people and their ways had been a pivotal feature of our story throughout. Also, we had always regarded ourselves as guests in another people's land, and had no inclination to treat our hosts with the inherent condescension so often exhibited by a certain element of other Brits 'wot lived there'.

Undaunted by such busybody discouragements and nuggets of 'insider' advice, I pressed on in the spirit of Coolidge, the thrust of his urgings being more pertinent now than ever…

> *'Nothing in the world can take the place of persistence.*
>
> *Talent will not; nothing is more common than unsuccessful men with talent.*
>
> *Genius will not; unrewarded genius is almost a proverb.*
>
> *Education will not; the world is full of educated derelicts.*
>
> *Persistence and determination alone are omnipotent.*
>
> *The slogan "Press On!" has solved and always will solve the problems of the human race.'*

Even if he had only nicked the idea from the lesson Robert the Bruce learned when observing a single-minded spider spinning a web in an awkward corner of a cave, what was good for Bruce in 1306 was still good for Coolidge in 1926, so there seemed no reason for me to question it in 2001. That's if we ignore what befell a random selection of such famously-persistent people as Joan of Arc, Napoleon, Gandhi and Adolf Hitler. But there are exceptions to every rule, so I girded my digital loins and began hitting the 'Email Send' button with a suitably resolute finger.

It had come as no great surprise that some of those publishers who did respond to my fiction offerings were inclined to take the usual line about humour being hard to sell. Yet no such qualification was made by the TV and film producers who got back to me. One, with an impressive list of BBC comedy series to his name, actually saw this aspect of the *Bob Burns* mysteries as an advantage, and added the stories to his list of proposals to be explored more thoroughly when pressure of work on his current 'slate' permitted. At the same time, he advised me about the harsh realities of his line of business, and how there was considerably more to it than just buying the rights to a book for 'cinematic development'. Indeed, before any binding commitment could be made, the normal routine was for the production company to assemble – for the perusal of TV networks, for example – a presentation package that comprised a detailed 'treatment' or synopsis, a pilot script, names of the 'talent' who had declared an interest in playing the lead roles, and ideally a director best suited to the particular idiosyncrasies of the project as well.

This advice was echoed by Marina Jessup, former head of development at the London office of one of Hollywood's leading studios, but now an independent producer in her own right. Of all the responses I'd had, hers was the only one that related specifically to *Snowball Oranges*, and she told me that if I cared to let her read the sequel when available, she would then be able to assess more thoroughly the potential of the premise as a feature-length film or, perhaps more likely, as a comedy-drama series for television. Sensing that my expectation level might already be heading towards the 'overload' mark, she quickly appended that, even if she did eventually decide to go with the idea, it could take a very long time, maybe even years, for it to materialise. And with so many rivals scrambling to grab a slice of a cake that was as elusive as it was small, raising the financial backing to fund the project might be the trickiest of all the many hurdles to be cleared. What's more, it had to be faced that the increase in production costs associated with *Snowball Oranges* being set in Mallorca wouldn't help in that regard either.

So there! If I hadn't been aware of such off-putting facets of the movie-making business before, I knew now.

Far from being disheartened, though, I actually welcomed the frankness. It was a tough, fiercely competitive game I was trying to be part of: no place for airy-fairy dreamers blinded by the limelight and bewitched by the stardust, and no place either for anyone expecting fame and fortune to come knocking at their door after the first submission of an idea. But in any case, I always had to bear in mind that helping the *promotion* of my books had been the overriding reason for my seeking to learn a bit about the disciplines of scriptwriting in the first place. It was proving to be an interesting excursion into a field of the business I fully intended to keep tabs on, though purely as an adjunct to the one in which, according to Izzie at Chestervale Publishers, I finally seemed to be making a bit of a mark. It was June 2001 and the publication date for *Mañana, Mañana* (née *Son of Snowballs*) was rapidly approaching, with promotional blurb and review copies having been sent out well in advance to key trade and media targets.

'Reaction is good – *except*ionally good!' an excited Izzie told me on the phone, before going on to reveal that translation rights had already been snapped up by the same foreign publishers quickest off the mark for *Snowball Oranges* at Frankfurt back in October. 'Imagine that!' she chirped. 'Bagging the lingo licences for the second book when the first one has only just hit their shops! Yep, and the agent who's handling a lot of that stuff for us says several other countries are as good as in the bag again too.'

Before I had a chance to express my surprise *and* delight, Izzie had started to reel off even more good news. Advance orders in the UK for *Mañana, Mañana* – now with the subtitle *One Mallorcan Summer* attached – had already outstripped the initial print-run of fifteen thousand copies (ten times the figure for *Snowball Oranges* when it came out) and showed every sign of continuing apace. On top of that, a number of valuable media contacts had already been lined up for interviews, and on top of *that* – wait for it! – the *Daily Mail,* one of the country's top-selling tabloid newspapers with a circulation of two and a half million, had just made an offer to serialise the books in two-page spreads over three days starting immediately after *Mañana, Mañana*'s publication.

I was flabbergasted – dumbstruck.

Izzie got the picture. 'It's OK, Peter, no need to say anything – I can guess what it must be like for an expectant father at a time like this. But once you've picked yourself up off the floor, you can make a start to writing *Snowballs Three*, because we'll most *cert*ainly be taking up our option. Oh, and another thing – to wet your new baby's head, we're throwing a little bash in London after close of play on 5th July. The bubbly's on Chestervale, so make sure you get there sharpish!'

* * * * *

Chapter Twelve
'DID SOMETHING SING IN BERKELEY SQUARE?'

*

The flagship branch of the Daunt Books chain occupies premises in Marylebone High Street that have earned it the reputation of being the most beautiful Edwardian bookshop in London. Its main hall, with atrium roof, stained glass windows and galleries fringed by oaken balustrades, hints at a cross between the library of a stately home and a book-lined chapel, where devoted browsers can seek refuge from the hustle and bustle of the outside world. The shop stocks an eclectic range of books, but has traditionally specialised in travel-related titles, which is presumably how Chestervale Publishers managed to persuade the management to lend them the use of a discrete corner in which to celebrate the publication of *Mañana, Mañana – One Mallorcan Summer.*

But being presented as the guest of honour (for want of a more appropriate description) in these surroundings just didn't seem right to me. Indeed, I saw myself as an impostor – a bit like a mongrel mutt gatecrashing a prize-giving ceremony at Crufts. Truth to tell, I didn't even regard myself as a 'travel' writer in the strictest sense of the word, my entitlement to membership of that august fraternity being limited to having taken my wife and sons to Edinburgh Airport for a one-way flight to Mallorca in 1984. Now, entering Daunt's hallowed premises, it struck me that only the work of 'legitimate' literary types deserved to be commemorated in such a place. Of a sudden, I was gripped by the same sensation of fruit bats doing aerobatics in my stomach that I'd experienced when climbing the stairs in Thin's venerated bookshop in Edinburgh a year earlier. Even the hum of voices emanating from the scene of this event seemed the same.

But as I approached the final wall of book shelves that separated the main body of the shop from the hideaway which was reserved, I presumed, for occasions such as this, it became apparent that there were certain important differences. Laughter! And the accompanying clunking of bottles! And the popping of corks! And the clinking of glasses!

'Aha,' I told myself with a smile, 'the Thin's gig was never like this!'

And neither it had been, for what was facing me behind that book-built room divider at Daunt's was not a challenge to entertain the customers or encourage them to buy my wares, but a gesture by Chestervale that was intended to give me a pat on the back for my contribution towards the success we had enjoyed to date, as well as 'wetting the head' of my new book. But it was also, I guessed, to help propagate their image as a small but upwardly-mobile publisher. For the owners of Chestervale, being young men with ambitions for their company, were sharp enough to make good use of any opportunity that might advance their cause, and would have seen the benefit of stamping their presence within this holy of holies of the London book-selling establishment. I was pragmatic enough to recognise this, particularly as they had already shown in contractual negotiations to be of a thrifty disposition, and were therefore unlikely to indulge in extravagant pursuit of rainbows – even those with an alluring orange hue.

Yet there was no mistaking the fact that they were putting my new book firmly in the spotlight this evening. Their three-strong team of publishing-trainees-turned-barmaids cheerily dispensed bubbly to the guests as they arrived, and their leader – once all of the twenty or so attendees were suitably refreshed and chatting away in little cliques typical of such gatherings – brought proceedings to order with a few pings of a fingernail on a champers glass. There followed a brief introductory speech, to which I replied equally briefly and with a suitably corny joke or two. Everyone tittered obligingly, then resumed chattering in their chosen groups.

And that's more or less how the event panned out. It was more like a polite cocktail party than some of the record business launch bashes I'd attended over the years. But it was all the better for that. There was no live performance of the latest bid for chart success to endure, no uninvited thunder-stealers trying to punt their own stuff, and no freeloading hacks hell-bent on pouring as much booze as possible down their throats while repeatedly promising massive coverage for '*What is it you're flogging again*?' in next Saturday's sports pages … or somewhere. Also, any business networking that took place between the Chestervale delegation and their peers was conducted so discreetly as to be noticeable by only the most nosy of flies on the wall.

After about half an hour, people began disengaging from their little groups to offer their thanks to the hosts and their best wishes to me, before forsaking the bookish tranquillity of Daunt's to venture back into the horn-honking, diesel-belching hurly-burly of a London evening – with some of them, for all I knew, heading off to their second, or even third, freebie drinks do of the day. (After all, not every freeloader has a '*Press*' ticket stuffed into the headband of his trilby!) Nonetheless, I was sure Chestervale had done me proud in their choice of venue and judicious selection of invitees, who could doubtless be relied upon to give *Mañana, Mañana* a leg up in some way or other.

But while fully appreciative of these good intentions, I still couldn't help doubting the commercial benefit of holding such get-togethers, no matter how strategically located or prudently convened. It appeared to be as much a case of 'seeing and being seen' as triggering any significant upturn in demand for what was being plugged. Then again, maybe I was unfairly judging the general concept by the example of those few lavish but relatively fruitless junkets I had witnessed in the music scene.

At least it seemed that not *too* much had been spent on this one, with even the most dehydrated of guests rationed to two glasses of bubbly. I tipped my hat to the provident policies of Chestervale's young chiefs. After all, it might well be revenue generated by the sale of my own books that would eventually cover the cost, and the money was better in their bank (and, hopefully, mine!) than in the pocket of a fizz bottler in north-east France.

*

If Daunt's was a jewel in the crown of London's impressive selection of good bookshops, the hotel I'd booked Ellie and me into for the night proved to be a wart on the nose of the city's hospitality sector. '*About as inviting as the Black Hole of Calcutta,*' commented one customer on a popular review website. I couldn't think of a more succinctly-apt description, and if I'd read it beforehand I would certainly have paid due heed by giving the establishment a wide berth. Unfortunately, though, I only recently stumbled upon that summing-up, and was amazed to discover that the place is not only still in business, but also attracting the same criticisms we had levelled at it some twenty-three years ago.

What had drawn me initially to the hotel was its location in an elegant Georgian terrace roughly midway between Marylebone and Marble Arch, which would be the starting point of a promotional trek around London that had been set up for the day after the *Mañana, Mañana* launch. Other deciding factors were the glowing endorsement I read in an 'official' guide to tourist accommodation in the capital *and* the surprisingly inexpensive tariff quoted. After the years I'd spent on the road as a musician, I was wise to the fact that there are no such bargains in the centre of any big city, least of all London. But those days had also taught me to be 'close with a buck', and old habits die hard.

'Looks quite nice,' I said to Ellie as we climbed the steps to the front door. I crossed my fingers, then added, 'You know, stucco walls and wrought-iron railings and everything.'

'It looks like something out of *The Munsters*!' was Ellie's curt response. 'Honestly, I wouldn't be surprised to find Lurch behind the reception desk.'

I coughed, apprehensively. 'Ehm, I think I'm right in saying it was actually *The Addams Family*. You're mixing Lurch up with Herman Munster, the Frankenstein freak in the other show.'

'Same difference! I mean, just look at the state of those windows! Filthy! And those net curtains! Shrouds whipped out of coffins, I shouldn't wonder! Look at the *holes*! Moth-eaten? Rat-gnawed more likely!'

I couldn't argue with any of that. Ellie was right on all counts, except, as it happens, her prediction that a Lurch lookalike would be manning the reception desk. For a start, there was no reception desk, and the 'receptionist' hovering inside the front door looked more like a leering Uncle Fester than Lurch – but of a less deathly pallor, and wearing a fez.

'Oh, very velcome indeed,' he smarmed with a bow and head wobble. 'You have make advance reservation, please? If not, ve can offer very nice basement room sharing vith some other –'

'*Yes,* I made a reservation,' I interjected smartly, then gave him the details.

'Place stinks,' Ellie informed me sotto voce while Uncle Fester rummaged in a wall cupboard. 'Pongs like a rabbit hutch. And the *state* of the carpet! Must've been hauled out of the rubble after the Blitz!'

'Please be coming, oh yes,' said Uncle Fester at length. He was brandishing a key and beckoning us to follow him upstairs. 'Ve have very lovely room for you. Very special, vith very lovely view from vindow and many vonderful facility for the gentleman and his vooman lady vife.' He led the way along a dingy corridor, opened the appointed door, ushered us through, then, with a cheesy smile and another head wobble, swiftly withdrew.

Ellie looked round the room and started to laugh. It wasn't a laugh of enjoyment, but a laugh suggesting a combination of disbelief and affront. If she had been of a weepy persuasion, she would almost certainly have burst into tears. But she wasn't so easily upset (she had spent all of her adult life assembling the armour, after all), so instead of turning on the waterworks, she turned instead to me and said, 'You won't be surprised to know that your woman lady wife isn't too impressed by your choice of overnight accommodation, dear – or should I call you *sahib*?'

I'd be the first to admit that I wasn't gifted with

Ellie's female ability to notice even the tiniest speck of dust on any given surface, yet I could empathise with what she was getting at here. Indicating the dilapidated furniture, peeling Victorian wallpaper and threadbare floor coverings, I conceded that even Lurch and Herman Munster would have turned their noses up at this apology for a hotel room.

'Or would've felt perfectly at home in it,' Ellie countered, swiping a huge cobweb off a corner of the window frame. 'Jeez! It's like a Turkish bath in here!' she gasped, before making a spirited effort to open the window, which stubbornly refused to cooperate.

'Hasn't budged since it was last painted,' I grunted, after stepping into the breach, hoping that my superior masculine muscle power would compensate slightly for my lack of perception in the dust department. But I failed.

'Hasn't seen a lick of paint this side of the First World War,' Ellie muttered, while flicking some yellowing flakes off an astragal. Then, gingerly, she pulled aside what might once have passed for a lace curtain and peered out. 'Might have guessed,' she shrugged. 'The lovely view from the window is the brick wall of a back alley.' She craned her neck to look upwards. 'Yes, and I'm sure there's a glimpse of sky somewhere up there among the fire escapes and chimneys. Breathtaking!'

'Yeah, as is the guff in here.' I stepped over and laid a finger on an ancient cast-iron radiator mounted on the wall by the door. '*Oo-ya!*' I yelped, whipping my hand away. 'Damn thing's boiling hot!'

'Just what's needed on a sweltering summer's night

in the middle of London,' sighed Ellie. 'Better see if you can turn it off before we suffocate.'

But, like the window, no matter how hard I struggled, the knob on the inlet pipe refused to yield.

'That does it!' I snapped. 'I'm going downstairs to demand another room from that Uncle Fester creep. The bugger must take me for a complete eejit!'

When I came back a few minutes later, Ellie was busy inspecting the bed clothes. 'That was quick. I take it from the look on your face that another room's out of the question.'

I nodded my head with an air of weary resignation. 'Yeah, not unless we fancy taking our chances in the multiple-occupancy basement.'

'No way! Sounds too much like the Black Hole of Calcutta!'

I checked my watch. 'Ten o' clock. Fat chance of finding another hotel around here at this time of night either.'

Ellie flapped a pillow slip in the expert way women do when making a bed. 'Oh well, we'll just have to grin and bear it. At least the sheets are clean, and I haven't found any fleas.'

'Could've been worse, then,' I mumbled, glancing forlornly at the fag burns adorning the front edge of a bedside table. 'I haven't noticed any cockroaches scurrying about either.'

Ellie casually informed me that, from what she saw when I was away, a spider probably ate them all. And I got the distinct impression she wasn't joking.

'Anyway,' she continued, deftly changing the subject, 'it's been a long day and I'm knackered. So,

I suggest a nice, refreshing shower before hitting the sack.'

'Good plan! You go first. It's getting more airless in here by the minute, so while you're in there I'll have another go at opening the window.'

'Well, good luck with that,' Ellie replied sceptically. 'But your best chance could be to chuck a brick through it.'

She was right again, so instead of expending any more sweat on a futile exercise, I sat on the bed and contemplated another cobweb I'd just noticed; this one bridging a one-metre gap between the top of the wardrobe and a wooden picture rail. It was quite an impressive feat of civil engineering by a bug that I calculated would have been capable of devouring one of those fruit bats my stomach had played host to of late, never mind gobbling a few measly cockroaches. I had a hunch this was the spider Ellie had been alluding to a bit earlier. She knew very well that I wasn't a fan of the larger specimens, and judging by its web, I reckoned this one must have been as big as a crab. I hoped it would remain respectfully in its lair during our brief stop-over within the precincts of its grubby domain.

Ellie had never been prone to screaming without good reason, so I feared the worst when I heard a loud screech coming from the shower room.

'*FLOOD*!' she yelled. 'Quick, Peter, the plug hole must be blocked! *Do* something!'

Sure enough, little waves of soapy water were lapping under the door and oozing onto the bedroom floor.

'Well, turn the bloody thing off!' I hollered. 'And put your dressing gown on before you come out. I'm going to get that smarmy Uncle Fester clone up here to sort these disasters out once and for all! I'm patience personified, although I say it myself, but enough is enough!'

Five minutes later I was back again. Alone. Ellie was perched on the edge of the bed waiting for me. She was wearing her dressing gown, but also a knowing look. 'So?' she enquired through the makings of a smirk.

'Yeah, yeah – laugh it up!' I bristled. 'I've just had the mickey taken out of me by a body double for a weirdo character in a loony TV show, and you seem to think it's funny! Well, let me tell you this, Mrs *Vooman Lady Vife*, I am *not* amused!'

Ellie sat tracing circles on her top lip with a finger, this time trying to hold back a titter. But the attempt only lasted a few seconds before a full-blown giggle escaped.

'S-sorry,' she spluttered, 'but you look so silly standing there with a rubber sink plunger in your hand...' She paused to wipe a large drip of hilarity from the tip of her nose. '...and holding it in front of yourself too, as if it's the Olympic torch or something!' With that, she dissolved into a paroxysm of unbridled glee.

Out of the corner of my eye, I caught a glimpse of my reflection in a full-length mirror on the wardrobe door. I could see why she had lost control, and I almost burst out laughing myself. Still, I held it together until Ellie had recovered her composure, then I said,

'Bugger told me the maintenance man was *off vork vith serious sickness, oh yes,* then gave me this damn plunger and apologised that it hadn't been placed in the shower for our personal convenience before we arrived.'

'That would be one of the wonderful facilities he promised, I suppose.'

'*Exactly* what I told him! Yeah, and I also told him, in no uncertain manner, that this hotel is an absolute disgrace, an insult to any self-respecting guest, stuck window and clapped-out radiator and crap furniture and everything.'

With eyes demurely lowered, Ellie nodded her head. 'Fair comment,' she replied in a small voice. 'It had to be said, and you said it.'

'Absolutely! But d'you know what he came back with?'

Ellie shook her head, but remained ominously silent.

'The bugger said, *Vot are you expecting for the much cheapness of price vot ve are charging you – the Taj Ma-fucking-hal*?'

That did it for Ellie. The cork on top of her mirth bottle finally popped and she collapsed into an even bigger fit of giggles than before. 'But did he call you *sahib*?' she wheezed. 'That's the main thing. I mean, *respect* – right?'

I glanced at myself in the mirror again, then nonchalantly tucked the plunger behind my back while Ellie crossed her legs and tried not to pee herself. I watched her for a few moments, and her reaction to the current drama reminded me of the nub of our well-practised maxim: when faced with challenging times, the best defence is laughter. And Ellie was providing more than enough of that for both of us, although I did allow myself a wry chuckle while plunging away gamely at the blocked plug hole after she had gone to bed. All my efforts turned out to be in vain, but as that other favourite saying of mine goes, you can't win 'em all.

*

Everything considered, we slept quite well for a couple of hours, due entirely to Ellie's ingenuity in improvising a bedside fan by setting up her hair dryer with the heat element switched off. Then, without warning, she woke me with a sharp dig in the ribs.

'Listen to that!' she whispered.

I blinked into the darkness, trying to remember where I was. 'What? What is it, for crying out? *I* can't hear anything.'

'Course you can – that squeaking noise!'

'It's nothing. Go back to sleep.' I pulled the sheet over my head and reminded her that we had another busy day ahead of us. I assured her that, in a dump like this, things were bound to go bump or squeak or rattle in the night, so ignoring them was the only sensible thing to do. But my entreaty fell on deaf ears.

She thumped me on the back. 'There it goes again! Rats! I knew it the moment I saw those net curtains – remember? Rats! I can't *stand* them!'

I raised myself up on one elbow and strained my ears, and sure enough, there *was* a faint squeaking noise. In all probability it would only have been a mouse under the floorboards or in the wall cavity behind the bed. Although the little creature was posing no threat to anyone, even the word 'mouse' would have had Ellie switching on lights, opening cupboard doors and looking under carpets, so some ingenuity of my own was called for if we were to get another wink of sleep before dawn.

'Oh yes, I can hear it now,' I said with a dismissive little laugh. 'Nightingale.'

Ellie sat bolt upright and I felt her eyes glaring at me in the gloom. 'A *night*ingale? What the blazes are you on about?'

'No kidding. You can't mistake that wonderful trill. Surely you recognise it from Mallorca – we heard it all the time there – in the orange groves at night and everything.'

'Yes, but that was Mallorca and this is London. You're not trying to tell me they get nightingales *here*!'

'Absolutely, they're ten a penny – in certain areas, that is.'

'Meaning?'

'Well, Berkeley Square's only a few blocks from here.'

'Berkeley Square? What's the connection with Berkeley Square, wherever it is?'

Fortunately, it was too dark for Ellie to see the grin spreading across my face. In an effort to keep from sniggering, I inhaled deeply and held my breath for a moment. '*Sure*ly you remember that famous old song, don't you?'

'I'm talking about rats,' Ellie grouched, '– the ones that gnawed holes in the curtains here. *That*'s what I remember, and nightingales have nothing to do with it!'

'But nobody ever wrote a song called *A Rat Squeaked In Berkeley Square*,' I ventured, the involuntary yodel in my voice betraying a measure of frivolity.

Silence reigned for a few tense moments, then Ellie grabbed a pillow and started walloping me about the head. '*That*! Was! *Not*! Funny! And I hope the giant spider comes and attacks you when you're sleeping!'

This stopped me in my tracks. 'Giant spider? You – you don't mean you actually –'

'Saw it? I couldn't miss it,' said Ellie, slipping effortlessly into matter-of-fact mode. 'It was creeping about on a huge web up by the wardrobe. Surprised you didn't notice it when you were looking at yourself in the mirror.'

I rolled my shoulders. 'Yeah, well, I was too busy trying not to look silly posing with a rubber Olympic torch in my hand, wasn't I?'

The recollection of that image prompted a little titter from Ellie, which inevitably enticed a companion chuckle from me. Pretty soon we were having a good-going laugh together, with all thoughts of rats mimicking song birds banished from our minds. Well, almost…

As was her wont, Ellie was sound asleep again in seconds, snoring away peacefully while I lay staring into the darkness, listening to what I tried to convince myself was really only the squeaking of mice in the wainscoting, and eventually nodding off despite what sounded suspiciously like the eight-to-the-bar thump of spider's feet slowly approaching from the wardrobe area.

I awoke with a jump, a panicky intake of breath and a strangulated yell just as the brute was about to sink its fangs into my throat. The sun was shining through the tattered net curtains, and Ellie was already up and about, fully dressed and busy packing our bag. She turned round when she heard me emerging from dreamland.

'Ah, good morning,' she chirped. 'I trust you slept well?'

'No – y-yes – n-no,' I stuttered, blinking. 'And you?'

'It's really good of you to ask,' she replied – a mite dryly, I felt, 'but if you must know, I didn't sleep well, because, my dear, your incessant *snoring* kept me awake all night! A nightingale sang in Berkeley Square, you said? Yeah … in your flamin' dreams!'

I rubbed my eyes and yawned a sigh. 'Oh, well,' I said to myself, 'at least the do at Daunt's went reasonably well last night, and today's another day. Press on, boy! Press on!'

* * * * *

Chapter Thirteen

'ACCENTUATE THE POSITIVE'

*

If there's anything more unpleasant than being stuck for fifteen minutes in a tunnel in the London underground it's being stuck in it for thirty minutes; and if there's anything more unpleasant than that it's being subjected to it in the middle of a heatwave; and if there's anything more unpleasant than that it's having to endure it during the rush hour in a train jam-packed with fellow gasping, sweating and (in several cases) fainting passengers. Indeed, such an experience might well have prompted Dr Samuel Johnson – if he had lived a couple of centuries later – to revise his famous assertion that *'When a man is tired of London, he is tired of life'*. Don't get me wrong, I'm not having a go at London in particular, or for that matter at any big city with a 'tube', but to a dyed-in-the-wool country bumpkin like me, living like ants pretending to be moles doesn't strike me as being something that comes naturally to members of the human race.

Even so, I had used the tube regularly when I lived in London and actually quite enjoyed escaping the traffic jams that blighted travel 'on the surface'. Mind you, these trips only happened once a week at most and never during the rush hour, so I often had a carriage pretty much to myself on the twenty-minute journey from Finchley Central to Tottenham Court Road. That was back in the early '60s, during my spell as leader of the Clyde Valley Stompers, when I would routinely visit our agent's office in Soho to hand over any fees that had been paid in cash after our latest performances on the road. And those early-afternoon jaunts on the underground bore no resemblance whatsoever to the sardine-can conditions Ellie and I experienced on that steamy July evening in 2001, and which seasoned London 'tube jockeys' probably regarded as no big deal, but merely a city-living blip that happens every so often.

We had hot-footed it out of what I now referred to as the Taj Ma-fucking-hal Hotel that morning without even venturing inside the glorified walk-in cupboard that served as the breakfast room; not because we weren't peckish (all we'd had to eat since sandwiches on the train from Edinburgh the previous day were a few 'picks' at Daunt's), but because the scene greeting us as we sneaked a peek through the half-open door wasn't one to instil confidence in the cuisine. Crammed together on either side of one small table were eight guys we took to be the occupants of the basement 'dormitory' Uncle Fester had referred to on our arrival the night before. Their slightly furtive demeanour suggested that they had either just slipped ashore from a banana boat at Tilbury Docks or had arrived without visas for a clandestine convention of calypso bands. Perhaps both. Whatever, despite everything, they gave the impression of being a cheery bunch, and I'm sure they would have proved entertaining company if we had asked them to budge up a bit to make space for us on their benches. No, what put us off partaking of breakfast was what our fellow guests were tucking into: some cremated bread slices masquerading as toast on a communal plate, a saucer containing a few tiny plastic tubs of Flora, and a jug of what looked like a brew made from the dregs of a hermit's billycan.

We gave the dormitory boys the thumbs-up, wished Uncle Fester happy haunting, and got the hell out of there. Rapidly.

*

Wanda, one of the young Chestervale team who had hosted the Daunt's event the previous evening, was waiting for us at Marble Arch as arranged. In her early twenties, she was tall and of athletic appearance – a good-natured soul who gave the impression that, when it came to chaperoning a Chestervale author on a whirlwind book-signing tour of London, nothing would be too much trouble for her. She had certainly made preparations to ensure the campaign ran smoothly, albeit that such preparations were of necessity limited to a list of the dozen or so bookshops to be visited, and an itinerary compiled to make every ensuing port of call as adjacent as possible to the previous one. Great in theory, though liable to be tricky in practice, given that getting from any 'A' to any 'B' in central London on foot, by public transport or (if you're lucky enough to grab one) by taxi, may make the best laid schemes of even meticulous planners *gang aft a-gley*, to rephrase what Robert Burns once said to a mouse in a ploughed field.

The purpose of today's exercise was not to undertake 'public' signings; those essentially relaxed occasions to which people bring their book to a table prominently located in the shop to have it autographed, and perhaps to exchange a few words with the author at the same time. Instead, I would more likely be directed to a back room, where there would be a stack of books awaiting my signature on the title page. Unglamorous, hand-aching work, perhaps, but the fact that such plentiful numbers of the books were in stock was proof of the shops' belief in their saleability, and adding a '*Signed by the Author*' sticker to the cover was reckoned to help in that regard too.

Chatting away as we strode briskly to our first stop, Wanda informed us that she had only recently opted for a career in publishing, having dropped out of a degree course in a totally unrelated subject. She didn't divulge what her eschewed subject was, but as the day and our expedition progressed, it became apparent that it probably hadn't been geography. In fairness, though, she did eventually get us to every shop on her list. With the best of intentions, she had arranged the schedule to prioritise the most important retailers in alphabetical order, so that a typical sweep through a notional square mile of London's West End involved making our way from Blackwells in Holborn to Foyles in Charing Cross Road, to Goldsboro's near Leicester Square, Harrods in Knightsbridge, Hatchards in Piccadilly, Stanfords in Covent Garden, then back to Piccadilly for Waterstones. Hither and thither and round in circles we traipsed, our pace set more by Wanda's youthful athleticism than by the physical limitations of a couple of sexagenarians (not *quite*, in Ellie's case!) silently suffering the after-effects of a night in the Taj Ma-fucking-hal Hotel.

To compound our tribulations, Wanda's timed-to-perfection schedule hadn't included a break for lunch, or even a few minutes to grab a burger on the hoof, so that by the time she headed off home, mission accomplished, we were in a state of near collapse – though still smiling gamely as we waved her goodbye. But while most shops were already putting up shutters, our book-promoting duties weren't over. We still had to have what might prove to be the most important meeting of the entire trip, or of any trip, already fulfilled or likely to happen in the foreseeable future. And newspaper offices never close.

So, we embarked on the two-and-a-half-mile, traffic-jousting journey from Piccadilly to Kensington, admiring Harrod's handsome façade as we passed for the second time that afternoon, and all the while watching the meter in the taxi guzzling the money we'd saved by not buying food all day.

The bright and airy expanses of the entrance hall of Northcliffe House, headquarters of the *Daily Mail* in swanky Derry Street, are a far cry from the popular image of the inky-stinky, tobacco-smokey squalor of a 'Fleet Street' news mill. And Susie Dowdall was the antithesis of the hard-nosed gossip ferret with a notepad in one hand, a cigarette in the other and a pencil behind her ear portrayed as typical of her profession in old Humphrey Bogart movies. Susie was the *Mail*'s deputy Literary Editor and had been responsible for acquiring the serialisation rights to *Snowball Oranges* and, after reading an advance copy, to *Mañana, Mañana* as well. But businesslike as she was in mien and attire, she came over as a warm and kindly person. Those qualities revealed themselves in her powers of perception...

'You must be exhausted after such a hectic day in this terrible heat,' she smiled after pleasantries had been exchanged. 'I'm sure you'd love a coffee.'

'*And* biscuits, *please*!' I blurted out like a latter day Oliver Twist.

Ellie winced. 'It's just that he usually carries a few in his sporran,' she tactfully ad-libbed, 'but he decided not to wear his kilt today.'

Susie laughed, then told me she totally understood, because she was seldom without a Hobnob in her handbag either.

We all laughed, and with the ice nicely broken, got down to the business in hand. Susie explained that the abridgement of the two books was virtually complete, but she wanted to check a few important details – *and* to put faces to the two main protagonists – before finalising the text that would be serialised in the paper, starting in just a couple of days time. And so we spent a most pleasant half hour, listening to how Susie and her colleagues had enjoyed working on the books, selecting and stitching together the passages they considered would appeal most to their two and a half million readers, and presenting the results in double-page lay-outs, together with some photographs depicting the spectacular landscapes where much of the action had taken place. Oh, and talking of photographs, if we didn't mind, she'd like one of her snappers to take a few shots of us while we were in the office – just to show how well we still looked almost a quarter of a century after our great Mallorcan adventure. We knew Susie was only being polite about our appearance, given what we had been through in the preceding twenty-four hours, but we trusted in the air-brush talents of her chums in the graphics department to work the necessary magic.

'Please do ask your publishers to send me a copy of the third book in the series when it's ready,' she said as she walked us to the escalator on our way out.

'Well, I've already started writing it, and the deadline is less than nine months from now, so you've given me even more encouragement to press on. Thanks very much indeed for your interest.'

'My pleasure, and I'll look forward to reading it.' Susie shook hands with us both, then dipped into her handbag and passed Ellie a small paper bag. ' A couple of Hobnobs for Peter's sporran when you get back to Scotland,' she winked. '*If* they survive that long!'

I had already discerned that Susie was a kindly lady, and I was now pleased to note that she had a good sense of humour as well. Her powers of prediction weren't too shabby either, because those Hobnobs had been scoffed before we reached the nearest tube station, with Ellie an enthusiastic accomplice in the process.

Taking the underground from Kensington across the centre of town during rush hour may seem like a fairly masochistic thing to do, but cost and time made the decision for us. Firstly, our 'housekeeping' fund had already taken quite a battering on this trip, and taking the tube offered a sensible measure of economy; secondly, we would have missed the train home if we'd tried to get to King's Cross station by any other means. Factoring in a breakdown on the underground somewhere along the line hadn't entered my mind, of course, but in the event we made it onto the Edinburgh express just before the 'Go!' whistle blew.

British Rail sandwiches never tasted so good. The trolley attendant must have thought we were refugees from a third world famine zone, for as soon as we had relieved his stock of everything that took our fancy, we got stuck into pigging out with a vengeance. No words were exchanged until our re-fuel had been completed, which coincided with an announcement that we were about to pull into York. We were half way home and feeling the buzz of elation that always comes to the weary traveller at such a moment.

'Can't wait to get a lungful of cool, fresh East Lothian country air,' I said to Ellie. 'After our experiences in London, I mean.'

'Yes, but not all Londoners live in a hell-hole hotel or need to use the tube every day, never mind get stuck in it.'

'Mmm, true enough, but it isn't a place for the faint-hearted all the same. It's all push-shove and hurry-scurry or get trampled in the stampede.'

Ellie had a quiet chuckle to herself. 'And you're a fine one to talk, I must say. All the years we've been together you've done nothing but what you're accusing Londoners of.'

I considered her point with a pensive nodding of my head. 'Yeah, but even so, I've mostly been doing it in the countryside, and there's a big difference.'

'And you should think yourself lucky for that! There'll be lots of city people who would gladly swap places with you.'

I raised my hands. 'Point taken. And I *do* count myself lucky in that respect, I promise you.'

There was no more to be said on the subject, so I sat silently watching the landscape scudding past while Ellie concentrated on reading about the ups and downs of Regency love life in Mills & Boon Land.

'I feel kinda guilty about dragging you around with me on these trips, you know,' I said after a while. 'It can't be much fun sitting about on your own in corners of libraries and shops while I do my book-plugging blethers and so on.'

Ellie glanced up from her novel and shot me a quizzical look. '*Dragging* me around?'

I realised immediately that I could have chosen my words more carefully. 'Ah well, not *actually* dragging ... but ... well, you know what I mean.'

Ellie leaned across the table and gave my hand a reassuring pat. 'Don't forget that we lived in London once as well, and there were many times, when you were away with the band, that I'd have given anything to be travelling with you, no matter what the hardships. And it was the same when you went away on record production work, but...' She paused to think for a moment. 'Well, looking after the kids and livestock had to come first, and I counted myself very lucky by then too – compared to sitting alone in a tiny flat in London.'

All I could do was stress that, even if I never actually *said* so, I'd always been grateful for her being there to hold the fort. And what's more, whenever I was away, I'd rather have been at home with her and the kids.

To which Ellie gave another little chuckle. 'So, if both of our wishes had been granted, we could always have waved as we passed each other half-way.'

I acknowledged Ellie's little joke with a smile. 'OK, but that would've meant we were heading in opposite directions, and life sent us off to pastures new together instead. Lucky again, eh?'

'Correct. And that's why you won't need to drag me along now. Rearing calves at Cuddy Neuk, picking oranges in Mallorca and doing up houses back here certainly became roller coaster rides at times, but we managed to have our fair share of laughs en route. And even if I can't lend a hand with actually *writing* your books, I'll happily muck in with the job of flogging them, wherever it takes us.' She patted my hand again. 'So, *tranquilo, hombre*! Relax! Keep the heid! I'll be there to make sure you change your socks every day, never fear.'

I was genuinely touched by that, but while I tried to think of a reply that wouldn't sound too schmaltzy, Ellie piped up: 'And before you say it, my chum Maggie *was* right: I either deserve a medal for stoicism or a certificate of flippin' insanity!'

*

Serialisation in a national newspaper probably boosted sales of my books more than all the other promotional efforts put together. A fortnight later *Mañana, Mañana* hit the No 1 spot on the *Whitaker BookTrack European Travel Books* chart (as published in the *Bookseller*, the UK's trade 'bible'), with *Snowball Oranges* in hot pursuit at No 7. This coincided with *Mañana, Mañana* being featured as 'Book of the Month' in the WHSmith chain of twelve hundred retail outlets throughout Britain, with special summer promotions also being set up nationwide by rivals Waterstones, Ottakars, Borders and Books Etc. All of this good news related to just over a year earlier when *Snowball Oranges* became a surprise bestseller with the backing of only a modest amount of promotional outlay. Chestervale Publishers had even been spared the expense of the 'bus fares' that had been mentioned figuratively in relation to whatever travelling I might undertake to counter competition provided by the more liberally-financed 'big boys'. Though being in no way smug, I did derive some quiet satisfaction from seeing *Snowball Oranges* out-selling books in a similar vein published by companies that had turned it down.

But there was neither time nor reason to dwell on such thoughts, because the moment had to be grasped to consolidate this success *and* build on it. If that meant keeping my nose to the grindstone more assiduously than ever, then so be it. It had been a long, hard struggle to reach this point, but no matter how gratifying the achievement, to ignore its fragility would be to risk throwing its benefits away. Which, to my astonishment, appeared to be what Chestervale suddenly decided to do...

Although they had been very quick to take up their option on a third book in the series (with a working title of *Snowballs Three*), and had urged me to crack on with producing the written goods in time for publication just twelve months after the release of *Mañana, Mañana*, Izzie contacted me out of the blue one day to inform me that this was no longer considered to be the best way forward. Instead of continuing with recollections of our Mallorcan adventures (for which I still had enough material for perhaps three more books), they now wanted me to write a set-in-Scotland prequel to *Snowball Oranges*.

My immediate reaction was that, while there *might* be a demand for such a book at some later stage, to stop the roll we were currently on would make no commercial sense. I reminded Izzie that she and her bosses had predicted the demand for a third Mallorcan book would match that achieved by the first two, so why the sudden change of heart? Surely, I reasoned, delaying *Snowballs Three* would jeopardise its chances of being taken up for newspaper serialisation, for which it was currently being considered in principle.

The same applied to my preliminary dealings with TV producer Marina Jessup, who had emphasised the attraction of building a project on a series of books as opposed to just one or even two. And apart from anything else, I had already started flagging up *Snowballs Three* during live events and in media interviews, prompting positive reactions every time.

My entreaties proved, however, to be in vain. The decision had been made, based entirely, I was told, on the company's grasp of the vagaries of the publishing business.

I could have responded by suggesting that the basic commercial rules of the publishing business were likely to be much the same as those of any other in which common sense dictates that you don't try to fix something that isn't broken. But I had established a really friendly and productive working relationship with Izzie and her young colleagues on the two previous projects, so I decided it was worth making an effort to understand their way of thinking on this one, no matter how illogical it might seem at first.

Izzie had been given the task of establishing contractual terms with me from the very start of my association with Chestervale, and had conducted negotiations in an even-handed and respectful way throughout. But now the prospect of wrangling over purely business matters with the person I'd become accustomed to working with on the creative side felt slightly uncomfortable, and I sensed Izzie felt the same way.

Apart from the need to discuss issues relating to the proposed set-in-Scotland book, it so happened that the original contracts for the first two books now required re-negotiating as well. In light of the unforeseen success of both books and the resultant flow of moneys into the Chestervale coffers, the modest royalty rates I had agreed to at the outset would have to be adjusted accordingly, if the partnership was to move forward on an equitable basis.

Again, Izzie was charged with the task of fronting negotiations, and while I had no reason to doubt the company's fairness, I took the precaution of having the terms of the contracts vetted by the Society of Authors. In the interests of fostering a spirit of good will, however, I had already resigned myself to settling for royalty percentages that would be a compromise between the optimal and minimum recommended by the Society, though in most aspects – particularly those pertaining to subsidiary rights – leaning more towards the lower of the two. And this was the area in which a glaring anomaly was spotted by the Society's advisors.

It's worth mentioning here, though, that there are two types of subsidiary rights applicable to overseas countries in which a book is *not* being translated into another language…

The first is an 'export' deal, whereby physical copies of the original UK edition are shipped to a distributor for marketing in a specific country. In such cases, the author's royalty is calculated in the same way as in the UK, as a share (typically between ten and fifteen percent) of the UK publisher's revenue from sales.

The second type of rights assignation, the one in which the Society of Authors had identified the aforementioned anomaly, grants an overseas English-language publisher a licence to manufacture the book and sell it as an item from their own catalogue in their own particular territory. In such an arrangement, the original UK publishers are not liable for the cost of printing or any other overheads, and this should be reflected in increased royalty points for the author. According to the Minimum Terms Agreement recognised by writers' associations internationally, the assignation of North American rights of this type should provide for the author to receive a royalty of, at best, eighty-five percent of the UK publisher's receipts, but with a minimum of fifty percent. Chestervale had allotted me eleven, which was even less than the median rate now considered appropriate for my home sales.

Given that North America is by far the biggest market in the English-speaking world, a book becoming a bestseller there can result in a financial bonanza, so a just share of the spoils is crucial. I chose to assume that Chestervale's decidedly one-sided division of those spoils had been an honest mistake, perhaps the result of the company never having had the rights to any of their books taken up by an American publishing house before. I didn't know, and I reckoned it was best to regard the matter as purely academic anyway. In the words of another old song: '*Accentuate the positive, eliminate the negative*'.

Consequently, as a mark of my gratitude to Chestevale for having given me my break as a published author – and in response to their assertion that, as a small publisher, they were governed by 'limited financial resources' – I accepted a royalty rate for North America of fifty percent, the Society's recommended minimum. Although this was considerably lower than the eighty-five percent top rate, it was well above the eleven percent I'd originally been offered.

And so we moved on.

But the words of caution about contracts that agent Bette Tanner had spoken at the London Book Fair the previous year came starkly back to mind: *'You can't be too careful – royalty rates, translation rights, options on subsequent books and so on. That's when having an agent is so important.'* Ironically, I'd had several offers of agency representation since the blossoming of *Snowball Oranges,* some of them from agents who had rebuffed my approaches before, and most of those clearly more interested in pocketing a slice of my existing earnings than advancing the prospects of finding a publisher for my fiction books.

For the present at least, I would continue ploughing my own furrow, while resigned to setting aside indefinitely the work I'd already done on *Snowballs Three,* and putting my mind instead to how I'd tackle its set-in-Scotland replacement. Firstly, though, there was a contract to sign, and I expected it to replicate the terms and conditions already agreed for *Snowballs Three*. Those, in turn, had reflected the cumulative success enjoyed by the first two books, so that the £500 advance royalty I received for *Snowball Oranges* had been upped to £2,000 for *Mañana, Mañana* and was to have been increased to £8,000 for *Snowballs Three*.

But these increments were being financed by profits realised by Chestervale from sales of my existing books, not by gambling on those still to come. As a consequence, the advance I received for *Mañana, Mañana* would already have paid for itself several times over. The same applied to the agreed advance for *Snowballs Three*. In short, the advances on royalties I was being paid for each new book were not really *advances* in the strictest sense, but reinvestments by the publishers of a portion of the proceeds my books had already generated. Those had grossed more than £150,000 for *Snowball Orange*s in its first year alone, and all in return for their gambling one *actual* advance of £500. Not a bad punt.

As someone who could occasionally be a tad 'close with a buck' myself, I had nothing in principle against the canniness exhibited in financial matters by the two young owners of Chestervale Publishing. But their approach also served to remind me that business is business, and now that my writing activities were developing fairly positively in that respect, it would have been remiss of me not to exercise due prudence as well.

I had opted to accept their plea of 'an honest mistake' for what might otherwise have been taken as an attempt to hijack the bulk of my North American royalties, but with the best will in the world, I could not bring myself to do likewise for the advance royalty as stipulated in the contract now being discussed. The first thing to strike me was that the advance which had already been agreed for *Snowballs Three* had been summarily reduced by three quarters to £2,000 for the set-in-Scotland book that the publishers, without seeking my opinion, had decided should replace it. It was time to get down to brass tacks.

* * * * *

Chapter Fourteen

'NOT ONE FOOT IN THE GRAVE'

*

I had never been under any illusion about how difficult it would be to earn a living solely from writing books, the career of a full-time author being as notoriously precarious, perhaps, as that of a professional jazz musician. But I had succeeded in the latter (for a while at least) and I hadn't had to resort (so far) to supplementing the former by working as a night watchman on a building site. That said, while the projected income from book royalties gave reason for optimism, we were still having to dip frequently into our 'housekeeping' nest egg, not so much to defray our own day-to-day expenses, but more to subsidise book-promoting activities that involved an increasing amount of travelling to distant locations. To date, no contribution towards the cost of these metaphorical 'bus tickets' had been made by my publishers, and this was one salient point of several that I intended to bring up when discussing their volte-face regarding the subject matter of my next book. First, though, I needed to find out what had prompted them to make such a puzzling decision in the first place…

The response I got from Izzie on the phone was virtually a repeat of their earlier assertion that it had been based entirely on the company's grasp of the vagaries of the publishing business, to which I gave my instinctive reply that this amounted to nothing but a totally negative exercise in attempting to fix something that wasn't broken. The silence that followed served to confirm that, irrespective of her own opinions, Izzie was obliged to implement the policies dictated by her employers. But why, I asked, would they want to cut significantly the advance royalty on my next book, which was tantamount to withholding essential feed from a point-of-lay goose that had already delivered two golden eggs? I was given the standard excuse that, as a small publisher, they didn't have the resources to offer big advances, which I countered by reminding her that any responsible publisher, large or small, has an obligation to reward its authors adequately for their efforts. And in my case, consideration should surely be given to the resources already being generated for Chestervale by the unprecedented profits they were enjoying from my first two books. Besides, I wasn't asking for fortunes up front, only enough to help sustain me while I worked to provide them with another new book in less than twelve months, and the proposed advance of £2,000 (already covered by their share of the *Daily Mail* serialisation fee alone) fell well short of that. Writing, I stressed, was my livelihood, not a hobby.

Stating this reminded me of a theory once aired by a respected book critic: *'Many of the people in publishing and agenting are frustrated authors themselves'*. While it was well known that a few members of those professions had indeed had their literary endeavours published – and often with limited success at best – I had never noticed any such inclinations in Izzie's attitude towards her day job. She was an editor first and foremost, and apparently content to leave it at that; other than taking responsibility for certain contractual negotiations, that is.

But what of her two bosses? They had formed the company with the primary purpose of publishing their own books, and as they still had aspirations to progress as authors themselves, could it be that, in some respects, they had subconsciously developed a tendency to treat the work of other authors as their own? If so, maybe their approach was along the lines of: 'You've been invited to *our* party, but we'll choose the games to be played and make up the rules as we go along.' Outlandish as this might seem, it made about as much sense to me, under current circumstances, as shunting a runaway success into a siding instead of stoking its boiler and speeding it on its way.

Putting such speculations aside, the reality of the situation was that, after all the confident predictions they'd made about the prospects of *Snowballs Three* replicating the advance orders of fifteen thousand copies notched up by *Mañana, Mañana,* they were now saying that a set-in-Scotland book would be a better bet, although they thought it would be unlikely to sell the four thousand copies required to 'earn back' the lower advance they were offering me. To my way of thinking, this begged two obvious questions: was this new lack of confidence simply a ploy to justify lowering the advance, or did they *honestly* believe the book would struggle to sell even four thousand copies? In either case, indications were that their faith in my being able to continue producing profitable books for them might now be in doubt. Could it be that they had come to regard me as a one-trick pony who had miraculously pulled a second trick out of his saddle bag, but would be highly unlikely to produce a third? If so, maybe offering to publish a book set in my native land was just their way of ending our relationship in a *considerate* way, while they developed other projects with the windfall funds I'd already helped provide.

As chance would have it, the very day before this confrontation took place, I'd had a call from a commissioning editor at one of the top London publishing houses to say that they were interested in exploring the possibility of publishing some of the fiction books I had submitted, but with the proviso that I would grant them first refusal on my non-fiction work as well. I thanked them for their interest, but explained that I felt duty bound to continue having my non-fiction published by Chestervale, so would be unable to accept their offer, tempting though it was. Normally, I would have been reluctant to use this to my advantage in the ongoing dialogue with Chestervale, but on this occasion I had no qualms, particularly since I had declined the offer purely as a mark of loyalty to them.

I got no direct reaction from the Chestervale management, either because they didn't believe I would turn down such an attractive proposal or because loyalty didn't feature as highly in their list of priorities as it did in mine. I had never forgotten the experience, almost forty years earlier, when I had been sacked by the management of the Clyde Valley Stompers for daring to ask that details of the band's burgeoning finances be shared with myself and my six colleagues, the musicians who generated the moneys in question. The management had thought that all they had to do was replace me as leader and their milch cow would continue to fill their bucket without kicking it over. To their surprise, however, the rest of the boys forsook their own financial security by walking out behind me. That show of solidarity made a profound and lasting impression, and taught me that true loyalty transcends all things material. But its reciprocation should never be taken for granted.

I continued my contractual deliberations with Chestervale on the assurance that their commitment to me was undiminished. As in all negotiations conducted in good faith, compromises were eventually made on both sides. The outcome in this case entailed my agreeing to a set-in-Scotland book as the next project, and to accepting a slight 'amelioration' of the reduced advance royalty. In return, Chestervale would pay all, instead of half, of it on signature of contract, thereby going some way towards covering my living expenses while writing the new book. A revised system of royalty calculation was also agreed, my percentage rising in increments of one or two points after specified sales targets had been reached.

Unavoidably, a degree of horse-trading had been involved, and there were occasions when I'd rather have had an agent acting on my behalf, especially since the bargaining process had included lengthy and at times quite blunt exchanges that resulted in delaying the completion date of the next book from April to August. At this stage, the fate of the months of work I had already done on *Snowballs Three* would be determined by the success or otherwise of its replacement. This was far from an ideal situation, and was the unfortunate outcome of Izzie and me spending valuable time 'negotiating' when we would have been better employed concentrating on the creative work we both enjoyed. But I had protected my interests as resolutely as I could, and hopefully without having too detrimental an effect on the rapport that had become a valuable element of our working partnership so far.

The priority now would be to get on with the job in a spirit of mutual trust, while the touchy topic of 'bus fares' would be put on hold for another day.

* * *

By early 2002 several more foreign language editions of *Snowball Oranges* had been published, mostly in hardback format and many with strikingly original jacket designs. It was both fulfilling and intriguing to see the people and situations I had described in English appearing in languages that were alien to me. For example, there were two Chinese versions, one printed in 'simplified' word-characters to cater for the majority of readers, the other in 'complex' or traditional characters for those considered to be of a more scholarly disposition. In either version, it was amusing to see a Scottish word like *dreich* (miserable, depressing, grey, drizzly) for which there would be no direct equivalent, appearing in splendid isolation in the middle of a row of Chinese 'hieroglyphics'. But irrespective of the language, I had the utmost respect for and trust in the skill of the translators, and always made a point of thanking them and the individual publishers involved. While I regarded this as no more than common courtesy, it was a gesture that would eventually pay dividends in the most unexpected – and disquieting – of ways.

Other developments that came with the onset of 2002 included the release of the audiobook edition of *Snowball Oranges,* as well as its publication in large print format. I had never given it much thought before, but a book being reproduced in large print enhances its chances of being stocked in public libraries, which in turn helps its promotion by word of mouth. The same applies to audio editions, although they have the added benefit of being a boon, not just to the visually impaired, but also to people regularly on the move, like long-distance truck drivers or deep-sea fishermen – and even, paradoxically enough, to night watchmen on building sites!

The Soundings division of Oxford-based Isis

Publishing had become established as front-runners in the unabridged audiobook business well before they bought the associated rights to *Snowball Oranges*, which marked the start of a productive and long-lasting relationship that would result in spoken editions of the majority of my books. Noted for their consummate professionalism and attention to detail, the Soundings producers chose versatile Scottish actor James Bryce to be the 'voice' of them all. Ultimately running to a typical playing time of ten hours per book, each recording involved at least a week of sentence-by-sentence concentration in the company's Whitley Bay studios. Great care was taken to ensure that the written text was followed to the word and that each inflection of speech and every nuance of accent came over exactly as a reader of the books might have imagined. No mean feat when taking into account the various foreign-language phrases and eccentricities of dialogue that are scattered willy-nilly throughout much of my writing. James 'Jim' Bryce proved himself to be a master of his art, only once having occasion to call me about a troublesome detail, which actually turned out to be a typo that had slipped through the proofreading net when the original manuscript was passed for publishing. Take a bow, Jim. Top man!

*

Sponsored by the ubiquitous bookshop chain, the WHSmith Literary Awards were presented annually for various categories of books that customers in the company's hundreds of retail outlets throughout country had voted for. Nominations were open to books in English by authors resident in the UK, the Commonwealth, the Republic of Ireland and the USA, and also to foreign-language works in translation. Quite a wide field to pick from, which made it all the more surprising to be notified that *Snowball Oranges* had been shortlisted. But it had, so while I didn't give myself any real chance of winning against what was bound to be formidable opposition, it would have been impolite not to attend the ceremony, which was scheduled to take place on 9th April.

So, Ellie and I set off again on the 400-mile train journey to London, bound this time for the opulent assembly rooms of the five-star Great Eastern Hotel, where we had arranged to meet up with Izzie and two of her newer Chestervale colleagues who, as recent recruits to the publishing game, were keen to avail themselves of a chance to rub shoulders with some of the great and the good of the current literary scene.

I had resolved to make this a purely social occasion, with no mention being made of 'business' issues. Enough time had already been taken up with those, and all of it eating into an uncomfortably tight schedule for completing the agreed set-in-Scotland book. Although a couple of fresh concerns had recently emerged regarding that project, this would be neither the time nor the place to address them. This was a night for celebration, even if only for being invited!

By that very token, it was just as well that I had approached the event with the old farm workers' motto very much in mind – *'Blessed are they who expect nothing, for they shall not be disappointed'* – because, as I expected, I didn't win anything. Consequently, another maxim I was happy to invoke was that the most important thing was not the winning but the taking part, especially since my selection hadn't been made by a panel of judges from within the inner sanctum of the literary establishment, but by countless members of the public I didn't even know and would be unlikely to ever meet. That was accolade enough for me.

While the elegance of the venue did ample justice to such a prestigious occasion, the glitz and glamour that would be taken for granted at an equivalent showbiz affair was absent. And no doubt deliberately so. This was no Tinsel Town extravaganza of red-carpeted exhibitionism, bejewelled celebs, jostling paparazzi, back-slapping hype and tearful acceptance speeches, but rather a sequence of reserved though sincere tributes to a selection of authors whose work had prompted a broad cross section of the book-buying public to register their appreciation and support.

Yet it was surprisingly informal in a way, with those guests seated at tables augmented by others milling round the periphery of the room. And it wasn't all culture-for-culture's sake verbalising from the platform either, with well-deserved plaudits for Ian McEwan's thought-provoking *Atonement* balanced by humour-spiced quotes from Pamela Stephenson's biography of her husband Billy Connolly, and some tasty tips from the latest cook book by TV's 'domestic goddess' Nigella Lawson.

As with the *Mañana, Mañana* launch at Daunt's bookshop nine months earlier, this get-together, though on a much grander scale, felt more like a casual cocktail party than a major awards night. I wondered if this was just the way that 'booky' people liked to hang out together, and if so, good on them. There were no signs of pretentiousness or the huddles of 'luvvies' that some of us might expect to see fawning over each other at such a gathering of creative types. That's not to suggest that opportunities to do a bit of lobbying and schmoozing were being ignored by publishers, agents and authors alike, but it was all done with due discretion after the main business of the evening had been wound up.

In a way, it reminded me of the bar at Edinburgh's Gorgie Cattle Market where, after the sale was over, farmers and dealers would gather to discuss the day's trade, celebrate or commiserate as appropriate and generally chew the fat to keep connections cordially cemented until next time.

No matter how discreet the moves in the Great Eastern Hotel, however, I suspected that a fair amount of scouting and 'fishing' was going on between people lingering in the bar. As would be expected, it was award-winning authors who were attracting most attention from would-be suitors, all of whom I instinctively took to be from within the ranks of the agenting and publishing fraternities. On the other hand, maybe most of these liaisons were just old acquaintances catching up, with no reason to either dangle bait or take it. Whatever, the atmosphere was congenial, and even though I turned out to be only an also-ran on the night, my presence *had* been noted by one established member of London's book-biz society; although it's only fair to say that, apart from the three Chestervale girls, she was probably the only person present who knew who I was anyway.

Bette Tanner of the Eltan Literary Agency had introduced herself to Elle and me at the London Book Fair two years earlier, shortly before *Snowball Oranges* was released. She had struck us as a pleasant person, not at all pushy, eager to stress the value of having a good agent when it came to contractual matters, but unfortunately showing no indication of being interested in helping find a publisher for my fiction books. I therefore assumed she was merely being sociable by approaching me again now.

I introduced her to Izzie and her colleagues, and she took what appeared to be a close interest in their respective roles, for although she might well have been accustomed to frying bigger fish, it would be prudent nonetheless to establish contact with up-and-coming publishing folk like them. Borrowing from the cattle-market analogy: the youngster selling a solitary calf today could be tomorrow's breeder of a pedigree herd. Meanwhile, Bette tactfully avoided mentioning anything to do with my own relationship with Chestervale, but as we said our goodbyes, she invited me to drop by her office next day…

*

Coincidentally, the Soho location of Bette's literary agency was but a stone's throw from the Great Chapel Street offices of Lynn Dutton, the band agent who controlled the affairs of the Clyde Valley Stompers back in the '60s, and where I regularly made my way by tube from our base in north London to hand over any gig fees that had been paid in cash during the band's latest travels. Even the geography inside the offices was pretty much the same: a narrow staircase up to the first floor, with a door leading into a small hallway with three doors off. The 'public' office in both cases faced the street, and would probably have been the living room of the flats that typically occupied such premises in times past. But that's where the similarity between the two agencies ended. The Dutton office was always a hive of activity, with musicians, managers and promoters coming and going while exchanging animated greetings and gossip in the passing, whereas the Eltan Literary Agency's front office was more akin to the reading room of a public library, complete with floor-to-ceiling book shelves, but without a trace of the public.

All was silent, except for the faint thrum of London rising from the street outside and the occasional trill of a phone ringing somewhere across the hall, where I presumed the business of the agency was being conducted within a similarly placid environment. We sat chatting over coffee with Bette for about fifteen minutes, during which she complimented me on the success of my first two books, asked about my immediate commitments and plans for the future, and generally gave the same impression of genuine interest that had been apparent during her conversation with the three Chestervale girls the previous evening. The big difference, of course, was that the Chestervale girls, with youth on their side, had career prospects unlimited by time, while I, in my sixty-second year, did not. Yet when I mentioned that I had elected to stick with Chestervale at the expense of accepting an offer from a major publisher, she said that she thought I'd made the correct decision. My writing career, she opined, would have a better chance of growing as an integral component of an upwardly-mobile young company than as only one of countless cogs in a large publishing machine. I could only take from this that she regarded the prospective longevity of an author-publisher relationship as yet another 'subjective' aspect of the literary game. And when I brought up the matter of having to haggle with Chestervale over royalty percentages and advances, she told me we had to remember they were still only a very small publisher, so such difficulties had to be regarded as par for the course and had to be dealt with accordingly.

'Which presumably,' I replied, 'is just one example of why it's so important to have a good agent, as you touched upon when we met at the London Book Fair.'

Bette nodded her acknowledgement of the fact, before confirming that the client list of her agency was full, though she would like me to keep in touch anyway. Circumstances, like the weather, were always liable to change when least expected.

Ellie patted me on the shoulder as we descended the stairs and emerged into the Soho sunshine. 'Well,' she winked, 'at least you can take some comfort from knowing she doesn't think you've got one foot in the grave – professionally, at any rate.'

'Hmm,' I replied, pensively, 'I'm not so sure my publishers would agree, though.'

'Not to worry,' Ellie breezed as I hailed a cab, 'I've a feeling London hasn't beckoned you down from Scotland again for nothing. Look on the bright side.'

'The *Moro* in Exmouth Market, please,' I called to the cabbie. 'And I've a feeling you could be right,' I told Ellie. 'When did I ever go to a Spanish restaurant looking any other way?'

* * * * *

Chapter Fifteen

'TV DREAMS AND BOOK-KEEPING NIGHTMARES'

*

I could see why Marina Jessup had suggested meeting in the Clerkenwell area of London, handy as it is for King's Cross Station where Ellie and I were to catch the evening train back to Edinburgh, and just far enough away from her Wardour Street office in Soho's 'Film Row' to be beyond eavesdropping lunchtime ears. As requested, I had sent her a copy of *Mañana, Mañana* when it was published the previous summer. She had emailed me a few weeks later to say she liked it a lot, and thought it added significantly to the 'televisual possibilities' of my Mallorcan memoir. Her intention was to discuss the idea with a colleague who shared her enthusiasm for this type of project, and although it was one that would take time to fully assess, she felt it would be a good idea to get together and 'talk about preliminaries' the next time we were in London. The WHSmith trip served the purpose nicely.

It's my guess that Marina had chosen *Moro* in preference to several other eateries in bustling Exmouth Market simply because it specialised in Spanish cuisine, so would probably make us feel at home – which it did. The aroma of wood-grilled pork and charcoal-roasted lamb transported us magically back to Sunday lunches spent in favourite country haunts in Mallorca, with even the uninhibited clamour of customers' conversation and the waiting staff's dramatically bellowed communications putting an authentic Spanish stamp on one small corner of north London. A view of the Mediterranean and a resident mosquito with a taste for Scottish blood would have been all it took to complete the illusion, but on balance I was more than happy to settle for the status quo.

In person, Marina proved to be pretty much as I had envisaged: forty-something, down-to-earth and with a warm, neighbourly disposition that was the antithesis of the popular conception of a movie business high-flyer. She was accompanied by co-producer Denny Joffe, a likeable character with the perkiness of a London cock sparrow. Together, they came over as the type of people who would brighten any company with their upbeat mien and easy-going turn of conversation. This was the spirit of bonhomie in which we spent the afternoon. And the more we talked, the more it became apparent that our belief in laughter being the best medicine was shared by Marina and had been the basis of her collaboration with Denny. It presented them with the intriguing challenge of how best to visually portray the mood of cheerful optimism that was such a dominant feature of our Mallorcan story.

'I believe it would make a *cracking* television series,' Marina enthused, '– a welcome antidote to all the gloomy, violence-laden stuff the public is bombarded with these days. Good, wholesome family entertainment to lift the spirits, and with that vital escape-to-the-sun element that so many dream of, but few are fortunate enough to experience in real life.' She added that, as with most book-to-screen adaptations, the narrative would be subjected to a certain amount of tweaking, twisting, exaggeration and moderation, although the distinctively *visual* style of my writing had already provided much of the ground work in that respect. If I was comfortable with this approach, she'd like to secure an option on the exclusive cinematic rights for a period of five years. A token fee of £1,000 would be paid up front, with a suggested £20,000 payable on the first day of filming. But, she immediately cautioned, the chances of the project ever progressing as far as that remained as slim as when she first noted her interest. This was a fact of life that had to be accepted in her profession, and it underlined the importance of only embarking upon ventures she was truly passionate about.

As laid-back as the meeting had been, things were moving fast and I was anxious to keep the momentum going, while at the same time not rushing into a situation I might live to regret. What I knew about the legal intricacies of movie options could be scratched on the pip of one of the pickled olives I was popping.

'Well, Marina, all I can say is I'm flattered by your

interest and extremely grateful for your belief in my material. I'll be only too pleased to cooperate in any way I can, of course, but where exactly do we go from here?'

She proceeded to explain that, before anything practical could be done, we would have to be joint signatories to a binding contract. Of necessity, this would be a lengthy and complex document (the standard template they used ran to some fourteen pages) which covered all legal aspects of the option, and although some of the specifics might seem unnecessarily pernickety, it was for good reason. Every clause had its origins in a long line of lawsuits dating back to the days of Charlie Chaplin and Buster Keaton. So, she stressed, it would be in my own interests *not* to sign the agreement until I had taken expert legal advice – and by that she didn't mean our local high street lawyer, who would be unlikely to have had sufficient, if any, experience of the subject. Most authors in this situation would either have an agent who specialised in these matters, or would rely on their publishers having an equally qualified member of staff. If I had no immediate access to either of these sources of advice (which I didn't|), she recommended that I should seek the guidance of the Society of Authors, who could be trusted implicitly – and, as I would already know, also provided the service to its members free of charge.

She went on to say that the next step would be for Denny, who had a proven track record in such things, to compose a treatment (detailed synopsis) of the opening one-hour episode, which would follow as faithfully as possible the storyline of *Snowball Oranges*, and would be augmented with a summary of how the series would progress from there. I would be kept informed and my opinion sought about each aspect until a 'complete package', including the names of actors earmarked for the lead roles, had been prepared for pitching to the TV networks. Thereafter, she and Denny would be hustling for the same elusive prize as every other script-toting man and his dog. And keeping every flexible part of their anatomies crossed as well!

*

In the end, Ellie's prediction that London hadn't summoned us down for nothing had proved to be correct, so our journey back to Scotland that evening was spent in a predominantly positive mood, though tempered with a degree of caution. We had gained *some* kudos from at least being shortlisted for an important literary award, had been asked to keep in touch by a respected literary agent who, if nothing else at this stage, had reinforced our favourable impression of her, and we had laid the foundations of what, with a large slice of luck, could prove to be a profitable relationship with a well-established TV production company. Now it was a matter of taking encouragement from all of that to press on with writing my next book, while continuing to devote as much time and energy as possible to promoting the two already on the market.

But Ellie, pragmatic as always, gradually diverted

the theme of our conversation away from the rainbow-chasing 'creative' side of my new career towards the fundamental matter of the proceeds we derived from it and, crucially, how they were being monitored. Ever since embarking on our farming endeavours at Cuddy Neuk all of thirty-two years earlier, Ellie had looked after our business accounts, keeping meticulous records of income from the sale of grain and livestock, together with outgoings for seed, fertilizer, fuel and cattle feed. On top of that there were the numerous comings and goings of record-business finances to be taken care of, and Ellie took it all in her stride. With typical modesty, she maintained that her job was made relatively easy by the accounting efficiency of our trading partners.

But now, such orderly book-keeping was not immediately apparent when it came to the question of my author's royalties, and this made Ellie slightly nervous. She had always left the nitty-gritty of contractual matters in my hands. To her way of thinking, the minutiae of legal mumbo jumbo meant little if the resultant earnings weren't paid into our bank account on time. Simple as that. And for her to fully understand and check the veracity of the current situation, I would have to provide her with a detailed list of what royalties were due from whom and when to expect them.

I confessed that I'd intended doing this as a matter of course anyway, but had allowed it to slip down my list of priorities because of all the other pressures that had been accumulating in the two years since the publication of *Snowball Oranges*. At that time, with only one book to consider, keeping track of royalty payments had been comparatively straightforward, and particularly so when only the original English-language edition was involved. The terms of the contract stipulated that Chestervale would do an 'accounting' of all sales achieved in the first six months of publication, and thereafter biannually for as long as the book remained in print. A slight complication was that, to give them time to factor in the value of any stock sent back by their distributors via sale-or-return arrangements and any losses incurred as a result, they were allowed three months grace after each accounting date before making the associated remittances. Still, it remained a fairly easy matter for me to remember when royalties were due. And this was also the case when my second book was published, even though its accounting dates differed from the first. I realised, however, that things would get progressively more convoluted as royalties from foreign-language, audio and large-print editions began to feed through, so it really had become imperative to make a detailed list of all relevant dates for reference going forward.

It wasn't that I doubted Chestervale's integrity in administering these various transactions, but I had already found their accounting system to be a mite 'haphazard', and more often than not any miscalculations tended to err in their favour – though purely by chance, I was sure. All the same, while I was resigned to making certain allowances for the fact that they were a small company, it was becoming a bit wearisome to have this trundled out as a reason for their inherently 'close' attitude towards the division of revenues and what might be seen as 'inefficiencies' in the way they were discharged. It was all well and good to have come to an agreement for my royalty percentages to be calculated on a rising scale, but if the trigger points were going to be missed along with the final payment dates, then we were heading for a state of confusion that would ultimately end in tears. And I had too much at stake to let that happen.

I had already discussed the issue with Izzie who had taken it to the bounds of her remit, so it was now for the company's owners to step up to the plate. Their response was to freely admit that their 'old abacus system' had become 'too creaky for purpose', and they intended to invest in a comprehensive upgrade, although that would take some time to complete. In the interim, I should rest assured that any 'minor discrepancies' in the content and timing of my royalty statements would be put right as soon as practicable.

With due acknowledgement of their candour, my reaction was to suggest that, in the interim, they might consider investing in a ten-bob pocket diary and a five-quid calculator. In the absence of a reply, it was left for time to tell.

Time, however, was a commodity in increasingly short supply, since even postponing the completion date of the Scottish book until August – to compensate for the three months spent working on the shelved *Snowballs Three* – had left me with an uncomfortably tight deadline to meet. Besides, I felt honour-bound to fulfil the personal appearances already set up to promote a book that would not now be published as originally scheduled – if ever.

By June 2002, there were already several book festival engagements between then and the end of the year entered in my diary: Wigtown in south-west Scotland, then Berkshire and Hampshire in the south of England, followed by a miscellany of 'reading' events in places as far apart as my home town of Haddington in East Lothian, Cromarty in north-east Scotland, Swindon in south-west England, Scarborough in north-east England, then yo-yoing up and down and criss-crossing mainland Britain to Perth, Sheffield, Selkirk, Lochcarron, Doncaster, Hull, Inverness, Reading, Ullapool, London, and finally back to another event in Haddington. All of these engagements had been made as a consequence of the interest created by *Snowball Oranges* and its follow-up *Mañana, Mañana*, so it remained to be seen what the public's reaction would be to news of a forthcoming book set in Scotland with no connection to Mallorca at all.

I admitted to being more than slightly apprehensive about the prospect, but I was grateful as always for having been asked to 'do a turn', so come what may I would honour the bookings and do my utmost to make the best of a tricky situation that had been created for reasons I still failed to understand. A publisher making such sweeping decisions is all very well if exercised from a distant office without members of the public seated a few feet away; but it would be for me to carry the can, and nowhere would I have to face a more savvy public than at an event referred to in a newly arrived letter, the gist of which read as follows…

Dear Peter

It is with the greatest of pleasure that I write to invite you take part in the Edinburgh International Book Festival 2002. This is the largest and most popular celebration of writers and the written word in the world ... with over 120,000 people attending over 500 events of every kind. We very much hope therefore that we may tempt you to come and join us… Among our authors taking part last year were Nobel Prize-winner V S Naipaul, seven Booker Prize-winners including Peter Carey, Margaret Atwood and Michael Ondaatje and many other major figures including Gore Vidal and Doris Lessing…

I greatly hope to welcome you in August.

Best wishes,

Catherine Lockerbie
Director

My immediate reaction was that I was having my leg pulled. Surely there could be no place for a spontaneous scribbler like me on the hallowed platforms of what truly was '*the largest and most popular celebration of writers and the written word in the world*'. What right could I possibly have to mix in the company of literary luminaries such as those named in the letter?

Well, I reasoned, the only way to test the authenticity of the invitation was to accept it, and this I promptly did. While waiting for a response, I told myself that the best I could hope for was that I was being offered a spot to provide some light relief during the 'comfort break' in one of the more serious events: a bit like a honky-tonk piano player thumping out a medley of toe-tappers while members of the audience repair to the bar during half-time at a symphony concert.

But no, I wasn't being pranked, as confirmed by Catherine Lockerbie in her reply. What she proposed was a *Travel and Exploration* event in the form of a chaired discussion to take place in the main auditorium on the evening of 15th August, featuring myself and celebrated South African novelist Christopher Hope, whose many awards included being short-listed for the ultimate accolade, the Booker Prize for Literature. His latest book, *Signs of the Heart*, was set in the Languedoc region of France, hence the 'travel' tie-in with my humble offerings.

This promised to be another testing step on what had already proved to be a long and steep learning curve for me, and while suspecting there might be another gastric visit from my familiar fruit bats on the night, I couldn't help but look forward with some relish to this new challenge. What a pity, though, that the publication of my third Mallorcan book, which I presumed had been a deciding factor in my being asked to take part in the first place, wasn't going to enjoy the benefit of such a rare promotional opportunity. And to add a touch of travesty to this regrettable state of affairs, its set-in-Scotland replacement, which in any case wouldn't be released until two months after the festival, would never have complied with the *Travel and Exploration* theme anyway.

A further incongruity was that the Edinburgh Book Festival engagement, although by far the most prominent I had yet undertaken, would be one that involved a minimum of outlay on travelling, the Scottish capital being only seventeen miles from my home base. But all of this served only to focus my attention at last on the matter of the accumulated personal expense involved in book-plugging travels during the previous two years.

Ellie wasn't slow to goad me into action. 'It's a vicious circle,' she said. 'The more popular your books become, the more invitations you get to talk about them and the more you fork out to make longer and longer journeys, not forgetting meals en route and overnight hotel bills. OK, that's maybe all in a good cause for everyone involved business-wise, but where in your publishing contracts does it say the author is responsible for picking up the tab?'

She needed no reply from me other than a shrug of assent. Ellie had made her point: it was high time I put my cards – or metaphorical 'bus tickets' – on the table.

* * * * *

Chapter Sixteen

'THE LADY CHATTERLEY CONNECTION'

*

I duly broached the subject of travelling expenses in an email addressed to Chestervale's co-owners, whom I had met only once, and then but briefly. In their early thirties, their ages slotted between those of our own sons, and my impression was that they were fine upstanding chaps. As stated earlier, I'd been told that their primary objective in setting up Chestervale had been to publish their own books, with their 'reverse highwaymen' approach reflecting a policy that would allow them to latch onto a passing opportunity, hope to bag a modest return without getting bogged down in long-term commitments, then revert to Dick Turpin mode to await the next likely target, while also utilising the time to further their own literary aspirations. In the main, travel related narrative material was what they were looking for, but as books in that genre tend to be reasonably long with correspondingly lengthy turnaround times between commissioning and publishing, to keep the till bells ringing in the meantime, a smaller, more 'transient' product needed to be added to their lists. They achieved this by diversifying into novelty and gift books aimed initially at the student market. Typical themes were along the lines of: '*How to chat up women*', '*Student grub recipies*' and even a dissertation on '*Why men are crap*'. I suspect that some of these books were written behind a screen of pen names by the partners themselves and even by a few of their young employees. It was all happy-go-lucky stuff, catering for a clientele that neither expected nor required the effort and expense of on-the-road promotion by the authors, who would probably be more than happy to remain in 'low maintenance' anonymity anyway. Quite an astute method of creating a comparatively fuss-free source of income from relatively low-budget publishing, and one that Chestervale would exploit with notable success in years to come.

But right now, they would have to come to terms with one notably mobile scribbler who might just be about to change his hitherto low maintenance spots.

*

I had always kept them informed of any promotional trips I planned to make (indeed, many of the invitations were relayed through their office in any case) and I had liaised closely with their sales people regarding the supply of books to be sold at the various events. This meant establishing if the hosts planned to sell the books themselves, or if they'd prefer to invite a local bookshop to do it for them, or, failing those options, if they'd like Ellie and me to bring stock with us. Many were the occasions when we could have done without the inconvenience of lugging a suitcase full of books on and off trains, up and down stairs and in and out of taxis, but we regarded it as a basic element of the job in hand, which was to promote my books and make the most of any sales opportunities, no matter how piecemeal.

And it was obvious that Chestervale's sales people felt the same way, even if the process might prove a bit 'fiddly' for them at times. By such means, after all, are word-of-mouth seeds propagated, and it was to those that my books owed a great deal of any success they were enjoying. But no matter how much revenue had been created by so modest an outlay, promotion, even the hands-on, foot-slogging variety I had been doing my bit to generate, did come at a price, and as Ellie had remarked, nowhere in my contracts did it state that the author should foot the bill. This was a matter that would have to be addressed before I embarked on the list of promotional journeys already entered on my date sheet for the last four months of the year, and it was this that comprised the essence of my email to Chestervale's management.

Maybe it was an issue they had never had to deal with before, or perhaps they hoped it was one that would resolve itself without too much hassle if left to the normal run of events. Either way, their eventual response was essentially an affirmation that my observations had been noted and would be given due consideration as soon as time permitted. I knew well enough that this could be a euphemism for '*We'll just ignore this in the hope that it goes away*', but if I allowed that to happen, it would be as good as agreeing to subsidise the publishers' responsibilities at the expense of our own 'housekeeping' reserves. And that was a situation that had gone on for long enough.

In an effort to inject some urgency into proceedings, I reminded them that in the past two years I had personally covered all expenses incurred while fulfilling 'reading' engagements in various parts of the UK, doing a stream of press, radio and TV interviews, making four trips to London and countless poster-delivering visits. All of that had set me back upwards of £1,500, not counting the expense of an extremely fruitful 'promo-cum-business' trip to Mallorca, and without taking into account the cost of Ellie accompanying me when needed, for example, to man the book-selling table at live events. I emphasised, however, that had my books not been successful, I would not be asking Chestervale to contribute one penny to the cost of my promotional efforts, past, present or future. But my books *had* been successful, resulting in unprecedented dividends for the company, evidenced by *Snowball Oranges* grossing £150,000 in its first twelve months from UK sources alone. Its sales had continued apace in the second year, with *Mañana, Mañana* following in similarly lucrative fashion, and with income from publication of the first foreign-language, audio and large-print editions now imminent as well.

All things considered, then, I respectfully requested them to address the matter of my out-of-pocket expenses without further delay.

As mentioned before, my inclination had been to empathise with their 'canny' approach to financial matters, particularly in our early dealings when they were taking a gamble on publishing my first book. But that gamble had paid off quickly and continued to deliver handsome returns. Surely there could be no excuse now for getting into an unseemly wrangle over reimbursing me with relatively small amounts of money. Still, it could be pretty much assumed that the clichéd *'We're only a small company'* would be offered once more as justification for any shortcomings.

I wasn't too surprised, therefore, that my email prompted a response which, though expressed sympathetically, was nonetheless dismissive. No mention was made of the £1,500-plus I had already forked out, but I was offered 'as a token of good faith' a contribution of £20 to help towards travelling expenses for each 'promotional appearance' in the future. A true token of good faith would have been to make a donation towards *past* expenses, but I had already resigned myself to writing those off, which constituted a sizeable token of good faith on *my* part. But I simply could not afford to adopt such a magnanimous attitude towards the list of upcoming 'appearances'. Unavoidably, the dates had been booked individually with each organising body, so no actual 'tour' itinerary could be arranged, with the result that separate journeys there and back would be necessary on most occasions. A total of almost six thousand miles would be travelled, mostly by train, with many dates requiring overnight stays. Taking the Berkshire round trip of eight hundred miles as just one example, no matter how penny-pinching I tried to be, a conservative £200 would be needed to cover my fares, accommodation and subsistence, which put Chestervale's suggested contribution of twenty quid into perspective. To make matters worse, I was informed that payment of such contributions would be delayed for up to six months to allow for 'normal' cash flow conditions pertinent to small companies like theirs.

I had always tried to give the benefit of doubt to Chestervale's owners when any potentially contentious issue involving money arose. No-one knew better than myself how, without the benefit of past experience, an element of unintentional discord can enter into such situations. I was no longer prepared, however, to accept 'small company' excuses, when even my local bank manager classified my own writing activities as merely a 'micro enterprise'. You can't get much lower down the corporate food chain than that, but it didn't relieve me of any obligation to conduct my affairs in a businesslike manner. And I was entitled to expect no less from anyone else.

From the start of our relationship, I had demonstrated that cooperation, gratitude and loyalty were my bywords, but anyone who took this as a sign that I might be a soft touch or passive milch cow would have been seriously mistaken. I had been through that mill in the music business forty years before and I wasn't about to fall into it again. Accordingly, I made it clear that from then on I would invoice Chestervale for legitimate expenses incurred in fulfilling all promotion-related 'appearances', and it would be for them to deal with those bills in whatever manner they thought proper. I also assured them that any expenses paid directly to me by event organisers would be deducted from my invoices, and all costs relating to occasions when it was necessary for Ellie to accompany me would be met in full by me. In short, Chestervale would be contributing not one penny more than they were obliged to, and if that arrangement proved to be unacceptable, they'd be putting the continuation of our partnership on the line. Business, after all, *is* business – even for spontaneous scribblers.

No objections were raised, so I could only hope that the way ahead had been swept clear of what I saw as totally unwarranted sources of friction. Inevitably, those choppy waters had spilled over into the writing and editorial areas that formed the foundation of our relationship. Although Izzie hadn't been directly involved in my exchanges with her bosses, I had kept her informed, and I'm sure they would have been doing the same from their side. An already tight working schedule had been further squeezed by the time spent in what had ended up as a take-it-or-leave-it situation, which wasn't ideal. But I had decided to let that particular sleeping dog lie and make the most of the few weeks now left to hit the delivery deadline for the set-in-Scotland book.

I had been asked to write it as a prequel to

Snowball Oranges, so I reckoned the most logical approach would be to make it an account of my life from early childhood until just before our fateful departure for Mallorca some forty years later. I still feared that issuing such a book at this point in time was premature, and indeed that many would consider it decidedly presumptuous on my part, since I was far from qualifying for the 'name' status on which the market for biographies thrives. But I had agreed to write it and therefore applied as much attention and dedication to the task as I had to any other.

I had named the book *Leaning Against the Wind,* a title that had virtually picked itself, given my family's ties with Orkney and the resolute character of folk born and bred in those windswept northerly isles. The title related primarily to an opening sequence in which, as a small boy standing atop a breezy bluff at Cuddy Neuk, my idolised grandfather treated me to a demonstration of that gravity-defying feat. Although my attempt to emulate him ended face-down in a cow pat (much to my grandfather's amusement and, eventually, my own), the full significance of the poignancy embodied in the very idea of *Leaning Against the Wind* would only become apparent as my recollections of the ensuing years came drifting back.

The misgivings I had about the commercial raison d'être for this book did dull my enthusiasm for writing it – for a while at least. But the more I became immersed in the process and the more I got used to the possibility that its eventual publishing might turn out to be a parting gesture on Chestervale's part, the more I allowed myself to become absorbed in the pleasure of recalling details that might otherwise have been committed to the fading pages of memory. However, while I enjoyed revisiting the many people, places and happenings that had featured in what had been an extremely eventful and predominantly fortunate sixty-two years, I had to avoid being self-indulgent. That would have killed stone dead any chance the book might have had of attracting any readership at all, for there's nothing more boring than being plied with personal bits and pieces that are of no interest to anyone but the writer and his granny. Equally, it would have been a mistake to deliberately spice up everyday happenings in hopes of elevating them from the mundane.

I therefore set out to present my story as an honest, down-to-earth, though essentially upbeat narrative about how life evolved from the early 1940s to the beginning of the '80s for one ordinary country lad, and encompassing many of the circumstances that would also have been experienced by my contemporaries. For me, the most valued aspects of the period had been a supportive family, a small circle of good friends and, in the fullness of time, a long-suffering wife. And although I'd never had a surfeit of material assets to build on, the benevolence of Dame Fortune had provided me with a ride on a roller coaster that had never remained at the bottom of the track for long.

So, having managed to pick my way along a puddle-strewn path with my feet reasonable dry for the past six months, I delivered the finished manuscript of *Leaning Against the Wind* to Chestervale at the beginning of August – all eighty thousand words of it. Izzie and her colleagues now had just two months to 'prep' the book for an October release, so they wasted no time in putting together an advance information sheet aimed at key targets in the book trade and media. Since Izzie had been editorially involved in the book's content from the start, she was suitably qualified to compose the required summary, a draft of which she sent me for feedback...

East Lothian is 'The Garden of Scotland' and the setting of this delightfully idiosyncratic story of country life. Often hilarious, always heartfelt and at times sad, here unfold the ups and downs of four generations of one farming family from the northerly Orkney Isles, who move to the little farm of Cuddy Neuk in the south of Scotland just before the outbreak of World War 11. A young Peter, the 'peedie boy' who sets his heart on filling his somewhat eccentric grandfather's straw-lined wellies, grows up to run the family farm and become a farmer father to his own sons, putting his ability to see the funny side of things to good use, as adversities crop up with intriguing regularity...

Presenting the gist of eighty thousand words with an acceptable degree of accuracy in just one short paragraph requires both a sensitive appreciation of the subject matter and the courage to be ruthlessly selective. Inevitably, many details will de sidelined, but if the mood created is sufficient to give the potential reader a fair impression of what's on offer, then that's the mark of a good précis. As expected, Izzie had proven herself up to the task, and I sent her my thanks and congratulations.

At long last, I could take a deep breath, leave others to put the new book to bed, and brace myself for tackling a full diary of events originally intended for the promotion of *Snowballs Three,* the opening chapters of which I still held 'on ice', but without any indication of when I might be asked to finish the job – if at all.

* * *

Scotland's capital, widely recognised as one of the world's most beautiful cities, has a resident population of just half a million, which is swollen to at least five times that number during the final three weeks of August by visitors from all over the globe, drawn by the cultural allure of the Edinburgh International Festival of the Arts. The 'main', or original, festival was launched in 1947 and features the world's finest exponents of classical music, opera, ballet and the visual arts, while its unashamedly nonconformist offshoot, known as the 'Fringe', has in time overtaken its more highbrow progenitor in terms of mainstream popularity, with ticket sales regularly topping two million for some three thousand shows. While the 'main' festival events are staged in the city's conventional theatres, concert halls and galleries, those of the Fringe, whether a solo stand-up comedy routine or a recital by an ensemble of unicycling ukulele players, may take place in any available space from the back room of a pub to an abandoned bus shelter. It's fascinating to note that many of the UK's biggest names in light entertainment got their first break by taking a chance on just such improvised platforms at the Edinburgh Fringe.

Finding suitable venues in one central location for the many facets of the Book Festival must also have posed a problem at the start. The solution the organisers came up with was an ingenious though controversial accessory to the neoclassical elegance of the city's *New Town*. Georgian Edinburgh hadn't been dubbed *The Athens of the North* without good reason, so any suggestion of pitching a tent in the middle of one of its most imposing open spaces would surely have met with shocked disapproval from officialdom and neighbouring residents alike. But what was actually proposed – and eventually materialised – wasn't just one tent, or even one marquee, but an entire village comprising an assortment of both. With due credit to the vision of the organisers, and despite the doubts of naysayers, leafy Charlotte Square Gardens proved to be a spectacular and much loved home for the Edinburgh International Book Festival for the next thirty-seven years.

For me, having only recently seen myself as something of a one-trick pony in a one-man travelling circus, entering this tented city (for it was too grand to be described as merely a village) was a humbling experience. My immediate reaction was one of admiration for the thoughtful way the grassy expanse of the gardens had been transformed into a vibrantly attractive 'arena' without detracting from the architectural dignity of the surroundings. This was sedate *Auld Reekie* wearing her jauntiest Easter Bonnet – even if slightly out of season.

Augmenting the three main 'theatres' was a selection of cafés, bars, a bookshop, a 'signing' tent and an authors' retreat, all clad in pristine white canvas and set around the perimeter of the 'village green'. On it, an abundance of deck chairs, tables and parasols had been provided for the convenience of those wishing to sit quietly reading a book, chat with friends over a glass or two of wine, or even tuck into the contents of a bring-your-own picnic basket with the kids *and* the family dog. Here was a shining example of how the world of books *should* be presented to the public.

The official publicity material for the festival described it as: *'A celebration of the written word, literature and ideas, bringing together leading and emerging international, British and Scottish authors and thinkers to inspire each other and audiences in an extensive programme.'* In practical terms, this entailed holding over 500 events of a diversity ranging from the most intellectually demanding to a festival-within-a-festival for children. With so many authors taking part, allotting them all a spot of their own would not have been possible, so it followed that many would be presented in a 'shared billing' format.

I suppose they must have fitted me in as 'definitely *Scottish*' and 'allegedly *emerging*', with a 'not proven' verdict in respect of anything to do with '*thinking*' or '*inspiring*'. This appeared to be in direct contrast to the qualities attributed to my fellow guest Christopher Hope, and served as an indication of how carefully assessed these pairings had to be. Much depended on the programme compilers having done their homework, and it soon became clear that Paul Johnston, an accomplished crime author tasked with being 'in the chair' for our session, had spared no effort in that regard himself.

Walking onto the stage, I could see that there were no empty seats in the tiered auditorium, which had a capacity of perhaps a couple of hundred, so the first thing that occurred to me was how different this was compared to my 'appearance' two years earlier at Waterstones bookshop just round the corner in Princes Street. No-one had turned up on that occasion, but I was sufficiently realistic to accept that the vast majority of those I was facing now were there because of their interest in the literary achievements of Christopher Hope. And this is where the skill in presenting such an ostensibly odd coupling came to the fore.

Once the three of us we were seated, Paul Johnston opened proceedings by briefly outlining any common denominators in the *Travel and Exploration* theme that applied to Christopher's writing and my own. Although it's unlikely that anyone present needed reminding of his gifts for description, Paul quoted from a review of Christopher's latest book, set in southern France, which the festival's director Catherine Lockerbie had written for the *Scotsman* newspaper: *'Christopher Hope is a superb prose stylist, with a deep understanding of how a place works upon a person ... He makes us taste and feel the lasting resonance of a simple meal of fresh bread, a twist of salt and fresh sardines in a damp, cold cottage in the Tarn.'*

There were mutterings of agreement from the audience – even a ripple of applause. Then Paul turned his attention to me, and I noticed an impish twinkle in his eye…

'But it has to be said, Peter, that you're no stranger to such praise yourself.' He referred to his notes. 'I mean, here's just one example, taken from a review featured in the publicity hand-out for *Mañana, Mañana,* your latest Mallorcan travelogue. It says, and I quote: *Kerr has an ability, reminiscent of D.H.Lawrence, to capture the overwhelmingly oppressive feel of physical fatigue on a hot day.'*

Paul glanced up at me, inviting a response.

'Yes,' I said, with a wink intended for all to see, 'but that's not necessarily related to digging irrigation channels through orange groves in the height of a Mediterranean summer. Take it from me, I've been just as knackered digging bullock shite out of a dung midden in the depths of a Scottish winter!'

It only took one raucous guffaw from a bloke in the back row to parry any sudden intakes of breath from elsewhere. Laughter prevailed, and although it was more restrained in some members of the audience than others, I was pleased to see Christopher having a quiet chuckle himself. No matter how tenuous the similarities between our personal observations of situation and circumstance might have been, the ice was broken and Paul now had carte blanche to steer the interview along a course as informal as he chose.

I found the question-answer-discussion format a pleasure, so the next hour literally flew by. Paul cleverly introduced topics that Christopher and I bounced off each other in ways that could be either empathetic or conflicting, but always good-humoured and, I think, entertainingly informative as well. The response from the audience at the end was enthusiastic enough to suggest that they had enjoyed our confab. But our host wasn't about to bid them farewell without revisiting an exchange he felt had been left unfinished. He turned to me again, and I noticed the mischievous glint had returned to his eye...

'In my introduction, Peter, I mentioned the book review that compared your descriptive work to that of D.H.Lawrence.'

I nodded my head, apprehensively.

'As you're doubtless aware,' Paul continued, 'although he's probably best known, by *some* at least, for writing *Lady Chatterley's Lover* – a novel infamous in its day for explicit descriptions of sex and the use of four-letter words – Lawrence was considered, by those best qualified to judge, as one of the finest travel writers in the English language.'

I half closed my eyes, bracing myself for the coup de grâce.

'I'm not suggesting,' Paul went on, 'that comparing your descriptive work with that of D.H.Lawrence is undeserved, as I notice it relates to just one of many five-star reviews your books have earned.' He paused and referred to his notes again. 'No indeed, it's just that, well, this particular review is credited to a magazine called ... let me see ... yes, called ... *Monoscope*.' He looked at me, his head tilted inquisitively. 'Frankly, Peter, I've never heard of it.'

A pregnant silence descended on the marquee.

The truth of the matter was that I had never heard of that particular magazine either, nor could I reasonably be expected to be familiar with many of the other publications, both in the UK and abroad, that had judged my books favourably. Paul knew this, of course, and it gave him all the more reason to tease – just to see how I would react.

'Well, Paul,' I sighed, lowering my eyes and shaking my head in an exaggerated show of self-reproach, 'as with all the other five-star reviews you mentioned, it's because I made that one up myself.'

I was joking, but was aware that not *every*one would have cottoned on. I glanced at the audience and saw a sea of facial expressions, equally divided between confused frowns, knowing grins and drop-jawed consternation. If ever I needed it, here was a perfect example of the subjectivity of humour. But as soon as a few people started to titter, more pennies dropped, and within a few moments the entire assembly had joined in a nudging, winking, chortling appreciation (genuine or fake) of my comeback to Paul's ribbing.

All in all, I had thoroughly enjoyed what would turn out to be my first of several Edinburgh Book Festival experiences, and any fruit bats that had been contemplating a flutter round my innards beforehand had been given short shrift by the pervading feeling of amity. As I had already learned, 'bookish' folk – that's to say the people who read books, work in bookshops for the love of it, or regularly make the effort to support book-related events – are the wind beneath an author's wings.

The majority of those who populate the 'business' side of things are of the same stripe, or so it may seem on the surface. However, I was soon to take the next step on *that* particular learning curve, resulting in a situation in which my commitment to this way of earning a living would be put to the test – once and for all.

* * * * *

Chapter Seventeen
'A THISTLY ISSUE'

*

Although book festivals are primarily a showcase for authors, they also attract the presence of publishers and literary agents, all of them keen to lend support to their creative clients, while also keeping an eye open for ways to consolidate and expand their own interests. Today's creative (and money-making) client may turn out to be tomorrow's has-been, and business, like life, goes on.

The morning after my own first appearance at the Edinburgh International Book Festival, I got a call from just such an agent, who happened to have been an active participant in subsidiary rights deals that had resulted in the publication of several foreign language editions of my first two books. We'll refer to him as Cephas, for reasons that will become apparent in due course. He was paying a visit to Edinburgh, he said, and would be delighted if I could meet him for lunch that very day. He'd leave it to me to suggest a place, but he'd prefer it to be reasonably close to Charlotte Square, as he had a couple of other people to see at the festival later in the afternoon.

I've never met a successful agent in any line of business who doesn't exude an air of confidence, whether it's an estate agent extolling the virtues of the 'sophisticated' (aka obsolete) plumbing in a clapped-out house he's flogging, an advertising agent doing the same regarding virtually anything he's being paid to punt, or a showbiz agent testing a record producer's intelligence (and patience) by playing him a demo of 'the next Barbara Streisand', who in reality sounds more like a whippet in the throes of a severe constipation attack. But in fairness, I had tended to put the literary agents I'd met in a less spiv-like bracket, although they had all possessed at least a modicum of the self-assurance that is clearly a prerequisite of their profession.

The Bar Roma, tucked away in a lane behind the west side of Charlotte Square, was one of Edinburgh's most popular Italian eateries: typically informal, irrepressibly cheery, conversationally clamorous, good value for money, and only a short walk from the entrance to the Book Festival. Perfect for purpose.

Agent Cephas turned out to be a genial gent in his fifties, casually but smartly attired, manifestly self-assured, but effortlessly adept at masking any suggestion of superiority. He had all the hallmarks of an agent, and he didn't beat about the *bruschetta* either! No sooner had we exchanged pleasantries over a plate of the Bar Roma's tomato-topped *crostini* than he got straight down to business…

'As you probably know,' he began, 'I'm first-and-foremost a conduit between publishers worldwide, selling translation rights of English-language books to my foreign connections on behalf of the original UK publishers. In your case, on behalf of Chestervale.'

He paused to order a *Pizza Calzone* stuffed with Parma ham and wild mushrooms (the most expensive pizza on the menu), while I plumped for a less 'robust' but equally pricey *Spaghetti alle Vongole*. Well, it isn't every day you're treated to lunch by a worldwide conduit, so why spare the baby clams!

'While representing authors is not our main line of business,' he went on between munches, 'we are always happy to consider the occasional one whose work shows international potential.' He took a discerning sip of the *Valpolicella Classico Riserva* he had selected (the house's best – no plonk-slurper, this conduit), then added that foreign reaction to my two books had convinced him that I could be one of 'the few'. However, to help him make a final decision, he would appreciate it if I could send him full details of all UK and overseas book sales *and* income to date, plus an idea of my plans for the future. He stressed that, as well as supervising the financial transactions of my existing books and seeking out more translation deals, he would undertake to develop my longer-term career prospects in whatever direction I chose to follow.

After so many years of struggling to find an agent, this all seemed promising – on the face of it. But one aspect bothered me right away: as agent Cephas would be working on my behalf as well as that of his existing publisher-clients, surely a conflict of interests was likely. When I put this to him – citing as an example a 'hypothetical' situation in which Chestervale and I might be haggling over the size of advance royalties – he confidently replied that, on the contrary, as both parties were being represented by his agency (albeit in *slightly* different capacities), he would be ideally qualified to act as an unbiased mediator. He smiled a reassuring smile. 'An honest broker, if you like.'

I *did* like – in theory anyway – though I could still envisage problems in practice. But why open cans of premature worms if it risked scuppering the chance of being taken on by a top agent? Better right now to sound him out about placing my existing fiction books with a publisher, since it was a foregone conclusion that they would be the basis of any future I might have as an author. For it had to be faced that the time would come soon enough when tales of our Mallorcan adventures had all been told.

I was, by Chestervale's own admission, the best-selling author they had ever had. Accordingly, I'd always believed the logical way forward would be for *them* to capitalise on the success of my non-fiction books by starting to release my fiction titles while my name was as prominent in the public eye as it might ever be. This would not only serve to establish a way forward for me, but would also add another few wagons to the gravy train towed by *Snowball Oranges* that had so fortuitously called at Chestervale's station. Still, all of my appeals to them had been rebuffed. In fact, it appeared that the more popular my books became, the more determined the owners were *not* to publish fiction. But it was their company and they were entitled to adopt whatever 'editorial' policy they thought fit. To me, however, it seemed they were missing a trick, and I couldn't fathom the thinking behind it.

When I related all of this to agent Cephas, his response was that, under such circumstances, publishers, like beggars, can't be choosers, but Chestervale, although small, could obviously afford to exclude themselves from that hard-up ilk.

And my response to this was that excluding themselves didn't tally with their attitude towards parting with money, whether for the calculation of advance royalties, or indeed observing royalty payment dates without delays caused by 'small-company cash flow problems'. If they weren't hard-up, why behave as if they were?

'The only answer is for you to be attached to an agent who's closely acquainted with their business practices,' said Agent Cephas, tapping the side of his nose. 'So, let's hope the breakdown of numbers you're going to send me will result in us tying the required knot.'

I said a silent 'Amen' to that, then settled back to a half-hour of small talk, dominated by Cephas quietly but pointedly blazoning his commercial credentials, and lubricated by an ample supply of his excellent choice of wine. Although I was no connoisseur, by the time coffees were ordered, I was in the mood to show that, despite being a comparative newcomer to his version of worldly wisdom, I wasn't entirely unfamiliar with lesser-known specialities of Italian libation myself...

'Would you like a *Grigio Verde* with your *espresso*?' I asked him.

'A *Grigio*...?'

'*Verde*. You know – g*rigio* meaning grey, and *verde* for green.'

Cephas, though having emphasised the advantages of being a multilinguist in his line of business, was plainly none the wiser.

I proceeded to elucidate: 'They're the colours of the Italian army uniform, I believe'

'But what's that got to do with coffee?'

'It's the name of a liqueur to go with it,' I said. 'Or rather a mixture – a favourite in Venice, or so I was told by an Italian waiter who hails from there.'

Agent Cephas was intrigued. 'A mixture, you say?'

'Yes – Italian *Grappa* brandy, fifty-fifty with *Crème de menthe* liqueur. Grey and green, see*?*'

'But *Crème de menthe* – that's French, surely...'

'So what?' I shrugged. 'If there isn't such a thing as an Italian green liqueur, nicking one from a neighbour is the next best thing, no?'

Cephas was inspired. '*Camariere!*' he called to the waiter. '*Due Grigio Verde, per favore!*'

'*Che?*' the waiter queried, clearly confused.

This prompted Agent Cephas to reiterate my explanation word for word, but in fluent Italian. Once he was satisfied that the waiter had finally got it, he raised two fingers and boldly appended, '*Due bicchieri ... GRANDI, eh!*'

'Ehm, I should warn you,' I discreetly advised the

agent, 'the old *Grigio Verde* may taste innocuous enough, but even a *wee* measure packs a helluva punch.'

I needn't have concerned myself. Without going into unnecessary detail here, I was left with the impression that if Cephas' qualities as an agent matched his ability to hold his drink, then being a client of his would be no bad thing. He also displayed a sharp eye for the main chance by toddling off to the Book Festival while leaving me to pay the bill.

I suppose it served me right for trying to get one up on a practised one-upper. I'd been mugged all right, but promptly persuaded myself to regard it as an investment: a small price to pay for laying the foundations of what I *hoped* might become a productive and lasting partnership.

* * *

The autumn of 2002 had always looked like being a busy one, if for nothing more than getting through the packed schedule of on-the-road dates that had originally been set up to promote the now-shelved *Snowballs Three*. Instead, I would be doing the rounds – all six thousand miles of them – beating the drum for *Leaning Against the Wind,* which Izzie had been 'prepping' for October publication since the beginning of August. Now, mid-way through September, she informed me by email that the title was being changed to *Thistle Soup.* I was both taken aback and puzzled, so phoned her right away.

'Why?' I asked straight out.

'We decided it's a much more *on-trend* title, that's all.'

'*We*? Who are *we*? I wasn't even aware it was up for discussion.' There was an awkward silence, so I stepped in to help Izzie out. 'Look, I realise that the naming of a book is ultimately the publisher's prerogative, but even as a courtesy, surely the author should at least be asked for an opinion before his own title is changed. I mean, you're a hundred percent familiar with what this book's all about: you caught the mood well enough in the blurb you wrote. Now, all of a sudden, the title's been changed to something that doesn't even make sense.'

'It's just that, well, no offence, but it was thought that *Leaning Against the Wind* wasn't catchy enough. It's not what the current market is looking for.'

'But irrespective of what you reckon the market is looking for, the title *Thistle Soup* bears no relationship to what I've written. Let's face it, it sounds more like some sort of sadistic cookery book, so where did the idea come from?' I had always got on extremely well with Izzie, regardless of any unavoidable bumps in the road we had encountered from time to time. I also had a very high regard for her as an editor, and had no wish to sour the relationship. But my well-tried keenness to cooperate was being severely tested here. 'On-trend, you said. What trend is that exactly?'

I was then informed that 'the girls in the office' had made the suggestion in light of the success currently being enjoyed by a book called *Umbrian Soup,* which Izzie, on being pressed further, loosely described as being a contemporary novel aimed mainly at a 'youngish' female readership. Oh, and it was set in Umbria, as I would have gathered from the title.

'In other words,' I replied with deliberate calm, 'a romantic holiday romp through the Italian countryside, straight off of the Mills & Boon "chic lit" shelf...'

'Well, yes, I suppose you could call it that. But the thing is, it has a catchy title that doesn't pigeonhole it in any way.'

'OK, but I presume the author has an existing fan base built on the popularity of one definite pigeonhole – namely women's romantic fiction.'

'Yes, she has actually.'

'So, they know in advance what to expect between the covers – no pun intended –whatever the title...'

'Yes, I suppose so, and I know what you're getting at, but it's the catchiness of the title that we want to exploit for your set-in-Scotland book.'

'Even if it makes absolutely no sense at all...'

Izzie ummed and ahed a bit, but it was obvious the conversation was going nowhere anyway. Chestervale were in their customary reverse-highwayman mode, hitching a ride on a passing coach flying the 'Popularity' flag, just as they had done when easing *Snowball Oranges* into the slipstream of an already successful book that also happened to have a citrus-flavoured title. I presumed the final decision had already been made to change the name of my new book to *Thistle Soup*, no matter how I felt, so there would be no point in spending more time discussing the matter. It was disappointing and slightly irksome to say the least, but going on about it to Izzie would serve no purpose. I'd have to make my views known to the company's owners. And, perhaps tellingly, an opportunity presented itself within the hour...

An email arrived from one of the partners advising me that a collage artist, whose work was 'currently much in-vogue', had been commissioned to design a cover for *Thistle Soup*, and the finished article had already been sent to the printers in anticipation of the book's publication in a few weeks time. A proof was about to be posted to me, along with a copy of the brief the artist had worked to. My comments would be appreciated.

The first thing I did was to dig out the note on that very subject that Chestervale had asked me to provide when the book was still called *Leaning Against the Wind*. Here's how it read:

Author's note:

I think it's worth mentioning at this early stage that the areas of the country featured in the book are not the 'Mountains, Heather, Glens, Stags and Lochs' type of Scotland popularised on shortbread tins and picture postcards. East Lothian, where most of the action takes place, has soft-rolling 'Lowland' landscapes with some spectacular sea/island features involving the Firth of Forth with its islands. I'd seriously avoid the temptation, no matter how great, to plump for a Highland 'Majestic Peaks' shot. It would be like using a pic of the Lake District for the cover of a book about Kent.

When I received the copy of the design brief that had been given to the artist, a quick once-over revealed its key words and phrases to be as follows:

Scottishness – Whisky, Haggis, Thistles.

The feel of the book – Combination of brightness and nostalgia – Cow getting stuck up a belfry.

The time gone by – old hoary Scottish grandfather smoking Woodbines – WW2 reminiscences: aeroplanes, open ranges and rationing.

Scottish influence is vital – Photographic shot of Scotland, with vibrant image of purple-and green thistle pasted in foreground.

Almost Monty Python collage-cartoon effect, but without the surrealism. Humour-collage effect of Bill Bryson's "Notes from a Small Island".

To me, this immediately conjured up an image of the Chestervale staff sitting round a table lobbing their individual ideas into a pot. It reminded me of the old gibe about a camel being the outcome of an attempt by a committee to design a horse. And so much for my plea to avoid resorting to hackneyed images of Scotland that were at odds with the essence of the book. Fair enough, they hadn't included heather, glens and stags, or references to specific shortbread tins, but haggis, thistles and whisky were in there to compensate. I felt sorry for the artist, who'd had to make something representative from guidelines as 'sundry' as this, and the photocopy of the cover when it arrived indicated that he had ultimately settled for a compromise that made no more sense than the title itself.

Despite my pleas to avoid them, heather-clad mountains provided the backdrop to a mock-up scene that I guessed had originally been inspired by the artist reading at least the opening chapter of *Leaning Against the Wind.* A prominent position was given to a young boy doing just that while standing tilted over the edge of a cliff. So far so good. Meanwhile, in the middle distance, an elderly man in a kilt (my 'hoary Scottish grandfather' wouldn't have been seen dead in one!) walked towards the stereotypical Scottish loch, which I had also suggested would be out-of-place, while in the bottom corner, a hen and cockerel added a rustic touch as they posed beside an outsize potato fork and a blue-and-white-striped Cornishware jar. Indications of creative licence being driven by approaching despair, perhaps? Still, at least there was no sign of a haggis.

But the most obvious deviation from Chestervale's brief was the absence of the v*ital* image of a purple thistle. And this is where the switch from the original title to the new one must have been presented to the designer. He had undoubtedly put a lot of thought into creating something he felt would satisfy Chestervale's curious requirement for taking an unspecified *Monty Python collage-cartoon effect* and blending it with the *Humour-collage effect* of England's green and pleasant land as seen through the eyes of an American.

So, what did the despairing designer do? He replaced the purple thistle he'd been asked to 'paste in the foreground' with a cut-out of a giant bowl, complete with wooden spoon. But unfortunately, although presumably not intended, the result looked for all the world like a wee laddie with suicidal tendencies pissing from a great height into a massive plate of soup. Purple, of course.

Yes, I felt sorry for the designer, and my natural tendency to at least *try* and look for a lighter side in awkward situations did allow me to have a wry smile at this one. I had been asked to give my opinion of the cover, and I did, with total frankness, while also bearing in mind there would be no point in creating a potentially terminal confrontation about something I took to be a fait accompli. I admit to feeling a bit miffed at being excluded from discussions regarding the change of title and ensuing 'presentational' decisions, for even though it wasn't my contractual right, being invited to contribute to the process in some small way would have been a mark of courtesy, if nothing else. This failure to communicate would have made it all too easy for me to jump to the conclusion that the whole affair had been handled in a blatantly offhand manner by the publishers, given that they weren't even confident of the book selling well enough for me to 'earn back' the correspondingly modest advance I'd been paid. And such thoughts did cross my mind.

But our younger son Charlie tried to set me straight on that point. Having worked for all of his adult life in the computer graphics department of a large advertising agency, he knew of many a lengthy board room think-in with miscellaneous 'creative' personnel brain-storming their way to a slogan that would best attract the public's attention, even if, or very often *especially* if, the slogan bore no obvious relationship to the product being advertised. '*Made In Scotland From Girders*' for example? That one worked spectacularly well, although it's likely that several camel-looking horses had been sent to the knacker's yard before celebratory glasses were raised to future sales of *Irn-Bru*.

Basically, Charlie was backing my own suspicion that the title *Thistle Soup* was simply the product of a get-everyone-involved scrummage of ideas that may well have been just one of several tackled on a Friday afternoon when Chestervale's small and youthful squad were already buoyed up by thoughts of the imminent weekend. Who was to say that all of them had even read *Leaning Against the Wind* in any depth? Think tanks need a plethora of ideas, period, and they do tend to come thick and fast when Friday night opening time at the pub round the corner is only half an hour away. Charlie had been there often enough to know!

I appreciated that he had been trying to spare his old man the aggro of fretting unnecessarily, and I readily agreed that *Thistle Soup* was indeed a catchy title, in much the same mould as *Snowball Oranges*, in fact. But we both knew the big difference was that both words in the latter title derived directly from the content of the book, whereas those in the former did not. What's more, while acknowledging the importance of the narrative's liberal seasoning of 'pawky' Scots humour, the sense of poignancy reflected in the original title of *Leaning Against the Wind* meant a great deal to his mother and me, and any hint of Friday afternoon flippancy towards that particular aspect would hurt. As it did. But he was right in what he had suggested: the title of the book was a done deal, so we should bend with the wind until we could see which way it was going to blow next.

* * * * *

Chapter Eighteen
'DECISIONS, DECISIONS?'

*

By the time *Thistle Soup* was published in October, its back cover had gained a tag line describing it as '*A ladleful of Scottish life – a brimming and lively broth of rural characters, drunken ghosts, bullocks in bedrooms and country superstitions*', which could be justifiably regarded as having been contrived to explain a title that was already contrived enough in itself. Also, the selected ingredients of the 'broth' had made relatively minor contributions to the overall flavour of the book, and didn't blend too well with Izzie's earlier précis, which had now become the main constituent of the back-cover blurb.

Here was another fine example of the subjectivity of humour. Perhaps the book's 'pawky' Scots wit I referred to earlier had failed to tickle the funny bones of whoever came up with the '*brimming and lively broth*' line, so they decided to highlight instead a handful of items that agent Libby might have termed more 'custard pie' than incisively-wry. And if 'incisively-wry' fails to enlighten, rest assured that seeking a definition of 'pawky' is as futile as asking someone to describe the shifting patterns in a kaleidoscope. Or, as Louis 'Satchmo' Armstrong used to say when asked to define jazz, 'Man, if you gotta ask, you ain't never gonna know!'

Anyway, when the first reviews of *Thistle Soup* appeared, it became obvious that plenty of people understood what the book was all about, in spite of how the cover *could* have influenced their judgement…

> *"It is wonderfully written, and you will also be treated to a ton of ticklish humour. A most enjoyable and heart-warming read"* … *"He transports you into the heart of some of Scotland's most beautiful scenery"* … *"memories of a quieter, simpler way of country life make you feel you are actually there"* … *"his infectious sense of humour is touchingly offset by some sad moments that he treats with an understatement that makes them all the more moving"* … *"this book contains bags of the Kerr wit and self-deprecating humour … wonderfully drawn characters and graphic descriptions of surroundings carry Kerr's readers right into his world"* … *"a real gem of a book"*.

And, boy, did I welcome those endorsements! As anticipated, there were other reviewers who bemoaned the interruption to the *presumed* Mallorcan series, and there were the inevitable wags who homed in on the front cover's illusion of a wee boy peeing into his soup, and took the associated piss. But the predominant responses to the book were reassuringly favourable, and would be manifested in sales of some ten thousand copies in the first month alone. A marked improvement on the maximum of four thousand in its lifetime the publishers had forecast when calculating my advance royalty!

Ironically, considering the circumstances into which it had been born, and given that its chances of amounting to much had been regarded as slim, *Thistle Soup* would go on to attract the enduring worldwide support of people who, like those who had made the Royal Scots Dragoon Guards' recording of *Amazing Grace* such an unlikely hit thirty years earlier, had been touched by an emotional quality that those who boasted 'a grasp of the vagaries of the business' had failed to recognise. In any event, it seemed that Dame Fortune had smiled on me again, even though my prospects as a full-time author were still in the balance.

Or were they?

At least I now had an agent to take on the task of navigating a way through my current career impasse, while also supervising the calculation and punctuality of my royalty payments. Agent Cephas had been as good as his word by promptly analysing the 'breakdown of numbers' I had sent him after our meeting during the Edinburgh Book Festival, and had been sufficiently convinced of my earning potential to offer me a place on his list of author-clients. I had taken time in the interim to make use of any reliable contacts I had to sound out his reputation, and as it was confirmed without exception to be beyond reproach, I'd had no hesitation in 'tying the knot', but first having checked the terms of his contract against those recommended by the Society of Authors. As could be expected from such a reputable operator, all stipulated conditions were met – and with the added attraction of his commission being quoted as ten percent, as against the fifteen which was becoming the norm at the time.

The 'breakdown of numbers' I had sent him was basically a copy of the list I'd made for Ellie: a note of what royalties were due from whom and when to expect them. But there were still some details that only Chestervale could provide, and my requests for them had met with assurances that the matter was in hand and a complete update was being prepared. Three months had now passed, but still no update. The details I needed related to advance royalties on subsidiary rights, mainly for foreign, audio and large print editions, half of which were payable on signature of contract, the remaining half on publication. As I knew the dates on which I'd signed the contracts, it followed that I knew when to *expect* the first instalments from Chestervale who, as my primary publishers, administered subsidiary rights on my behalf in exchange for a share of the royalties: typically between fifty and sixty percent. However, I had no way of being sure when the foreign editions in particular had eventually been published, so had to rely on Chestervale being on top of that side of things *and* for keeping me informed.

Purely by chance, I then received from an overseas

publisher a cheque for fifteen hundred pounds, which was the 'on-signature' half of the advance royalty on my second book, and should have been sent to Chestervale. It was from a company dealing directly with them, instead of via an agent, and paying the money to me had been a genuine mistake, which I rectified immediately by forwarding Chestervale their share. But the speed with which this advance had been remitted by that particular publisher didn't square with the delay associated with their payment of the equivalent advance for my first book – or at least with my *receipt* of it. Negative thoughts began to creep into my head, and although it was against my nature to go behind the back of anyone I was working with, Chestervale had been given ample opportunity to provide me with the relevant information, so I felt an exception was warranted in this case.

And that was when the simple gesture of having personally thanked the various publishers who had taken up subsidiary rights proved its worth. I contacted them again now, on the pretext of needing certain details for tax purposes, and asked them to confirm the dates on which they had paid my advance royalties during the past couple of years. They all obliged without demur.

It took a few weeks to gather and assimilate all the information, covering as it did the separate publication dates of the two books in several different countries. What became apparent at an early stage, however, was that a pattern was developing of late and often miscalculated payments by Chestervale. The miscalculations were of no immediate concern, as any alleged complications involving currency exchange rates or mix-ups in respect of individual contractual percentages could be easily resolved, if the will was there. But the delayed payments were a different matter entirely. The accepted rule within the industry was that the author's share of subsidiary-rights royalties received by the primary publisher should be forwarded to the author 'promptly on receipt'. The relevant clause in Chestervale's contracts interpreted this as 'within thirty days', and I had readily agreed to that. After all, they were a small company and needed a bit of time 'to do the books'.

But there's a big difference between thirty days and eleven and a half months, which is how long it took for my share of the advance royalty on one subsidiary publication to be credited to my bank account. Other examples emerged, involving delays of between a few weeks and ten months, and totalling revenues of some £40,000 collected by Chestervale. To give them a fair chance to explain these 'anomalies', I had kept them informed of the details as they came in, and they finally confessed, entirely of their own volition, to being in breach of contract, and quickly followed this up by offering me £1,000 'as compensation'.

The significance of this offer was related, I guessed, to a standard contractual clause which stated that if the publisher committed any such breach, the author, or a firm of chartered accountants on his behalf, would be entitled to examine the relevant books and records of the publisher, and to take copies of same to present as evidence, if required, in court. While I mulled this over, matters took yet another unexpected turn…

I had sent agent Cephas copies of all my correspondence with Chestervale right from the start, simply because the primary reason I'd undertaken these 'enquiries' in the first place was to tie up all royalty-related loose ends before handing everything over to him. He had remained noticeably detached throughout, making no comment one way or the other. I saw no reason to suspect anything untoward in this, as it was my responsibility to provide, by whatever means, a clean slate for him to work on. It was only much later that I found out he'd known all along about many of those late payments, because, in his capacity as Chestervale's foreign rights agent, *he* had been responsible for administering them! Yet, in his capacity as as *my* agent, he'd elected not to offer his support during my frustrated efforts to have them explained by Chestervale. There was a whiff of collusion about this. I'd have to tread carefully.

Perhaps in hope of pre-empting any audit of their books that I might decide to initiate, Chestervale had eventually sent me comprehensive extracts from their accounts, itemising all receipts and payments of subsidiary-rights royalties generated by *Snowball Oranges* and *Mañana, Mañana*. This was when I discovered that certain royalty payments which passed through the 'conduit' of agent Cephas had been seriously late to arrive in the Chestervale coffers. Crucially, those encompassed most of the lucrative foreign-language editions. Why Chestervale hadn't picked up on this, only they knew, but whatever the reason, they had then contrived to make matters even worse by proceeding to delay payment of *my* share of the income – often by many months.

As if this weren't already complicated enough, Chestervale now had to pay my royalties, not directly to me as before, but through my agent, Cephas. The first instances of this to be tested in practice related to advances emanating from subsidiary-rights contracts I had negotiated with Chestervale myself, and in which Cephas had not been involved in any way. Yet it took him up to five months to process the associated moneys, which totalled several thousand pounds. When I queried this, he put the blame down to a 'banking anomaly' that had taken some weeks to resolve. For 'some weeks' read 'five months'. And although all Cephas had to do was allow a couple of days for his bank to clear the incoming Chestervale cheques before forwarding the funds to me, when he did finally part with the money, he had actually deducted a ten percent agent's commission first! This had amounted to almost fourteen hundred pounds in one month alone, and was totally inconsistent with his own professional association's code of practice, which stated that it was 'understood' that agents should undertake as a courtesy such 'reprocessing of moneys due under previous contracts not negotiated by them, and not expect compensation'. Immediately after I confronted him with these examples of what amounted to blatant pick-pocketing, he instructed his office to refund the fourteen hundred pounds and told me he thought it best that he should now 'withdraw' from being my agent. Jumping before being pushed, was how I saw it!

So, to summarise, a major part of the subsidiary-rights earnings from my books had been 'mismanaged' in one way or another by my publishers *and* an agent who was acting on their behalf and, latterly, on mine too. He was taking *two* slices of ten percent from the same pie, which made a mockery of his apparent undercutting of the fifteen percent agent's commission currently being accepted as 'normal'. The reason I had subsequently dubbed him Cephas was that, like the eponymous biblical disciple, he claimed to have the ability to be all things to all people (*'an honest broker, if you like'*), although there was nothing honest *or* saintly about this parable of chicanery. Getting him off my back had been essential and, as it transpired, surprisingly easy. But deciding what to do about my association with Chestervale was going to be a different story altogether.

*

My immediate thought was that Chestervale had been in cahoots with Cephas, but if that had been so, what benefit would Chestervale have gained by Cephas withholding funds due to *them*? Surely this was more likely to be a case of Chestervale indulging in a fairly casual approach to book-keeping and blithely ignoring the fact that such a cavalier attitude was detrimental to their financial well-being, and also, more crucially, to that of the author whose books were generating those selfsame funds.

Something other than sloppy book-keeping may have been involved, however, when it came to Chestervale themselves withholding royalties they had received on my behalf – several times over and not just from from Cephas. According to more than one latter-day Socrates: '*A mistake repeated more than once is not a mistake any more; it is a decision.*' If we take that proposition as applicable to Chestervale's 'sloppy book-keeping', it's easy to arrive at the conclusion that their directors were more calculating than cavalier. As US President Coolidge might have said: '*Nothing is more common than unsuccessful businessmen preoccupied with candour*'. And I had always been under the impression that the Chestervale partners were earmarked for success.

No matter which way I looked at it, the fact remained that they had been using my earnings as the equivalent of interest-free loans, involving amounts they had not divulged to me, and which I could only *hope* they would eventually repay. And in full. Thousands of pounds were being garnered by them, during which time I had been obliged to dip into our hard-earned 'housekeeping' nest egg to live on while continuing to meet writing deadlines, and also to help finance an increasingly hectic schedule of promotional work.

All of this had only come to the surface because I had been paid one tranche of an advance royalty in error by an overseas publisher. So, did this serve to confirm my suspicion that Chestervale's sole motivation for publishing my orange-related book had been to snatch a passing whiff of lucrative lemon? Their vacillating over *Snowballs Three* and their intransigent attitude towards *Leaning Against the Wind* (alias *Thistle Soup*) gave the impression that it may well have been.

But then it dawned on me that there might be another way of looking at this. Instead of taking it all at face value, which would almost certainly end negatively for both parties, I could try accentuating whatever positive aspects remained and use them to build on the foundations that had already been laid. Bluntly, why cut off my nose to spite my face, even if it currently had '*MUG*' written all over it?

Although it may only have been because I didn't *want* to believe the worst, I still couldn't bring myself to accept that Chestervale Publishing was an intrinsically deceitful organisation. For, to be fair, how many of us can genuinely claim never to have repeated a mistake to our own advantage? OK, it's true that Chestervale had been inclined to make a habit of it, and there *was* that suspicion of some kind of collusion with agent Cephas. But he had been eliminated from the equation, so why not leave the dust to settle until we could see more clearly which way the wind was blowing now?

After all, the excellent working relationship I had developed with editor Izzie and her young colleagues wasn't something to be casually cast aside, and although I didn't know their two bosses all that well, as a Scotsman I had always had a soft spot for their 'canny' attitude towards money – just so long as it wasn't furtively 'borrowed' interest-free from me, of course! Then again, if I chose to be vindictive, I could 'go public' with details of this unsavoury affair, thereby denting, if not totally wrecking, the professional reputations of both Chestervale *and*

Cephas. But such a course of action would never have been my intention, although neither of them had any inkling of that at the time.

As a prominent member of the international agenting community, the last thing Cephas needed was to have his questionable methods exposed, so his speedy 'withdrawal' from representing me had had an element of panic about it, and I was content to leave him stewing in his own juice.

As for Chestervale, it was possible that the money they had offered as 'compensation' for having breached our contracts had actually been aimed at dissuading me from spilling the beans to *their* professional peers and associates. But it wasn't just a surge of big-heartedness that prompted me to politely decline their offer. On the one hand, all I wanted from them was what was legally due to me: not a penny more, but not a penny less. *And* on time. Yet on the other hand, I knew from past experience in different walks of life that asserting your rights against members of the so-called 'establishment' can do you more harm than good. On any level, the David who has the nerve to confront Goliath can be too easily seen as a trouble-making upstart who should be kept in his place. Permanently.

Even so, I'd leave the way open for reconciliation with Chestervale, on the assumption that they were prepared to abide by the recognised rules.

*

Editor Izzie had told me a couple of years earlier that *'there's nothing like a tight deadline to get an author's creative juices flowing*'. Now, in 2003, it had become apparent that there's nothing to sharpen a publisher's focus like being faced with the reality of having let an odds-on 'earner' slip through their fingers. Because an odds-on 'earner' is what *Snowballs Three* seemed destined to be, judging by the feedback I was getting in readers' letters and at literary events all over the country. Healthy demand for this next book in the *Snowball Oranges* 'series' was also being expressed by the overseas companies already on board, and none more positively than the publishers of the English-language edition in the USA.

I got the impression that their view was that the book-buying public called the shots, and if a publisher was getting signals that they'd hit on a theme with legs, they shouldn't spend time deliberating 'the vagaries of the business', but do what the jungle drummers were telling them before they beat it in another direction. It wasn't that they didn't like *Thistle Soup* (they had already contracted to publish it in the States), but Chestervale's timing of its release seemed to have puzzled them as much as it had me. Their reading of the situation had then been backed up by *Snowball Oranges* featuring in the current year's national Book of the Year Awards in Los Angeles. This is what their publicity department had to say about it…

'The American Book of the Year Awards were established to recognise the achievements of authors in a wide range of categories. Shortlisted

in the Narrative Travel category, a jury of booksellers, librarians, reviewers and other industry professionals selected "Snowball Oranges" for the bronze prize, based on the originality of the book's narrative, the value it has added to its genre, and its ability to entertain.

We regard this as a tremendous achievement The competition, particularly in the travel book category, is massive in the USA, so to win such a prestigious award (even the bronze!) really does take some doing. And it couldn't have happened at a better time – coinciding with the American publication of the sequel "Mañana, Mañana", which is already receiving rave reviews and looks like becoming one of the best-selling travel books of recent years in America.'

Chestervale were quick to issue their own press release on the back of this publicity windfall…

'The bunting is out and the corks are popping at Chestervale! There are 100,000 books published in the States every year, and although we had every faith in "Snowball Oranges" when we heard it was shortlisted for this award, we knew it was going to be up against some serious competition, which makes this win a truly remarkable achievement. We are thrilled that Peter's talent has been recognised in this way.'

I was asked for an accompanying quote…

'It was a big enough surprise when I finally got "Snowball Oranges" published after eight years of rejection, so even having it acknowledged at such an eminent event seems quite surreal – in the nicest possible way!'

Serendipity! Dame Fortune had done me a timely favour – yet again. And sure enough, this stroke of good luck did sharpen Chestervale's focus. It was time, they decided, to shunt *Snowballs Three* out of the siding they'd left it in and get it back on track. But quickly!

* * * * *

Chapter Nineteen

'VIVA MALLORCA!'

*

It was a relief to learn that the three months I'd already spent writing the initial chapters of *Snowballs Three* weren't going to be wasted after all. Throughout the recent 'detour' it had appeared increasingly likely that I'd be looking for another publishing vehicle to hitch a ride on if I wanted to continue on my way, but I knew that finding one wouldn't be easy. I hadn't forgotten the impression I'd formed at the London Book Fair when starting out on this journey three years earlier: although I was now a published author, I was still a small fish in a very big pond. But tellingly, it seemed the Chestervale decision-makers had now come to the conclusion that small fish capable of tipping the scales profitably aren't that easy to catch either. So, enter pragmatism, pushing a bicycle built for two.

It was now the summer of 2003, and as pleased as I was that a commitment to work for our mutual benefit had been made verbally, important details relating to the original contract for *Snowballs Three* would have to be revised before I actually got down to writing again. I had put the recent administrative 'mistakes' behind me, but felt compelled to insist that the subsidiary rights involved would no longer be assigned to Chestervale. The most significant aspect of this meant that, in future, the right to negotiate and manage all foreign language contracts and associated moneys would be retained by me. Although this may have proved a difficult pill for Chestervale to swallow, they assented without protest and also volunteered to reinstate the original advance royalty of £8,000 for *Snowballs Three,* which had been summarily cut by almost three quarters for *Thistle Soup*. What's more, 'as a mark of good will', they offered to pay two thirds of the advance (instead of the usual half) on signature of the new contract. I thanked them sincerely, while bearing in mind that their 'largesse' was funded by healthy revenues already being earned from sales of *Thistle Soup,* never mind those still rolling in from *Snowball Oranges* and *Mañana, Mañana*. However, to cement this new spirit of conciliation, I volunteered in turn to pay them 25% of future royalties received from the American publishers of the English-language editions of my books, as their initial interest had been conveyed to Chestervale direct, and not through any agent. I made this gesture despite the Society of Authors' recommended base rate in such instances being only 15%, and not forgetting that Chestervale had originally allotted themselves 89% – by mistake!

But such matters were all part and parcel of how our association had panned out, and my publishers enjoying robust financial health would be to my ultimate advantage too, provided I got my fair share of the spoils without having to resort to such 'investigative' measures again. And this prompted thoughts of swapping my conciliatory hat for a practical one. Administering this side of the business myself would take time – of which ongoing writing, illustrating and promotional activities already demanded every available moment – and it would also require book-industry know-how and access to vital contacts I simply didn't have. In essence, attempting to function as my own agent would not be a realistic proposition.

Fast rewind again to the London Book Fair and Bette Tanner's words of caution: *'You can't be too careful – royalty rates, translation rights, options on subsequent books and so on. That's when having an agent is so important.'*

On that occasion and the two others on which we had spoken to her since, both Ellie and I had come away feeling that Bette was basically a decent sort of person, regardless of her reputation as an agent, which, according to all available sources, was without blemish in any case.

'Ah but,' you'd be entitled to point out, 'Cephas also came with a glowing seal of approval from his peers, and look how reliable *that* assessment turned out to be!'

'Which just goes to show,' I'd be inclined to reply, 'that you should never undervalue your own first impressions. Think Parma Ham pizzas and *Grigio Verde*!'

And I hadn't forgotten Ellie's reaction after meeting Bette for the first time either: 'I'm not a bad judge of character, and I actually got pretty good vibes from that lady.'

'Yeah, she came across as all right to me too,' I'd said.

Those gut feelings came back when we eventually met for that relaxed, no-axes-to-grind chat in her office. Her parting words then were to confirm that her agency's client list was full, though she would like me to keep in touch anyway. Circumstances, like the weather, she'd said, were always liable to change when least expected.

Fast forward to the present and a timely phone call to Bette, in which I brought her up to date on the recent whirlwind of events…

'So,' I said in conclusion, 'I've cleared the air with Chestervale, but I now need to get on with the job of writing, and I can't do that *plus* try and look after all the tricky contractual stuff you marked my card about back at the London Book Fair.'

'In other words, you want to know if I'll be your agent, right?

'In a nutshell.'

With all the frankness we had come to expect from her, Bette reiterated her previous opinion that remaining contracted to Chestervale was the wisest thing to do, since my writing career would still 'have a better chance of growing as an integral component of an upwardly-mobile young company than as only one of countless cogs in a large publishing machine'. This didn't disguise the fact, however, that from an agent's point of view, it also meant that the laborious task of finding me another publisher had been obviated. But in fairness, Bette *had* made it known from our very first meeting that it was my non-fiction material that appealed to her, and she now confirmed that finding a home for my fiction titles was not an undertaking to which she could devote the required attention. She meant no disrespect to the books – there just weren't enough hours in the day. This being the case, if I was happy to have her agency's involvement limited to taking care of the business side of my writing for Chestervale, she would also make an effort to offer her *personal* opinion and advice on any 'other work' I might produce in the future.

So there I had it. Bette was in a position to cherry-pick, and although she'd put it to me in the most gracious of ways, I could either take the one she'd picked or leave it. As things stood, I had little option but to accept, though time would tell that it was the right decision for all that.

Meanwhile, it had always been clear that Bette subscribed to the view that, in my fiction work at least, some of the humour 'got in the way' of elements she otherwise enjoyed. As one reviewer would ultimately note, '*A spade's a spade, and that's what you get with Peter Kerr ... with his repertoire of humorous observation ranging from gentle, to dry, wry, mischievous, satirical, schoolboyish and even, just occasionally, to ribald*'. What it boiled down to, I suppose, was that Bette didn't really *get* that aspect of my writing. But did this matter in the wider scheme of things? After all, there's no sense of humour of any kind required for vetting the fine details of legal documents, or indeed for sieving the minutiae of royalty returns. The most important consideration for me was that a weight had been taken off my shoulders. I could now look forward to picking up the creative pieces with Izzie and crack on with completing *Snowballs Three* in time for publication in the spring of 2004.

* * *

As ever, a mood of optimism and fun had pervaded the initial chapters of the new book, for that was at the heart of all our Mallorcan experiences and had never been dampened by any temporary downturn in our luck. Now, in keeping with the positive perspective generated by my revised working partnership with Chestervale, a new hint of elation crept into my writing, boosted by the feeling of support afforded by my recent hook-up with agent Bette. Consequently, a suitably celebratory title for the book was called for, and I reckoned *Viva Mallorca!* seemed to fit the bill perfectly. All interested parties agreed, while a subtitle of *One Mallorcan Autumn* fell naturally into place as the narrative unfolded, and also served to extend the season-by-season theme that had already been established for the 'series', no matter how inadvertently.

Now, for the first time, the pressure of hitting the deadline for delivery of the manuscript seemed to lessen as the appointed date approached; the reason being, I suppose, that the task of writing a light-hearted story of any stripe can only come across as honest and uncontrived if the prevailing atmosphere is right.

Izzie and her fellow 'Chestervale Troops', as I called them, entered enthusiastically into the swing of things by giving *Viva Mallorca!* all the 'prep' required, and in record time too. A month before the early-May publication date, I was sent a draft of the advance publicity notice that would be sent out to targetted trade and media contacts, and would also serve as the gist of the book's back-cover blurb. It read as follows…

Autumn has arrived for the Kerrs on their little orange farm on the Mediterranean island of Mallorca…

The year's third quarter, the magical 'Season of Winter Spring' as the Mallorcan country folk call it, finds Peter under the sharp eye of his long-suffering wife Ellie, while he struggles (not particularly keenly!) to shake off the relaxed Spanish 'tranquiloness' he has now mastered all too well. Old friendships are re-established and new acquaintances made as the family is introduced to the island's champagne-swilling Filthy-Rich Set, and their eyes are opened by just how the other half lives!

Meanwhile, rustic remedies like vinegar rubs and smouldering donkey dung mosquito repellents, the banter of colourful local characters and the enticing aromas and irresistible flavours of Mallorcan cuisine – with background support from dogs, thunder storms, parrots and canaries – help make this an autumn such as they have never known. And all recalled with an abundance of the infectious good cheer we have come to expect from this author. Viva Mallorca!

Word duly got round, and if the resultant influx of invitations to do live 'readings' during the rest of 2004 was anything to go by, any pent-up interest in this book had survived the recent 'delay' in its publication. Advance orders were already approaching the 7,000 mark, so it appeared that Chestervale's re-kindled faith in the 'product' I was turning out for them was destined to be amply justified. And for this I heaved a relieved sigh, content in the belief that from now on whatever proved good for my publishers would also prove good for me.

But for the present, I had those promotionally-important invites to handle, and their range made any previous 'tours' look like a walk in the park…

*

Birmingham's National Exhibition Centre (or NEC as it's popularly known) is the largest such venue in the UK, having 18 interconnecting halls and 34 conference suites, and with a seating capacity of 15,000 in the principal 'auditorium' alone. I had been asked to take part in the *Viva España 2004* show, sponsored by the *Telegraph* newspaper and scheduled to take place over three days from Friday 7th to Sunday 9th May. Clearly, the title of my new book fitted neatly with that of the exhibition, which the organisers described as Europe's biggest annual celebration of all things Spanish.

'They've slotted me in between performances of the Juan Ramírez Flamenco Dance Company and the world-famous Andalucian Horses of the First Equestrian Theatre, so I'll be taking a pair of castanets *and* a shovel!' I quipped to a reporter from the *East Lothian Courier* before I headed south.

In the event, I needed neither, because the NEC is so vast and the gamut of stands, stalls and displays covering the floor of the main hall for this extravaganza were so diverse that the heel-clickers, hoof-tappers and I never came within an *'Olé!'* or *'Gidddy up!'* of each other. The carefully arranged programme stipulated that I should spend certain periods of each day signing books and meeting the public on the stand run by London's iconic Spanish Bookshop, with half-hour breaks morning and afternoon set aside for being interviewed in the 'theatre' by the exhibition's host, TV presenter Nadine Dereza. The entire experience, which had to be meticulously timed, amounted to a master class in keeping-to-your-own-lane by everyone involved, and also provided an all-expenses-paid opportunity to publicise the publication of *Viva Mallorca!* that would prove to be as rewarding as it had been unexpected. Also, the mix of meet-the-public and talk-to-the-public that had been arranged not only kept me on my toes for the three days but also endorsed the fact that even an inveterate mumbler like me can be made to communicate in a surprisingly fluent way when being asked all the right questions by an interviewer of the professional class of Nadine Dereza, who had obviously taken the time to read my books, understand the intricacies and note all the points that would serve the occasion best. I learned a lot from her.

After such a slick engagement, maybe it was inevitable that the next phase of the book-promoting campaign would seem a tad shambolic by comparison. Then again, maybe it was just that Chestervale's promo people and I got our communications in a tangle, no matter how well-meaning our intentions. For, somehow, we managed to prepare and approve an itinerary that involved my travelling back the 240-plus miles from Birmingham to East Lothian to host a literary lunch in Gullane's plush Greywalls Hotel, only to leave the very next day for meet-the-author events at bookshops all of 460 miles away in the port of Southampton and the adjacent towns of Christchurch, Bournemouth and Poole on the southernmost coast of England. And the day after that I was back in East Lothian for a book-signing date at the ever-supportive Kesley's Bookshop in my home town of Haddington, with just enough time to draw breath before packing my bag again for a return trip to the deep south the following morning.

Ellie had kept me company every inch of the way on this madcap bout of yo-yoing, and never with a murmur of complaint. Yet, one tell-tale sign had recently prompted me to suspect that I was taking too much for granted. On a whistle-stop, one-day tour of libraries in Staffordshire, I had been doing an afternoon 'reading' on a particularly wet and miserable day, and the librarian had mentioned before I started that, although there was a full house, she recognised quite a few of the audience as down-on-their-luck individuals who regularly came in on days like this 'just to get in from the cold and have a little snooze'.

Sure enough, shortly after I started my talk about the pleasures of life in sunny Mallorca, I heard an ominous sound coming from the back of the room: a gentle purring sound at first, but gradually getting louder until it was a full-blown, lip-flapping, nostril-rasping snore, terminating in a stifled yelp as the secret snoozer suddenly woke up. I recognised the voice which then exclaimed, '*SHIT! WHAT A BLOODY NIGHTMARE!*' It was Ellie, now trying to hide her blushes as a ripple of sniggers spread through the audience. I couldn't resist having a good chuckle myself, knowing as I did how proud Ellie was of her reputation as a staunch *dis*believer in the use of strong language!

But this had been a clear indication that Ellie needed a break from all this traipsing about, and our younger son Charlie was quick to step into the breach before I embarked on the next round. Being my 'road manager', as he put it, would give him a few days' breather from the tedious half-hour train commute between his North Berwick home and the Edinburgh advertising agency where he worked as a computer graphics artist. Well, at least the *first* leg of our tour would comply with his idea of what was in store…

With due credit to Chestervale's sales people, what they had arranged for me had been well thought-out geographically. However, in deference to my own 'on the road' experiences stretching all the way back to my days as an itinerant jazz musician in the early '60s, they had left it for me to make the travel arrangements and book the necessary hotel accommodation. Even more mindful than usual of the need to keep costs to a bare minimum (Chestervale were chipping in for some of them!), I paid particular attention to the accommodation aspect, since ways of skimping on travel were strictly limited in any case. Thankfully, everything went pretty much according to plan. Initially.

Straight off the Edinburgh plane at London's Gatwick Airport, we headed, as per Chestervale's instructions, to Waterstones' bookshop in the terminal building, where a pile of books was waiting to be signed. And straight from there we nipped along to WHSmith's outlet in the same retail hall to do likewise for them. In both cases, the deed was done, not in view of the public, but in back room storage areas, which reminded me of identical undertakings fulfilled on a traipse around selected central London bookshops the day after the launch of *Mañana, Mañana* a couple of years previously.

But as mundane and hand-numbing as these tasks were, they were all in response to invitations that would not have come my way three years earlier. And in the case of a bustling international airport like Gatwick, anything that might help catch the eye of even a fraction of the millions who passed through every month was worth getting an aching hand for. So, I assiduously scribbled my moniker on title page after title page, while obliging members of staff sat beside me slapping '*Signed by the Author*' stickers on front cover after front cover. Charlie, in the interim, had entered smartly into road manager mode by selecting an open-fronted bar which was handy for both shops, then sat enjoying the passing show. And a pint. I empathised, and would gladly have joined him in lifting a glass to counter the repetitive strain condition now affecting the muscles of my book-signing arm. But we had a tour schedule to follow, and time was of the essence.

* * * * *

Chapter Twenty
'TO EACH THEIR OWN'

*

Tenterden is a town of some eight thousand souls, nestling deep in the Kent countryside about 45 miles east of Gatwick as the crow flies. In the absence of passenger-carrying crows, we were obliged to make the journey by train, or rather by 'trains' plural, since there was no direct link.

It was four o' clock in the afternoon, a good hour before the start of the evening stampede that would see hoards of commuters piling out of London and heading for the many 'dormitory' towns of Kent. So, the seventy-minute journey from Gatwick to Tonbridge was completed in relatively soporific comfort, with my 'road manager' proving his worth by waking me up in time to change trains for the quaintly-named village of Headcorn, situated about fifteen miles further on, along a line fringed by the orchards and hop plantations that proliferate in this, the 'Garden of England'. In fact, if I'd allowed my mind's eye to substitute fields of golden grain for orchards and hop plantations, we could almost have been in my home county of East Lothian, the appropriately named 'Garden of Scotland'.

We were met at Headcorn railway station and driven the nine miles to Tenterden by Glen, the manager of the town's bookshop, a rural outpost of the nationwide Ottakar's chain. The business occupied two floors of a medieval building in the centre of this most vibrant of English country towns, long known as the 'Jewel of the Weald', an area densely forested in ancient times, but now a predominantly pastoral landscape stretching from the vineyards of east Kent all of 150 miles westward to the rolling Hampshire hinterlands of Portsmouth.

The Woolpack, or 'The Woolly' as its known locally, is a 15th century inn just a short walk along Tenterden High Street from Ottakar's bookshop, and on being dropped off there prior to my 'reading' event, I was both relieved and heartened by first impressions. All I'd had to go on by way of recommendation when booking a room was a brief description in an old RAC handbook and a hunch that the modest price quoted would suggest nothing less welcoming than a dyed-in-the-wool '*olde worlde*' pub of the sort that embodies the very essence of rural England – log fires, oak beams, horse brasses and all. My intuition hadn't let me down.

'I think I'll just chill out here while you're doing your book-store spiel along the street,' said Charlie, leaving me to check the whereabouts of our room while he checked the 'hospitality credentials' of the bar. 'You know what I mean, Padre – spread the hardships of life on the road and all that.'

To be honest, I couldn't fault Charlie's logic. I'd probably have suggested the same if our situations had been reversed. On such occasions, I had always felt a bit guilty about Ellie sitting by herself in a quiet corner (if one were available) reading a book while I 'did my turn' for the assembled patrons. But keeping a low profile was her preferred way, while killing time in the nearest pub most certainly was not. Consequently, there must have been many a time when she was bored to the back teeth listening for the umpteenth time to my 'book-store spiel', no matter how much I shuffled the pack or how many times I produced a surprise ad-lib from up my sleeve. As in her days as a jazz musician's wife, record producer's wife, farmer's wife and orange-picker's wife, her contribution by way of providing unstinting support for my attempts to earn a living by writing books was immeasurable. But she had now turned sixty, and her old friend's wisecrack about her either deserving a medal or a certificate of insanity had never been more relevant. Our sons knew she needed a break, and as Charlie was currently best placed to provide it, he hadn't hesitated, though warily reserving the right to make 'campaign strategies' which also fitted his own particular way of life. And if keeping a bar stool warm for me while I undertook book-promoting chores was how he chose to go about it, then that was absolutely fine by me. I appreciated his company.

As it transpired, the atmosphere at the Tenterden bookshop echoed that of the inn. The Ottakar's chain (at that time numbering well over a hundred throughout the UK) was well known in the trade for the attentive nature of its staff, as well as being understandably popular with its customers. Indeed, it was said that many of them regarded their local branch as more akin to an independent, owner-behind-the-counter store. That had certainly been the impression given in those I had visited to date, several of which had also been located – in compliance with company policy – in smaller centres of population than had hitherto been regarded as commercially viable by other major retailers. True to form, then, staff and customers combined to make my visit to their Tenterden premises among the most easy-going and satisfying I'd experienced in my three years of treading the book-shop boards.

And on my return to 'The Woolly', I was presented with yet another pleasant surprise. For Charlie hadn't just kept a barstool warm for me, he had exhibited his road-managerial potential by fixing us up with a chunky wooden table for two, strategically located in a corner between the inglenook fireplace and the bar.

'Have a gander at the grub menu if you want, Don P,' he said, handing me the bill of fare, 'but I reckon the *Chicken, Ham and Leek Pie* will take a bit of beating. Comes with mashed tatties and all the trimmings. Yeah, I've been watching the other punters – mainly locals, for sure – and that's what they're all scoffing. That's a good enough ad for me, and good ads are hard to find, believe me!'

I accepted the benefit his adman's experience and left him to make the one-metre trip to the bar.

'I've asked them to put a decent bottle of wine on ice an' all,' he winked on his return. '*Sauvignon Blanc* – the white.'

I squinted at him. 'The *white*?'

'Yeah, the *Sauvignon Blanc* red can be a bit … well, heavy with chicken. Know what I mean?'

I massaged the tip of my nose to hide a smirk. 'But *blanc* – that *is* "white" – in French, I mean.'

Charlie grimaced. 'Fuckit! That'd be why the barman gave me that "are you taking the piss?" look.'

'Yup, most likely.'

'Never could get to grips with the French lingo,' Charlie shrugged. 'You know – spelling the word for "white" like the Spanish *blanco*, but leaving the "o" out and pronouncing it *blong*. Nah, bonkers lingo, French – at least Spanish words sound like they look.'

'Well, yeah, mainly … but there are exceptions too, to be fair. For instance, there was that cracker your mother came out with when she wished a Mallorcan shopkeeper a "Happy New Arsehole" instead of a "Happy New Year".'

Charlie gasped, delightedly. 'You're joking! How the hell did she manage that?'

'Just because she pronounced the Spanish word for "year" as if it didn't have a little wiggle above the letter "n", which meant she said *an-no* – "anus" – instead of *an-yo* – "year".'

'Wow! That's miles better than my *blong* blooper!'

'Hmm,' I nodded sagely, 'especially since the poor guy had just had a haemorrhoids op.'

Charlie slapped his knee. 'An absolute classic! Good old *Madre*!' he spluttered into his pint. 'Gotta admit, she could certainly come out with some lulus!'

Since our return back home, apart from recollections of linguistic clangers we had all dropped in Mallorca, and which were providing a few self-deprecating anecdotes for my books, we had automatically stopped using most of the every-day Spanish words that had become second nature during our three years on the island. Words like *gracias* and *de nada* – 'thank you' and 'you're welcome'.

For some reason, however, neither of our sons had lost the habit of referring to Ellie and me as *Madre* and *Padre*, which hadn't been an affectation back then, and was no more so now. It had become and remained second nature, that's all. And their tendency to address me occasionally as *Don Pedro* – or *Don P* for short – was a relic (though with a slight twist) of our time living in Mallorca as well.

The use of the designation *Don* before a man's name in Spain was traditionally reserved for addressing persons of wealth and social standing, such as the nobility or even royals. But time has gradually eroded all such forelock-tugging conditions, until nowadays the application of the *Don* tag is seen as only a slightly more formal version of the common or garden *Señor* (Mister). It still has a distinctly 'elite' ring to it, though, which means that its interpretation, depending on the respective attitudes of addresser and addressee, can either be taken as fitting or frivolous – not to mention flippant or facetious. The dreaded 'subjective' word strikes again!

Coming from a long line of dirt-on-their-boots peasant farmers and wage-slave coalminers, I was clearly too well-bred to be regarded as noble, or even royal, but our elderly neighbours in the valley didn't know this when we first arrived in their midst. To them, we would more than likely have been just another example of the idle-rich foreigners who were already starting to buy up 'rustic' properties like Ca's Mayoral, purely to use the house as a holiday or retirement home, with no interest in maintaining the orchards that had been the beating heart of these little farms since time immemorial. Consequently, although our neighbours had appeared courteous and welcoming from the start, there was a palpable hint of reservation about their attitude towards us. We guessed it was due to a suspicion that, since we had chosen to adopt a farming lifestyle widely rejected by members of their own younger generation, we must have left our brains at the airport. But once these elderly Mallorcan country folk realised we weren't totally *loco* and were actually hands-to-the-plough *campesinos* like themselves, the invisible barriers came down.

'*Hey-y-y-y-y, Don Pedro! Cómo va su vida?*'

'How goes your life?' What a pleasant form of greeting: the Spanish equivalent, more or less, of 'How's it going?', yet somehow just a bit more gracious. In 'street' usage of the English version, for instance, the word 'pal' or, more currently, 'buddy' would probably be appended. But it was the prefix rather than any notional appendage that mattered the morning our jovial old neighbour Jaume hailed me over the drystone wall that separated our two farms. It was the first time I'd seen him since surviving a prolonged tasting session of his home-made wine the previous lunchtime, an experience that also taught me the importance and, in this case at least, the inevitability of taking a siesta.

I couldn't remember leaving Jaume's house, but if the grin now lighting his face was anything to go by, I could safely assume that I'd managed to perform the task without knocking over anything of value. His tongue-in-cheek demeanour also suggested that whatever dignity I had succeeded in maintaining while weaving my way homeward through his lemon groves had been sufficient to earn me the 'title' of *Don*. Anyhow, the boys readily adopted it as the basis of my new nickname, and it stuck – even if Ellie delighted in defining me as more of a *Quixote* than a *Juan*!

Despite her avowed aversion to pub pies, I'm fairly certain Ellie would have enjoyed the Tenterden Woolpack's 'just-as-granny-used-to-make' *Chicken, Ham and Leek* version. She would also have relished the simple luxury of sleeping under a patchwork quilt in a comfy-cosy, old fashioned bedroom, followed by a breakfast of the celebrated 'Full English' variety (although she would have treated with circumspection the hearty helping of baked beans corralled within a phalanx of fried eggs, crispy bacon, plump pork sausages, black pudding, horse mushrooms, bubble-and-squeak, cherry tomatoes and fried bread that Charlie wolfed down as if he were competing for Scotland in the Gluttony Olympics). A relaxed post-breakfast stroll window shopping along a country-town high street would have completed Ellie's idea of a tolerable 'tour base'. But like all good things, this one had to come to an end, and I'm absolutely certain she would *not* have enjoyed what followed…

*

Our next port of call was London, and the route plan provided by Chestervale was straightforward enough. We were to make our way back to Tonbridge railway station via Headcorn, then, instead of changing for Gatwick, take a north-bound train to Dartford and change there to head westward for a short stopover in Greenwich, where a batch of books was waiting to be signed – again at a branch of Ottakar's. According to the plan, getting to Greenwich should have taken us about an hour and a half, allowing for time spent waiting for connections. In the event, it took us almost twice as long, and in all conscience, I couldn't lay *all* the blame at my road manager's door.

I had gone over the day's itinerary for him at breakfast, with the emphasis on a 'reading' engagement at Stanfords travel bookshop in central London that evening. I'd also mentioned, though doubtless more fleetingly, that there would be several book-signing sessions to fit in en route, the first of which would be in Greenwich on the eastern outskirts of the metropolis. Maybe every detail had been too much for him to ingest along with the sausages, black pudding, fried eggs and so on, or perhaps I hadn't adequately explained the cat's cradle layout of the rail network on the final approaches to our destination; but for whatever reason, he confidently led the way onto the wrong train at Dartford, and I trustingly followed. We disembarked at London Bridge station an hour later, having overshot Greenwich by some six miles and already ninety minutes late for my Ottakar's appointment. So much for our 'straightforward' route plan.

But Roy, the shop's manager, was the very epitome of his company's reputation for affability when I eventually stumbled in, panting. It wasn't to be a public signing in any case, he smiled, so no harm had been done.

Except, I silently mused, to my blood pressure *and* fingernails.

'Man can't survive on nibbled fingernails alone,' Charlie breezed after I'd finally accomplishing my first mission of the day. 'I noticed a Spanish grub joint called the *San Miguel* along the street there, so, as your road manager, I suggest we make a pit stop to top up our tanks with some Franks.'

Franks – or *Frank Zappas,* to give them their unabbreviated handle – survive as an example of the rhyming slang Charlie had picked up while attending an international school in Mallorca. And the idiom did indeed contain an egalitarian, hands-across-the-sea vibe in that it married the name of an American rock idol to the generic term for a miscellany of humble Spanish titbits known as *Tapas*. Charlie had also managed to maintain, selectively, the Spanish *mañana* attitude to life that he'd taken to like a duck to water in Mallorca. He adopted it again now.

'*Tranquilo*, Don Pedro. Don't get your sporran in a twist,' he advised while we were heading for the *San*

Miguel, which happened to be within plank-walking distance of the *Cutty Sark*, the last and fastest of the legendary sailing clippers that once plied the China Tea trade from one side of the globe to the other, and now lies berthed as a tourist attraction on the south bank of the Thames at Greenwich. 'Let's face it,' Charlie continued, 'if the captain of that old tub could find his way round the world with only the stars to guide him, surely finding our way to your next stop in London won't be a problem for *us*.'

I looked skywards and shrugged. 'No stars.'

Charlie produced a piece of paper from his pocket and held it in front of my face. 'Train times.'

He then revealed that, while I was busy signing my name in Ottakar's back room, he had been in the front shop chatting to one of the sales girls, who took time between serving customers to copy down all we needed to know from the local railway timetable.

'All part of a road manager's job,' he winked. 'Yeah, and anyway, I think she fancied me.'

With that, he swept into the eatery, calling over his shoulder as I followed fretfully in his wake, 'Don't worry, Padre – I've checked, and the next train to Charing Cross doesn't leave for half an hour. Plenty time to down a wee *ración* o' Carnegies, eh?'

Again, I couldn't fault his logic: why stand about on a draughty railway platform when we could be sitting in convivial comfort enjoying a platter of Carnegies? (That's Meat Balls, by the way. *Carnegie Halls* – get it?)

Eddi, Chestervale's petite but dynamic new PR lady, was waiting for us at Charing Cross station as arranged, and duly commenced to make up for time already lost by shooing us along to Blackwell's local book store for my next signing commitment. What followed that afternoon was a bit like a shuffled re-run of the whirlwind dash round key London retail outlets Ellie and I had made in the slipstream of Eddi's athletic predecessor Wanda. On that occasion it had been copies of *Mañana Mañana* (working title *Snowballs Two*) I was signing, and although I was now three years older with correspondingly less puff in my pipes, at least keeping up with Chestervale's latest fleet-footed pathfinder wouldn't be hampered by the after-effects of a seriously disturbed night in the Taj Ma-fucking-hal Hotel. Also, it was encouraging to learn that the interest shown by those same shops in *Viva Mallorca*! (working title *Snowballs Three*) was as keen as it had been in its forerunner – with, apparently, the 'intervention' of *Thistle Soup* having had no adverse effect on the nascent set-in-Mallorca series. In fact, they reckoned *Thistle Soup* had created a complementary following of its own, which amounted to reciprocal good news all round.

*

Stanfords, which has been trading in London's Covent Garden since 1853, has long been recognised as the biggest and best retailer of maps and travel literature in the world, being patronised over the years by travellers, explorers and adventurers of all persuasions from Florence Nightingale to Ernest Shackleton, Scott of the Antarctic, Amy Johnson and even (though in a fictional capacity) Dr Watson of Sherlock Holmes fame. The company also sponsors specialist Travel Writing Awards and a Travel Writers' Festival which routinely feature the foremost *serious* scribes in the field. Not without good reason, therefore, did I wonder why I had been invited to 'give a talk' to what would surely be a gathering of equally serious customers. And as I looked across Long Acre at the shop's distinctive rococo façade, the all-too-familiar flock of fruit bats congregated for a flutter round my innards.

But, as had happened in similar situations before, my worries proved to be unfounded. It's just a simple fact that not everyone who has a passion for reading about the exploits of the Dame Ellen MacArthurs and Colonel John Blashford-Snells of this world would personally try sailing solo round the globe or navigating the lengths of the Congo and Blue Nile Rivers, whereas a fair proportion of them might consider themselves capable of emulating the likes of me, who had done nothing more daredevil travel-wise than take his wife and kids twenty miles to Edinburgh Airport for a three-hour, one-way flight to Palma Mallorca. Thus, a savvy but supportive assembly of Stanford habitués made me feel less of an impostor and more of an inspirational trail-blazer, albeit of the least gung-ho variety. It was all good-natured stuff, with the audience happy to contribute to proceedings with a mix of pertinent questions and leg-pulling banter. I thoroughly enjoyed the evening, as did Charlie, who had been so taken with the atmosphere on arrival that he eschewed his intended one-hour exile in the nearest pub in favour of staying put to 'savour the *craic*', as our Irish friends might say.

This was to be the first of three consecutive Stanfords engagements in different parts of England, the previous two days of independently arranged promo activity having been Chestervale's way of getting the most from *their* contribution to the cost. I fully concurred with that and, as already noted, my main way of supporting their canny approach had been to book modestly priced hotel accommodation for the four nights involved. However, that policy did not extend to giving another chance to the dreaded Taj Ma-fucking-hal. On a London visit subsequent to our one-and-only experience of that establishment, Ellie and I had discovered another small hotel which, although centrally located in an almost identical Georgian terrace, had every essential attribute that the 'Taj' lacked, right down to bedrooms overlooking leafy municipal gardens as opposed to the brick wall of a grubby back alley. After such a hectic day, Charlie and I were in need of a good night's sleep, and it was comforting to know that, with no man-eating spiders or 'mice' impersonating Berkeley Square nightingales to bother about, we were fairly sure to get one.

So, I'd scored two successes out of two on the choice-of-hotel front. This gave good reason to be thankful, but as we were still only half way into the tour, something told me it would be best to avoid giving myself *too* hearty a pat on the back, just yet. Meanwhile, the itinerary Chestervale's 'troops' had prepared for us was proving to be as well-considered as it was comprehensive.

*

The next stop on the sweep round Stanfords 'chain' of three stores was set for Bristol, and the two-hour train journey west from London had been scheduled to allow for a live radio interview on BBC Bristol's Keith Warmington Show before my bookshop engagement in the evening. Again, Chestervale were making the best use of my time to reach out to the biggest audience possible within the confines of a limited budget. And as usual, I had backed up their efforts by booking a hotel that was both reasonably priced and conveniently located. I was pretty pleased with what I came up with…

Tucked away within the maze of narrow streets and lanes that typify Bristol's 'Old City', I suppose the accommodation I had chosen was really more of a 'hostel' than a hotel: a basic but welcoming resting place for on-the-hoof back-packers, well favoured, for example, by young Australians going walkabout in Pommyland. Although Ellie would have baulked at sharing a bathroom with the adjoining 'dorm', I waived any reservations I might normally have harboured by adhering to the generation-jumping relationship I had always enjoyed with our sons. If young Charlie saw no problem with such 'chummy' toilet facilities, then I wasn't about to show myself up as some sort of prudish dinosaur. Even so, I did make a furtive point of engaging the lock on *our* side of the communal bathroom door before hitting the sack that night. Any neighbouring Aussies caught short in the wee small hours would just have to make do with a bit of 'bush' improvisation. Their bedroom window, I calculated, would have opened onto a convenient 'Old City' alleyway anyway, so no worries there, sport!

But all things considered, the accommodation served our purpose well. It was but a short walk to Stanfords bookshop, and even closer to the plethora of bars, cafes and restaurants that have long made Bristol's St Nicholas Street a magnet for the peckish, parched and light of heart. As I set off to do my 'book-store spiel', I left Charlie happily watching the comings and goings from a seat in the forecourt of a building that had once housed a fish market, but now prided itself on being one of the most popular bars in the area. I liked the feel of the place too, so agreed to join him after what would prove to be another satisfying hour chatting to a group of people with reading interests in travel-related subjects broad enough to accommodate the more 'frolicsome' of the genre.

'Pub across there seems to be doing brisk business,' Charlie informed me when I came back. 'A bit more lively too. You can hear the laughing from here – music an' all.'

So you could indeed, and as it was getting a bit chilly for bending the alfresco elbow, I followed Charlie's lead and headed over the street towards a welcoming doorway surmounted by an elephant's head carved in stone.

'Pub's called The Ellie. That's short for The Elephant, by the way,' Charlie disclosed as he held the door open. 'But nothing to do with Madre.' He hooked a thumb over his shoulder. 'Barmaid in the other pub there told me she had a hunch we'd like it – whatever she meant by that.' He tapped the side of his nose, then winked. 'I think she fancied me, though.'

It took but a few seconds inside The Ellie to realise what that barmaid had *actually* meant, and I was struck by how naive I'd been for not having realised it long before this. For those prone to jumping to a certain type of conclusion, the sight of a man in his sixties going about with a chap at least half his age could mean only one thing, and the barmaid's knowledge of 'normal' goings-on in The Ellie would have triggered her suspicions about Charlie and me. It seemed that the clientele jumped to the same conclusion the moment we walked in, with glances of approval directed exclusively at Charlie, I should point out. Clearly, a six-foot, good-looking young man of sporty physique was just the sort of new blood The Ellie's regulars liked to see, the accompaniment of his ageing 'partner' being of no particular consequence.

The room was packed, the babble of carousing competing with the racket of a karaoke session in full swing up at the far end. There, a dapper, business-suited gent of diminutive stature and mature years was belting out a medley of Tom Jones' greatest hits, adding visual embellishment to the lyrics with a bold if somewhat incongruous attempt at emulating the Jones boy's trademark hip gyrations and pelvic thrusts. His predominantly male audience was lapping up the performance with bawdy laughter and lewd exclamations of encouragement.

Meanwhile, the barman, who was as camp as a field full of wigwams (we'll call him Pocahontas) must have noticed my bewildered look.

'Gentleman Jeff,' he said with a sideways nod in the direction of the karaoke corner. 'One of our best customers. Lovely, *lovely* man! Oh yes, and com*plete*ly queer as well – despite the butch clobber. Now, what'll it be, my lovelies?'

I was about to say we had a bus to catch, but Charlie got in first. 'Pint of lager for me, please, and a glass of white wine for Don Pedro here.'

'Oo-oo-oo! Don *Ped*ro, is it? Hmm, *very* cosmopolitan, I *must* say!' Pocahontas looked me up and down with mock approval, pouted, then sashayed off to fix our drinks.

'What the hell are you thinking about?' I hissed at Charlie.

'Well, it didn't say anything about "Gays Only" on the door, so we may as well have a drink now we're here. Anyway, the place is buzzing – great atmosphere – and nobody's gonna bother us if we don't bother them.'

He was probably right, but I still couldn't help feeling like the proverbial sore thumb. While Charlie stood pint-in-hand absorbing the 'great atmosphere' and grinning from ear to ear, Pocahontas could be heard calling out a jubilant '*Bingo!*' every time he rang up a sale on the till. I sipped self-consciously at my wine, feigning fascination with what I took to be the remnants of some kind of wooden framework on top of the bar. Our eagle-eyed bartender minced over to elucidate.

'Poofters to the left, lesbos to the right,' he said, not in any disparaging way, but more as a statement of fact from one member of the club to another.

'Sorry?' I queried, confused.

'The glass partition that used to be here. The bad old days of segregated drinking. Hmm, but we live in more enlightened times, don't we, my dear? Male, female and whatever else between or beyond. Anything goes now, doesn't it?' Pocahontas gave me a blatantly lascivious wink. 'To each their own, ducky, and anybody else's too, right?'

He shimmied off before I had time to respond, which was just as well, because I was stuck for words. I glanced along the bar and my eyes lit on the rear view of a shapely young women in a red mini dress who was engaged in intimate conversation with Charlie. In the karaoke corner, Gentleman Jeff began belting out the chorus of *She's A Lady*, just as Charlie, having concluded his impromptu tête-à-tête, headed back towards me.

'You look a bit flushed,' I told him po-faced. 'I take it *she* fancied you as well, did she?"

Furtively, Charlie moved in close and whispered, 'Fancied, yes. She, no. I mean, check the front view, Padre!'

Sure enough, now that the young woman had turned to face us, a Zapata moustache and designer stubble lurking beneath the overhang of a jet-black Brillo hairdo left little doubt that, contrary to the lyrics of Gentleman Jeff's ongoing song, Charlie's latest fancier was no lady.

Right on cue, a beaming Pocahontas materialised

at the other side of the bar. 'Just as I said,' he lisped, 'male, female and whatever else between and beyond. Mmm-hmm, and it takes one to know one,' he added hand-on-hip. 'Same again is it, my lovelies?'

At which point we beat a dignified retreat to the street, from where we could hear his falsetto giggles terminating in a triumphant yell of '*BINGO*!', while Gentleman Jeff performed a valedictory rendition of *It's Not Unusual*.

Brows raised, Charlie and I looked each other in the eye. 'To each their own,' we said in unison, then made straight for our lodgings. With 'straight' being the operative word.

*

The three-hour trek north to Manchester by train next day gave us plenty of time to reflect on events in Bristol's Elephant pub the night before. As was our familial wont, we had a good laugh about what we managed to convince ourselves had been a deliberate misunderstanding. We had been the gullible victims of a mischievous bartender whose cross-dressing chum had pranked Charlie big-time. Fair enough, we had fallen for a caper they'd envisaged the moment they set eyes on us, but it had all been harmless fun, and we didn't mind being the butt of their little jape, no matter how uncomfortable it had been for us at the time. After all, as I knew well enough already, there's nothing more subjective than humour.

I had learned another lesson, nonetheless, and I resolved to be more aware of the misconceptions a certain type of person thrives on. Yet I had no intention of allowing that to stop Charlie and me going about our business in public without enjoying each other's company and displaying it as freely as any father and son are entitled to. If anyone chose to see anything 'abnormal' in that, then they had a problem, not us.

I had chosen the hotel for our overnight stay in Manchester on the recommendation of a local booking agency, the lady on the other end of the phone having listened to my explanation of the need to be reasonably close to Stanfords bookshop before suggesting an establishment in Canal Street, which she assured me was only a ten-minute walk away. She had paused before adding somewhat hesitantly that The Rembrandt, or 'The Rem' as it was popularly known, had become something of a legend in its time – as I might probably know. I assured her that I hadn't even heard of the hotel before, but legend or not it complied with all essential requirements, so I'd be grateful if she'd book a twin-bedded room for me and my son Charlie.

As we climbed into a taxi at Manchester's Piccadilly railway station, I gave the driver details of our destination then tried to tell myself that what might have been taken as a smirk tugging at the corner of his mouth was nothing but a nervous tic. And when we checked in at the hotel, I did my best to ignore what could have been construed as knowing nods and smiles from the other guests (all male) sitting round coffee tables in the lobby.

We were directed to a semi-basement room in an annex round the corner from the main building. It turned out to be simply but comfortably furnished, with no apparent shortcomings other than the obvious lack of a window with a view. So, as it was a sunny evening and there was time to spare before my scheduled 'spot' at Stanfords bookshop, we decided to head back round the corner to the front of the building overlooking the old Rochdale Canal, on which bargees once delivered and shipped their cargoes to and from workaday Manchester, but where people now sit enjoying a refreshment in the shade of trees that haven't taken the strain of a mooring rope for half a century or more.

I sat marvelling at this oasis of tranquillity tucked away in the centre of such a lively city, while Charlie flicked through the pages of a visitors' guide he'd picked up in our room. After a couple of minutes, a chap with a portable tape recorder slung over his shoulder approached from a nearby table, where I'd noticed him embroiled in an animated exchange with the two men seated there. He said he was a reporter from a radio station. Then, without so much as a by-your-leave, he thrust a microphone in my face and asked what I thought of how a certain character in a popular TV soap was being depicted. When I told him, politely, that I'd never seen the show, therefore wasn't qualified to make any judgement, he looked at me as if I'd just claimed to be a visitor from of Mars.

'But you *must* have watched it,' he insisted. 'I mean, we *all* do, and *every*body thinks the way they're portraying him is really unfair. Yes, and it's only because he's supposed to be –'

I held up a silencing hand. The guy was beginning to annoy me, and placid and patient as I pride myself on being, I couldn't resist telling him, politely again, to bugger off and leave us to enjoy the peace and quiet. He rolled his eyes skyward and stomped off in a state of high dudgeon, bemoaning bloody Scotch cavemen and muttering something about *Donald Where's Yer Troosers*.

Charlie gave me a nudge. 'This explains all,' he said, pointing to a page in his guidebook. 'Look, it's right there...'

It took only a swift scan through the relevant paragraph to relieve me of the thought that I might have been veering towards paranoia in suspecting that an affinity existed between recent happenings. This is the gist of the piece...

> *'Manchester's famed Gay Village, which is reputed to be one of the most thriving in Europe, is centred on Canal Street, where The Rembrandt Hotel enjoys an enviable location overlooking the eponymous old waterway and leafy Sackville Gardens. The hotel, with its adjacent REM pub and lively Tropicana nightclub, has been serving the gay community for decades.'*

I looked at Charlie and hunched my shoulders. 'As you say, this explains all: the "legend" word used by the booking agency, the smirky looks of the taxi driver and the guys in the lobby, and now the bamboozled radio bloke.'

'Dead right. And not forgetting the Bristol shenanigans last night.'

'Yep, and who knows how many others have

jumped to the same conclusion over the past three days?'

Charlie glanced past me with a wry smile on his face. 'And in case you're in any doubt about what we've wandered into, take a look at that.'

I turned my head and followed his gaze to a sign on the wall. It read *Canal Street*, as would be expected – except that the letter 'C' had been neatly painted over.

We allowed ourselves a quiet chuckle, before declaring for the second time in twenty-four hours: 'To each their own.'

For good measure, I also quoted Charlie's words of wisdom from the previous evening: 'Nobody's gonna bother us, if we don't bother them.'

And it could be taken as read that we had no intention of bothering anyone. 'Live and let live' had always been a principle I subscribed to, and I saw no reason to go back on it now.

*

After that evening's Stanford's event, rather than risk drawing unwanted attention to ourselves in the hotel bar, we stopped on the way back for a nightcap at a little pub that had a down-to-earth, unpretentious look about it. As I commented to Charlie, it reminded me of the type of no-frills working men's boozer my father used to frequent back home. Inside, although the lighting was subdued, it was possible to catch enough of the general atmosphere to confirm that impression – at least to the extent that the customers were predominantly men, none of whom paid us any particular heed as we made our way across the room.

It had been another long day, and I was looking forward to taking the weight off my feet, but every chair at the scattering of tables was occupied, so we just stood cowboy-style with our elbows on the bar, sipping our drinks and talking about the ups and downs of our mini road trip, now drawing to a close. We'd had a satisfying journey, all things considered, but were now looking forward to embarking on the final leg tomorrow morning. Talking as a seasoned vagabond, I assured Charlie that returning home was always the most enjoyable part of going away.

'I'll drink to that,' he smiled, and clinked his glass against mine. Then, of a sudden, he dug me in the ribs, jerked his head sideways and said, 'That bugger there just groped me!'

'*Groped* you?'

'Yeah, grabbed my arse and gave it a squeeze. Twice!'

I nodded my head, slowly. 'Hmm, I did wonder about the pinkish-blue lighting in here. We've obviously wandered back inside the boundary of Manchester's famous Gay Village, as your guidebook calls it.'

'Well, to each their own,' Charlie said with a stoical shrug. 'No harm done and no big deal.'

I was mentally weary, physically fatigued and altogether in no mood to pander to the intrusive impulses of anyone, least of all a sly, wandering-hand merchant trawling for targets in a public bar. In legal terms, what had just happened was a sexual assault, and the perpetrator needed to be put in his place.

'OK, Charlie,' I muttered out of the corner of my mouth, 'head for the exit – but dead casually – and I'll catch up with you in a minute.'

'No, honestly, Dad, it's no big deal. There's no point in –'

I put a finger to my lips and nodded towards the door. 'Just go, Charlie, OK!'

Albeit with some reluctance, Charlie did as instructed, while I turned to the creep who had been standing next to him. I smiled and offered my hand, which he took, a bit too readily, I thought. I then quietly but firmly advised him, on pain of having his sleazy, perverted fingers rendered permanently unfit for purpose, never to take such liberties with a son of mine again. I squeezed his hand with the kind of vigorous kneading motion I recalled being administered by tyro sadists in primary school. They called it a Knuckle Grinder, a simple but enfeebling form of torture which used to elicit yells of agony from the juvenile victims back then, and provoked an eye-watering grimace, complete with lip-biting yodel, from the adult recipient now.

Although the aggressive way I had reacted was totally out of character, I felt quite proud of myself for having taught a lesson in appropriately paternal fashion to the molester of my offspring. And I told Charlie as much when I joined him at the door.

Charlie flashed me a wan smile. 'Ehm, there's just one wee problem, Padre…'

I cocked an apprehensive ear.

Charlie cleared his throat. 'You, um-ah, you taught the lesson to the wrong guy.'

I froze. 'Wrong ... guy?

Charlie winced and nodded his head. 'Mm-hm, 'fraid so. The groper left the building right after he did the deed. I tried to tell you, but –'

'Yeah, yeah, yeah, I get the picture,' I cut in, then took a quick look over both shoulders. 'Right, Charlie, let's get the hell out of here before the bloke with the knackered knuckles bugles up the cavalry!'

* * * * *

Chapter Twenty-One
'THE FOUR SEASONS'

*

I suspect Charlie was somewhat relieved to return to the relative sanity of the 'flamboyant' corridors of advertising, while I pressed gamely on through the ostensibly 'sedate' paths of the book business. And after our hasty withdrawal from Manchester, I'd have precious little time to catch my breath before setting off again.

Essentially, it was the nagging worry about *not* being able to earn enough from writing books that kept me motivated. At a recent festival at which I had been on stage with a panel of three other authors and a poet, we were asked what provided the inspiration for our writing. The others gave answers describing at some length the levers that released their creative brakes, while my concise response was: 'The fear of being skint'. The reaction from audience and fellow panellists alike ranged from awkward smiles to looks of dismay at what they took to be my flippant attitude towards 'the art'. But my reply to the question had been made in absolute honesty and in no less genuine a spirit than the lyrics of an old Bing Crosby song:

'When my bankroll is getting small,
I think of when I had none at all,
And I fall asleep counting my blessings.'

We were making a living now, if only a modest one, but I realised how fragile our position was in such a fickle occupation, so was happy to hit the promo road whenever invited. Which was the outlook that had taken me on the just-concluded campaign trail with son Charlie. Ellie, true to form, had meanwhile made use of her break from accompanying me to keep herself busy in other ways. Creating a 'normal' home life had been her priority over the years, and she had managed to achieve it against a variety of odds – though, due to circumstances over which she had no control, never for long. Consequently, she decided there was likely to be no better time than the present to put that right, once and for all.

'A house is not a home without a dog,' she blithely declared when I walked in the door. 'Meet Archie and Jocky!'

We had always lived in a dog house (figuratively speaking), apart from the years we spent doing up temporary abodes to sell on. Our fellow occupants had generally been Collies or Boxers, so this was the first time I'd been welcomed over the threshold by two little bundles of wire-haired mischief with faces like the three dots on the end of a coconut. Border

Terriers are by nature fearless, single-minded, hardy, of cordial disposition (most of the time!) and brim full of energy, but also make cheery companions for any humans who match up to their exacting requirements (accompanying them down fox holes mercifully excluded!).

The exploits, adventures and misadventures of Archie and Jocky could provide enough material to fill a book of their own (and it may, someday), but it's sufficient to say here that Ellie's decision to draft them into our family had been well-considered, though not obviously so at first. Her thinking was that sitting hunched over my computer for hours on end was bad for my health. Dogs needed regular exercise, so that's why she had bought this pair of nine-week-old live wires.

'Aw, just look at their cute wee faces,' she drooled. 'Who could resist taking them for walkies four or five times every day?'

'I get the logic, Ellie, but it isn't very practical, is it?'

'Why not?'

'Well, for starters, I *do* need all the time I can find for writing, and then there's all the away trips we have to make.' I hesitated, struck by a sudden thought. 'Unless, of course, you've decided not to go with me again.'

Ellie gave me one of her 'don't be daft' looks. 'All taken care of. Any time I *do* go with you, I've arranged for a nice lady to dog-sit for us. She's already been introduced to the puppies – fell in love with them – can't wait for the next time we go away.'

Ellie now dealt in like manner with my concern about 'walkies' biting into my writing time. She informed me that, for anyone who depends on thinking a lot, medical evidence proves there's nothing better than exercising your dog to accelerate the process. To head off any possible argument, she promptly added that she'd seen this in a magazine at the hairdressers – or on a daytime telly programme – or somewhere. End of debate.

But it wasn't the end of her formula for creating a 'normal' way of life – or as near normal as possible. Instead of just looking at the back of my head every time she passed the little upstairs study she called my 'playpen', Ellie had decided to spend a day or two each week being productively occupied herself, but doing something completely different from all the DIY chores that had been her lot until recently.

Even during our busiest years farming at Cuddy Neuk, Ellie had made a point of helping out occasionally at a friend's dress shop in Haddington. She loved clothes and also enjoyed meeting people, so now that she had some time on her hands, she had decided to make the arrangement slightly more formal. Apart from getting her out of the house when I was engrossed in my work, it would earn her some pocket money of her own, and that would be 'nice'.

I knew Ellie well enough to guess that much of the pocket money would go right back into the dress shop's till in exchange for any 'staff-discount' clothes she fancied. And I saw nothing wrong with that: she was entitled to spend her own money as she chose, and in any case she thoroughly deserved to spoil herself now and then. She had worked long and hard for the privilege. But I had a hunch there would also be a more pragmatic motive behind her decision to 'take a wee part-time job'. Dipping periodically into our contingency nest egg had been necessary to keep our bank balance out of the red throughout the latter part of our house-renovating period, and subsequently during our experiences with late and miscalculated royalty payments as well. We trusted that those difficult times were well and truly behind us, but were sufficiently realistic to accept that preparing for the worst is a sensible way to balance hoping for the best. Although she didn't say so, I was pretty sure Ellie would be planning to squirrel away a *reasonable* share of her dress shop income to help out should similar 'cash flow' problems ever occur in future. I counted myself lucky – yet again.

* * *

Early sales of *Viva Mallorca*! built briskly on the solid foundation of orders notched up in advance of publication, and the first reviews added both retail impetus and a renewed sense of urgency on Chestervale's part to keep this lucrative snowball rolling. They didn't delay in taking up their option for the fourth book in the series, with a completion deadline set to allow for publication in June 2005. As had become the pattern, I would have about nine months to provide them with a ninety-thousand-word book, plus the customary black-and-white drawings to head each chapter. It was a demanding enough task when factoring in all the promotional commitments already agreed for the existing books, but made even more so by news that Izzie would no longer be my editor.

She had decided to quit the publishing business to pursue a new career in nursing, which, on the face of it, may have seemed an odd change of direction. But perhaps honing a manuscript does employ skills similar to those required to help poorly patients attain a better state of health. Although she would be a hard act to follow, it seemed there was no lack of university graduates keen to cut their editorial teeth under Chestervale's tutelage. While I would have welcomed the continuation of my partnership with Izzie, I now had to prepare myself for establishing equally productive relationships with her successors.

It was a foregone conclusion that *Snowballs Four*, like its three forerunners, would have a particular season of the year as its main theme, and as only one season remained to be covered, a subtitle was assumed before the main title was even thought of – or, for that matter, before a word of the narrative was actually written. In any event, it followed that *One Mallorcan Spring* would also be the last in the series. Disappointed as I was, I had no alternative but to accept Chestervale's unwavering policy of not publishing fiction, even though to do so in my case would have given them an opportunity to make further capital out of a 'brand' they had helped nurture and which was currently attracting an unforeseen measure of recognition – in a dozen different languages to boot.

I already had three fiction manuscripts ready for

any publisher prepared to take them on, and since my new agent Bette Tanner had made it clear she could do little to help in that regard, I now redoubled my own efforts, but without diverting my focus from the crucial tasks of completing and promoting the breadwinning *Snowball Oranges* series. Hectic times indeed, but all the more stimulating for that.

Press on, boy! Press on!

*

The Palma Book Fair (*Fira del Llibre* in Mallorcan) is held in early summer, when the island's capital plays host to dozens of booksellers who leave their shops and take to the street to meet their customers. The *Fira* takes place in the city's most elegant boulevard, El Paseo del Borne, where throngs of book lovers stroll from stall to stall between columns of shady old plane trees. The *Born*, as local folk refer to it, not only features some of the most striking classical architecture in the balconied houses that overlook the street, but also boasts a glittering array of stores and boutiques bearing the names of such world-famous fashion houses as Mulberry, Zara, Carolina Herrera, Louis Vuitton and Rolex. With a choice of cafes, bars and restaurants to suit all tastes and budgets never more than a few steps away, El Paseo del Borne is an upmarket bazaar capable of seducing even the most restrained of shoppers.

It therefore came as no surprise that Ellie promptly pronounced herself sufficiently refreshed to tag along when I received an invitation to take part in the current year's event. For me, the week-long sojourn turned out to be something of a working holiday, insomuch as there was no travelling involved once we arrived in Palma, leaving me enough free time between engagements to make a start to writing the next book.

The *Fira* itself, rather than conforming to any 'staid' image of a book festival, was more akin to a bunting-bedecked village fête, but on a grander scale and with an atmosphere befitting this vivacious Mediterranean city. Apart from one informal speaking event and three magazine interviews, the official 'working' aspect of my visit entailed nothing more time consuming than being on duty under the awning of one of the stands for a couple of hours each day, chatting to predominantly English-speaking tourists and expats who had either read my books or wanted to know something more about them.

In the interim, Ellie busied herself soaking up the opulence of the local shop window displays, though steadfastly exercising her powers of self-restraint by yielding *not* to temptation. Well, maybe just once or twice, she ultimately confessed, 'but only a teensy-weensy bit*'*, so I could rest assured our 'housekeeping' nest egg had not been gratuitously plundered.

Even if I wasn't *entirely* assured, I was certainly rested, and felt ready by the end of the trip to face the hurly-burly of commitments awaiting me back in the UK. But one other positive outcome of our fleeting return to Mallorca had been the result of a visit we made to the valley in the lower slopes of the Tramuntana Mountains where we'd once lived. As feared, in the seventeen intervening years many of the orange groves on little farms like our own had been neglected by their new owners, mainly well-to-do foreign retirees who had no interest in the age-old Mallorcan farming traditions that we ourselves had tried so hard to maintain. It was a regrettable sign of the times, but as we reminisced about our own experiences at Ca's Mayoral, my thoughts were drawn to the subtitle of my current writing project and its connection with one particular incident during our first spring on the island…

My memories had all but faded of the day a few months earlier when a freak blizzard turned our unpicked oranges into exotic snowballs and transformed every palm tree in the valley into a grenade burst of cotton wool. Then, to my dismay, I heard Ellie shout:

'Peter! It's snowing!'

'Would you credit it?' I'd muttered through clenched teeth, 'Only two falls of snow in living memory, and both since we arrived. Looks like we've brought a Scottish jinx with us!'

As deflated as I'd been by her piece of meteorological bad news, Ellie was cheerfulness personified when she came into the storeroom where I was stacking crates. Looking as happy-go-lucky as Dorothy skipping down the 'Yellow Brick Road', she was swinging one of the little wicker baskets we used for orange-picking. But, significantly, it didn't contain any oranges.

What had put her in such a joyful mood was having just witnessed a phenomenon that transforms the island's countryside into a shimmering 'snowscape' for a few days every year. But this wonder of nature has nothing in common with the wintry scenes traditionally depicted on Christmas cards. Indeed, it signifies the exact opposite. It's almond blossom time – the arrival of Mallorcan spring.

Ellie thrust her basket at me. 'See,' she chirped, 'I've brought you a basketful of snowflakes!'

And that's how, all those years later, the memory of that day provided a title for my new book, a title which also happened to chime with the subtitle already chosen. So, *A Basketful of Snowflakes – One Mallorcan Spring* it was destined to be.

But that was for the future, and *Viva Mallorca! – One Mallorcan Autumn* was the book demanding all the attention I could give it right now. The next stop on the campaign trail happened to be another festival, though as reserved and demure in some ways as the *Fira del Llibre* had been easy-going and colourful. Yet the Warwick Arts Festival, justifiably regarded as one of the premier cultural events in England, did not lack a spirit of experimentation in its programming.

As already mentioned, it had become a fairly common feature of the less formal of my 'reading' engagements (which means most of them!) to have some Spanish music playing in the background as the audience arrived. This was normally provided by a CD player and tended to favour the exuberant guitar-thrashing of the Gipsy Kings rather than, say, the delicate artistry of a classical guitarist like the legendary Segovia. And this suited the mood of those occasions just fine. But it would not have struck a chord with what the directors of the Warwick Arts Festival had in mind.

Very few have had the distinction of being suggested as a possible successor to Segovia, the undisputed maestro of Spanish classical guitar, but the musician I had been booked to appear with at Warwick was one of that rare group. Brazilian-born Fabio Zanon was still only a young man, but had already graced the platforms of concert halls and recital rooms in some fifty countries worldwide. He was held in the highest regard by the cognoscenti of serious guitar music, and members of that elite fraternity would almost certainly have comprised the vast majority, if not all, of the audience facing the stage I found myself sharing with him. To be absolutely accurate, though, the stage was not a stage as such, but an altar, the focal point within the medieval chantry chapel of a magnificent half-timbered building known historically as The Lord Leycester Hospital.

The organisers of the event had thoughtfully provided Fabio and myself with rooms in the same accommodation the previous night, which had given me an opportunity to have a chat with the young *senhor* over breakfast next morning. His inherent modesty manifested itself in a laconic approach to conversation, and he came across as essentially a rather shy, private person: the antithesis of someone whose life revolves around communicating with the public. Clearly, Fabio Zanon was content to let his guitar do the talking. But being endowed with such a rare talent did not prevent him from having a considerate, indeed generous, attitude towards lesser creative beings with whom he chanced to perform from time to time.

In my own case, this resulted in his decision to give prominence in today's programme to a *pièce de résistance* for solo guitar by acclaimed 19th century Spanish composer Isaac Albéniz: an opus which was named, appropriately enough, *Mallorca*. I was as mesmerised as the audience by this virtuoso performance of a wonderfully atmospheric piece of music, evocative of the serenity of the island, yet also containing a jaunty, lightsome passage depicting the irrepressibly genial character of its people.

'Follow *that*, Don Pedro!' I said to myself as I took my place behind the lectern and looked into the eyes of row up row of classical music buffs who were presumably more than a tad puzzled by my presence. After all, the nearest I'd ever got to playing classical music was my contribution of some jazzy clarinet licks to the Clyde Valley Stompers' 1963 rehash of Prokofiev's *Peter and the Wolf*. And, on the spur of the moment, referring to that was exactly how I introduced myself. The audience, much to my relief, responded with a burst of laughter – not of the knee-slapping variety, but with a decorum befitting our presence within a place of sanctity. Thereafter, it became obvious that devotees of serious music are no less accommodating towards an affable interloper than their counterparts in the world of books.

That being the case, I stuck to my usual policy of being myself, relating whatever anecdotes I felt suited the occasion and, in this particular instance, making sure I didn't swear. This approach held up well until, buoyed by the receptive mien of the audience, I started to tell the story of Ellie's New Year faux pas when she dropped a linguistic clanger by trying to wish a haemorrhoidal Mallorcan shopkeeper a Happy New Year in Spanish. The word 'arsehole' slipped out before I remembered where I was, but I immediately sought divine forgiveness by looking heavenward and mouthing a silent apology. Anyway, the gathered congregation took it all in good part by allowing themselves another burst of deferential laughter, and I hope the recipient of my apology had a little chortle to Himself as well.

During the second half of 2004, there were ten more engagements to fulfil, including the Edinburgh, Lincoln, Glasgow 'Aye Write' and Inverness Book Festivals and involving the now-familiar pattern of zig-zagging and yo-yoing up, down and across the country to library and bookshop dates which, although more modest than festivals in their scope, were all just as valuable in their way. To round off what had been an exceptionally busy and eventful year, one commitment remained: one that promised a complete change from the normal routine and, on the basis of a change being as good as a rest, one that could possibly provide us with a bit of a breather as well…

It had been at the end of doing a 'turn' at the Basingstoke Word Fest in Hampshire the previous year that a gentleman with a businesslike look about him approached me and introduced himself as the entertainments director of a major cruise line, based 'down the road a bit' in Southampton. He said he had liked the evening's format of having the audience seated at tables with a glass of wine, which was reminiscent of holidays in Spain, he thought. This had convinced him that 'something along those lines' could fit in with a programme he was putting together for a Spanish-themed cruise scheduled for the latter part of the following year. Would I be interested in coming along as a featured speaker? I would of course be paid a fee, he stressed, in addition to enjoying all the entitlements of full passenger status – for two.

There could be no denying that this sounded a really attractive proposition, particularly for anyone inclined towards a relaxing life on the ocean wave. And although it was a pastime that had never appealed to Ellie and me, it would have seemed discourteous to have rejected out of hand such a generous offer. It was on this basis, then, that I welcomed the opportunity to wind up my book-promoting efforts for 2004 by taking to the high seas on a two-week cruise aboard a luxury liner bound for the Canary Islands

* * * * *

Chapter Twenty-Two
'A LIFE ON THE OCEAN WAVE – OR NOT'

*

For anyone whose familiarity with ships is limited, as mine had been, to hopping on ferries for an hour or two between the likes of Dover and Calais, confronting a luxury cruise liner for the first time can be a jaw-dropping experience. The vessel in this case looked for all the world like a floating apartment block, its decks towering above us as our taxi pulled up on the quayside at Southampton. But if the exterior seemed daunting, the interior was truly breathtaking and worthy of being described as on the palatial side of luxurious. The great hall, for want of a better name, was in the form of a vast and lavishly appointed atrium, with a grand staircase and glass lifts connecting several 'floors' that housed four dining rooms, eight bars, a casino, theatre, show lounge, night club, shopping centre, library, cyber study, a gym and many other facilities essential to cruise clientele of a discriminating cut – or at least those sufficiently flush to give the impression.

For me to claim I felt at home in this environment would be pretentious in the extreme, yet it took only a cursory tour of the ship to see how fans of cruising are attracted by the opulence of a vessel such as this. For some, it's a way of life enjoyed on a regular basis according to the measure of their affluence; for others, a once-in-a-lifetime treat paid for out of savings hard-earned over many years.

But it wasn't for me to judge the social or financial status of the one thousand or so passengers whose holiday I was sharing as a paid guest. My brief was to 'inform and amuse' them by talking about and reading from my books at appointed times in the theatre or show lounge every day the ship was at sea. I would also be expected to welcome opportunities to chat with those who felt so inclined, and to generally enter into the spirit of conviviality the company prided itself on promoting. As luck would have it, I can be as gregarious as they come when circumstances dictate (how else would I have survived the life I've lived so far!) yet I also value my privacy. But given a reasonable balance of the two, I reckoned this latest book-promoting venture would work out just fine. As indeed it did, for not everyone on board subscribed to the '*All good pals and jolly good company*' concept that cruising conjures up in the minds of the uninitiated – myself included at the time.

It's true that a wide choice of activities and entertainments – from line dancing sessions to West End style shows – was laid on for passengers from morning to night, but havens of peace and quiet were also provided for those who preferred shipboard solitude, or just needed an occasional break from sampling the wide choice of entertainments and activities.

During the fourteen days of the cruise, eight would be spent in the scheduled ports of call: Vigo (north-west Spain), Lisbon (Portugal), Cadiz (south-west Spain), then all the way south to the African coast and the Spanish Canary Islands of Lanzarote, Gran Canaria, Tenerife and La Palma, stopping for a day at the Portuguese island of Madeira on the return voyage to Southampton. This left only six days 'at sea' for me to do my talks. A pretty cushy number, you might say. And so it was, but not before the Bay of Biscay had put its stamp on proceedings.

This mighty bite out of the Atlantic seaboard of Europe, bordered by the coasts of France to the west and Spain to the south, has an age-old reputation among seafarers of being the lair of some of the most violent storms to plague the seven seas. Like most people, I had heard stories about gigantic waves driven by hurricane-strength winds sinking ships in the Bay of Biscay, but that was when ships were but little wooden tubs compared to the thirty thousand tons of welded, riveted and bolted steel we were shrouded in now. This thing was built to withstand, with no more than a gentle roll, anything the sea could hurl at it, thanks to the hi-tech stabilisers, computer-controlled gyro whatsits and all the rest of the up-to-date gizmos vessels this size are equipped with. And anyway, cruise lines always relied on pinpoint, satellite-generated weather forecasts to ensure hazardous conditions would be avoided wherever they occurred. Better another day or two in port than risk compromising passengers' safety at sea. As a seasoned landlubber, that was my reading of the situation anyway.

I was awakened by a phone call to our cabin on the morning following our first full day out from Southampton. It was the cruise director, the company executive in charge of all those onboard entertainments and activities we touched on earlier…

'Good morning, Peter. I hope I'm not disturbing you.'

'No, no, not at all. What can I do for you?'

'Look, I'm really sorry about this, because I realise this is a day off for you – you know, with everyone due to disembark when we dock at Vigo a bit later.'

'Well, I haven't got anything planned, so…'

'OK, I'll come straight to the point. The captain has just had a report of a potentially troublesome weather front approaching the Bay of Biscay from the south. The path of the storm is a bit tricky to predict, but it looks like we could be heading right into it.'

Perhaps it was just my imagination, but no sooner had he said that than I could have sworn I felt the ship tremble slightly. Or maybe it was just my knees.

'It's good of you to let me know,' I said, making an effort to sound unconcerned. 'I'll unpack my sou'wester.'

The cruise director gave a polite little laugh. 'Quite – your sou'wester. Good idea, and fairly appropriate too, as it happens. But no, what I was actually going to ask is if you'd mind doing an unscheduled talk today. OK, I know it's not in your contract, but if you could see your way to –'

'It's all right. Don't worry about it. Anything I can do to help out will be no problem at all. But, just to satisfy my nosiness – is the speaker scheduled for today ill? Nothing serious, I hope.'

We had been introduced on our first evening on board to the two other featured speakers: one a retired lecturer in anthropology, the other a professor of architecture. I had made a point of watching their individual 'spots' at the first opportunity, and had been impressed by their professionalism and preparation, which included PowerPoint 'slide show' presentations of their respective subjects, focusing of course on the Spanish theme of the cruise. They made my largely ad-lib routine seem rather haphazard by comparison, yet I was now about to have this more 'casual' approach upheld in a way that was both unexpected and much appreciated, even if slightly foreboding too.

The dilemma, as the cruise director went on to explain, was that he had to take reasonable precautions in case we *were* caught in a storm, but without creating unnecessary 'apprehension' among the passengers. The captain had already decided that to alter course towards the port of Vigo as originally intended would mean presenting the ship broadside on to the run of the sea, resulting in an inevitable 'rocking of the boat', which some passengers might find a bit 'uncomfortable'. So, erring on the safe side as always, appropriate alterations were being made to the entertainments programme for today: specifically the curtailment of any activities that involved the risk of stumbling – like line dancing sessions or keep-fit lessons, for example – and replacing them with more sedentary attractions – like talks.

The upshot of this preamble was that the director, going on past experience of such situations, was of the opinion that what was required was a talk that would be more 'diverting than edifying' in nature. Storms at sea, he confided, were always liable to prompt passengers to react in this way, which was why he hoped I might step into the breach today.

Two hours later, I was standing on stage in the Las Vegas style show lounge, telling happy tales about our life in Mallorca and feeling eerily like a member of the band that played gamely on while the Titanic sank. My audience amounted to about twenty brave souls who, like me, had bounced their way along corridors and staggered up and down stairs to reach here. (In the interests of safety, all lifts had been put temporarily out of commission). What had started half an hour earlier as a gentle rolling of the ship had now developed into a slow-motion see-sawing movement, a bit like the nodding and rearing of a giant rocking horse being spurred on by a sadistic kid. Through the lounge windows I could see the watery horizon appearing and disappearing as the ship bucked and dipped, with every so often the view totally obliterated by lashings of flung spray and blown spume.

I chattered gamely on, suspecting that those passengers remaining stoically at tables surrounding the dance floor were either seasoned 'storm troupers' who took this sort of drama in their stride, or were first-timers glued to their seats by fear. Nature was tossing this thirty thousand tons of steel around like a rubber duck in a jacuzzi, and the effects were getting more violent by the minute. Of a sudden, the bow of ship could be felt plunging into a trough between the oncoming waves, followed by a deep whirring sound as the stern rose out of the water to leave the propellers with nothing to propel but thin air. Then there was a loud thump and the ship palpably shuddered in response to a massive breaker battering against its hull.

Looking down at the dance floor, now tilting at ever more jaunty angles, I realised how prudent it had been to cancel today's line dancing session! But had opting for my 'diverting' talk proved equally astute? Well, all I can say is that nobody threw up during the entire forty-five minutes of its delivery – including, surprisingly, myself.

* * *

2005 began with an already exacting list of events planned to build towards the release of *A Basketful of Snowflakes* in June. But with a March deadline set for delivery of my completed manuscript, time was tight, so all of those events had been limited to locations requiring only one night's stopover, if any. The longest journey was the relatively easy 190-mile round trip for an engagement at the Winter Words Festival in scenic Pitlochry. The town's famous Festival Theatre sits amidst one of the most stunning landscapes in Highland Perthshire, with a backdrop of lush woodlands and breathtaking views over the River Tummel valley. This would be the first such engagement I'd undertaken since the Canary Islands cruise, and although that trip had given us an opportunity to take in many wonderful sights in exotic places to which we might never otherwise have travelled, it took but a moment on arrival in Pitlochry to realise just how uniquely beautiful Scotland is. We were glad to be back home, and were in no particular hurry to venture so far away again.

Nevertheless, just a few days later, I received an invitation to go as a speaker on *another* cruise, the director of the last one having recommended me to the specialist agency involved. Despite mainly pleasant recollections of the voyage to the Canaries, the Bay of Biscay 'episode' was the one that endured most vividly, prompting Ellie to admit that the very thought of it still made her feel seasick. Consequently, my immediate reaction was to thank the agency kindly for their invitation, but to politely decline. Even so, after only a surprisingly short consultation with Ellie, the decision was made to accept. Why the sudden about-turn? Firstly, because the trip was set to start and finish in Scotland, setting out from Greenock, only fifty miles away on the west coast, and returning to the east coast port of Leith, just a forty minute drive from our Haddington base. And secondly, because the destination was to be the rugged Atlantic coast of Norway, Scotland's nearest neighbour across the North Sea and a country that held a special fascination for me due to its historic links with the Orkney Isles, home of my mother's side of the family since the year dot. But an equally persuasive factor was simply that Ellie had long had a wish to visit the Norwegian fjords. Here, then, was an opportunity to do just that, and at no cost to ourselves. What's more, the dates were set to follow hot on the heels of the deadline for completion of my new book, so if any extra incentive to hit the target were required, signing up for the Norway trip would serve the purpose nicely.

But this isn't a book in which I ever intended to expound the attractions or otherwise of luxury cruises: it's an account of the life and times of a spontaneous scribbler who somehow became a published author who somehow gained a reputation for being an 'unrefined' public speaker with a feel-good factor woven into his ramblings. In this latter respect, I suppose I provided an easily-digested alternative to the more scholarly fodder dished up by retired academics and intellectuals who, together with an assortment of emerging and superannuated 'celebs', comprised the bulk of the booking agency's roster. But whereas many of those speakers might have had enough time on their hands to regard cruise ship engagements as freebie holidays to be enjoyed whenever they fancied, I had a living to earn, and for someone who isn't much good at writing on the move, spending even the occasional two weeks away from the 'playpen' is hardly conducive to keeping the wolf from the door.

I'll say no more about our Norwegian trip, except that sailing silently in the moonlight through mountain-flanked fjords with waterfalls tumbling as if from the sky is a truly awe-inspiring experience; and exploring saga-steeped (and troll-inhabited!) Viking havens an opportunity not to be missed by those with an interest in Nordic history and folklore. As with the ports of call on our Canaries voyage, you can read more about these places where you will and visit them if you so decide. For me, however, a firm decision had to be made, and not even an invitation a month later to chatter my way round the Caribbean could sway me from drawing a line under my book-plugging life on the ocean wave.

But short and sweet, and occasionally turbulent, as that chapter of my life had been, I gained lasting benefit from it in two distinct ways. The first was that the voyages, and in particular some of the colourful characters encountered on them, had provided me with a wealth of material for what I envisaged could be a fitting addition to the two humour-laced crime novels I already had in the can. The other was the result of a casual conversation I'd had with an elderly lady towards the end of the Norwegian trip…

She had just bought copies of my books from the ship's souvenir shop and had asked me to sign them. As I did so, she remarked that the travel aspect of my stories was what interested her most, having had incurably 'itchy feet' all of her life, caused mainly, as it happened, by the lure of cruising. The thrill of waking up in a different port every morning was an addiction she'd had no inclination to control, until now. For no discernible reason, she had finally come to the conclusion that, when you got right down to it, every quayside looked pretty much the same as the next. All she wanted to do now was get back home to her faithful old dog, who had waited patiently for her return, too often and for too long.

This touched a nerve. Archie and Jocky, our little Border Terriers, had been with us for about a year now and had become cherished members of the family. I had tried to stifle the pangs of guilt I felt on leaving them at kennels when going on those cruises. The look of bewilderment on their faces as the gate closed, 'abandoning' them on the inside while we drove off, haunted me all the time we were away. And the tail-wagging, yelping, twirling, jumping, panting, face-licking welcome they gave us on our return banished any doubt that they'd missed us.

We totally empathised with that elderly lady's way of thinking, which helped establish the most conclusive reason of all for limiting our future business commitments to those that allowed us to put 'family' considerations first. However, as things currently stood, the publication of my next book was destined to be the last, so how to avoid devoting too much time to anti-familial matters was likely to be the least of our worries. But no matter how rational our intentions, fate, in typically unpredictable fashion, was about to dictate what lay ahead for us anyway.

* * * * *

Chapter Twenty-Three
'TWO WATERSHEDS AND A PADDLE'

*

From the back cover of *A Basketful of Snowflakes – One Mallorcan Spring*...

"It's the peak of the orange harvesting season on the Kerrs' little farm in the entrancing Tramuntana Mountains of Mallorca, and the family are trying to relax into their new life on the sunny Spanish island. But it's also crunch time and, after an eventful first year, hard facts have to be faced. Will all the work they have invested provide them with a decent living, or will their dream turn into a nightmare? Whether or not, the Kerrs' sense of humour remains irrepressible amid the 'snowfall' of almond blossom as the balmy spring season progresses..."

*

When *A Basketful of Snowflakes* was released in the

summer of 2005, the five years separating it from the first book in the series seemed to have passed in a flash, compared at any rate to the confidence-sapping eight years it had taken to find a publisher in the first place. Our old friend Dame Fortune, backed up by a few of us lesser mortals, had created opportunities to make an international success out of easy-to-read family stories that combined escapism with a mix of adventure and fun. I had grabbed those opportunities with both hands, resulting in a flurry of promotional activities crammed between deadlines for the completion and delivery of successive manuscripts and illustrations. Time had indeed flown.

Doubts and concerns about what now lay ahead for my writing career (and income!) were given a welcome shove to the back of my mind by reactions to the publication of this fourth book in the series. If it was to be my swansong, I would give it every chance of being a memorable one. To help things along, the book's advance sales had compared favourably with those of its predecessors, and this was soon being reflected in the first reviews…

> *"Far from having to worry about sustaining his style in another book or finding more fresh content on his favoured themes, Peter goes from strength to strength. Even the humour is better, raising a laugh from the most po-faced."* (TOP Magazine, Spain)

> *"You can almost smell the almond blossom. Curl up with this great book and the sun will shine instantly!"* (Waterstones.com)

> *"Poetic the title may be, but this is Kerr in his usual gutsy style, continuing with the fourth in his series about starting a new life in Mallorca. His larger-than-life personality jumps off every page."*
> (The Good Book Guide)

Thus, without need for any formal 'launch', *A Basketful of Snowflakes* took off with flying colours, and I threw myself with renewed gusto into the now-familiar promotional whirl. This varied between visits to small rural libraries and yet another appearance at the Edinburgh International Book Festival. This time, director Catherine Lockerbie lent her continuing support to my efforts by pairing me with Joan Lingard, one of Scotland's most respected novelists. She had just published her fifty-fifth book, *Encarnita's Journey*, a literary *tour de force* set in Spain and Scotland, which was presumably the common denominator responsible for what could be regarded as a fairly unlikely 'double billing'. Anyhow, the event was warmly received by the audience and I had a hunch Joan Lingard enjoyed the experience as much as I did. Yet again, I counted myself extremely fortunate to have been included in such distinguished company.

Coincidentally or not, a few days later I received a request from Chestervale to write a *fifth* book in the series. Taken aback as I was by this sudden U-turn, I could understand their motivation: to them, it must now have made more commercial sense than ever to keep this highly profitable snowball rolling. But as much as I needed a financial straw to clutch at myself, there were certain practicalities that could not be ignored. Not least of those was the fact that there are only four seasons in the year, and they had all been featured in the subtitles of the books already published. Then there was the matter of available material…

Of the lengthy list of amusing stories, nail-biting situations and quirky anecdotes I had to draw from, I had made it a rule to feature only those I believed to be the strongest, and I saw no reason to change that policy for what could be judged as simply squeezing the last juice from a golden orange. Filling a fifth book with padding and spurious 'happenings' would only serve to demean what had become a well-regarded quartet of books, and I had no intention of allowing that to happen, no matter how tempting the advance royalty.

But Chestervale's young chiefs weren't to be so easily dissuaded. With a weather eye always open to the main chance, they devised a way round this dilemma that had the makings of a good earner *and* the possibility of actually adding value to the series. Why, they asked, didn't I write a book beginning with the reasons behind our decision to end our Mallorcan adventure, and segue the narrative to details of our return to Scotland, all the while extolling the attributes of both places and maintaining the usual feel-good factor throughout? Although it would have been easy to pick holes in the suggestion, I had to admit it had the potential to be developed into a much-needed lifeline. And if sympathetically handled, it could turn out to be a logical adjunct to the series, insomuch as it would give me scope to fully reveal the background to our return 'home', while *Thistle Soup* already explained why we left in the first place. The more I thought about it, the more the idea appealed, and even a title immediately suggested itself. I got down to writing *From Paella to Porridge* with due haste and the enthusiasm of a canoeist who has just been thrown a paddle to help him avoid the entrance to a notoriously noxious creek.

*

Pillion Press was one of several smaller outlets I had recently targeted in my ongoing and seemingly endless drive to find a home for my fiction books. There were striking similarities between Pillion and Chestervale in that I had made contact with both just as they were seeking to expand their catalogues: in Pillion's case with books in a genre popularly referred to as 'cosy crime'. Although my two *Bob Burns Investigates* mysteries were more quirky than cosy, they were sufficiently lacking in gratuitous violence and graphic blood and guts to tick enough of Pillion's boxes. And the stories had the added attraction for them of being peppered with a liberal seasoning of, wonder of wonders ... humour!

Now, instead of having just one book to promote in 2006, I was to have two, with Pillion promising to take on more of my ready-to-publish material if the first *Bob Burns* book made the grade. I would certainly have to keep my nose to the grindstone, but although I had now turned sixty-five, the age at which most of my contemporaries were settling down to enjoy retirement, I was raring to go. Having worked against the odds to build a lasting future in other fields, I was no stranger to disappointment, so couldn't have been happier with my present lot. That old roller coaster looked set to climb again, and I was itching to get on board.

As Pillion Press were still in the early stages of their development, it was pretty much taken for granted that publicising my side-step from non-fiction to fiction would have to be done within the confines of a modest budget. But that didn't faze me. I had travelled that path on many occasions, and this time it would be made considerably easier, ironically enough, by the fact that I already had a full diary of events lined up to promote the last of my *non*-fiction books. Admittedly, we would still have to do our bit to distribute posters and spread the news to media contacts, but at least I wouldn't be faced with the hard graft of breaking new ground again. Meanwhile, the book's most effective promotional asset of all would prove to be the one that those rejecting it had constantly ignored: its subtitle – *The Mallorca Connection.*

Which takes us back to the start of this stroll down memory lane in early 2000 and the creation of an irksome circle that had finally been squared. While the six years since then had certainly flown by, the following eighteen would seem to have had rockets attached. Or maybe it's just a sign of growing old! Whatever, the watershed that fate had created for me in 2006 opened the floodgates in terms of hard work.

Even though I'd never lost faith in *The Mallorca Connection* being capable of attracting a worthwhile readership on its own merits, I can't deny that it was following in the slipstream of the *Snowball Oranges* series that helped it attract the required degree of 'discoverability' on which every new book depends.

All of the many promotional events I committed to in 2006 had been booked on the back of initial reaction to *From Paella to Porridge,* which was summed up by *The Scots Magazine* book reviewer as follows:

> *"A brilliantly observed account of a Scottish family's transition from a Mallorcan farm back to Scotland. The Mallorcan episodes are a joy. I recommend it. Thoroughly."*

Since I reckoned it would be unlikely to appear too out of place if I slipped a short but carefully-worded plug for the first *Bob Burns* yarn into these talks and interviews, that's precisely what I did. And it didn't take long for the effects to show. Early sales, although never realistically expected to set the heather on fire, were soon notching up very respectable figures, and reviews followed in like manner...

> *"A fantastic story, with some nice humour too. A delightful read – a classic murder mystery."* (Audible UK)

> *"Whodunnit fans will love this – a murder hunt with funny and frightening results."* (Sunday Post)

"A rare combination of suspense and comedy." (The Scots Magazine)

So, ever mindful of former US President Coolidge's assertion that *'Nothing in the world can take the place of persistence'*, and having followed his advice to *'Press on!'* through thick and thin, I was finally seeing a door open that had remained stubbornly closed for longer than I cared to remember.

The publishers of audiobook and large-print editions were quick to confirm their ongoing support, while Pillion Press, true to their word, undertook to publish the second *Bob Burns* mystery the following year. Subtitled *The Sporran Connection,* here's what some critics had to say...

"I giggled uncontrollably. Kerr has a rare talent for producing the most ingenious satire. A thoroughly enjoyable, fast-moving novel." (Welsh Books Council)

"A really gripping page-turner that's peppered with laughs." (Amazon UK)

"Well off-the-wall and very much tongue-in-cheek. Escapist and liberally laced with humour." (Edinburgh Evening News)

No doubt encouraged by such reactions, Pillion also snapped up my *Cuddyford Chronicles* town-meets-country romp, now re-titled *Fiddler On The Make* in recognition of main protagonist Jigger McCloud, a puckish fiddle-playing 'rustic' with an eye for a fast buck *and* the ladies. Once again, reviewers reacted with an encouraging thumbs-up...

> "*A delicious, delightful and devilishly funny gem of a novel.*" (Stornoway Gazette)

> "*This is a hoot – pure fun, an observation on the absurd.*" (Welsh Books Council)

> "*A strong sense of place, coupled with a tightly written plot and a delightful cast of characters.*" ('I Love A Mystery' Magazine)

It was indeed very gratifying (as well as a great relief!) to see my belief in those first fiction efforts endorsed by at least *some* readers who had become followers of the *Snowball Oranges* series. I realised, however, that there were also those who didn't take easily to this change in direction. They would much rather that our 'living-the-dream' family stories had continued, but as already stated, I firmly believed that to do so would inevitably have led to scraping the barrel for content.

While it's true that you can't please everyone, my inclination to include a Mallorcan element in my fiction would, I hoped, help retain a fair proportion of the following that had taken so much time and effort to attract. The folks at Pillion Press also subscribed to this line of thought and backed their hunch by commissioning two more books incorporating just such a link. Their catalogue was expanding fast, and

I was only too pleased contribute!

I jumped at the chance to breath life into a couple of 'based-on-reality' ideas I'd been keeping on ice for some time. One was the *Bob Burns* mystery that had suggested itself to me during the first of the luxury cruises I detailed earlier. And I can honestly say, with no offence to cruising devotees intended, that I had more fun writing *The Cruise Connection* than I'd had on the actual trip! Here's what a few critics thought of the result:

"A fast-paced and hilarious voyage on the high seas." (Xpat Magazine, Spain)

"Good escapist stuff. Wry, droll, observant, whimsical, mischievous, yet quietly sardonic as well." (Amazon UK)

"Peter describes a cast of outlandish characters with gentle mockery. Anyone who has been on a cruise will recognise the types." (Nautical Magazine)

The other 'true-to-life' story I decided to write was inspired by a young tour rep I'd noticed at Mallorca's Palma Airport one day while I was waiting for friends. He was a fresh-faced lad of about twenty, I guessed, all togged up in his company's blue blazer and white slacks, and making a brave attempt at rounding up and herding onto coaches an unruly mob of just-landed, alcohol-fuelled clients. He was doing all right, smiling and keeping his cool, but still managing to look totally out of place.

He immediately struck me as an ideal model on whom to base a light-hearted romantic adventure. I eventually cast him as a young Scottish veterinary student who takes a year's break from university to work as a guide in Africa, hoping to find time to study the wildlife while there. But because of an administrative glitch, he finds himself instead in Mallorca, thrust in at the deep end of the madcap package tour business – a hapless fish out of water, for whom the nearest thing to wildlife appears to be the hordes of holidaymakers disgorged by 'gannets' (charter planes) newly arrived from the UK.

And so *The Gannet Has Landed* became my eleventh published book, and although a marked change in subject matter from any of the others, reviewers took to it in a much-appreciated sprit of generosity…

> *"A gentle, amusing romance, with enough travel elements to make the discerning reader consider discovering the real Mallorca."* (Dumfries & Galloway Standard)

> *"A great tale. Kerr writes with a speed and efficiency which gives his story great momentum. His dry wit is a delight."* (Welsh Books Council)

> *"Makes fiction seem like real life. An outstandingly good writer with an exquisite sense of humour."* (Amazon UK)

It was now 2008, and with all current writing

commitments honoured and hopes fading of any mutually-acceptable non-fiction projects being agreed with Chestervale, I now faced an open-ended period of waiting until Pillion Press decided what they'd like me to do next on the fiction front. Until very recently, this state of affairs would have filled me with apprehension, if not full-blown panic, but with royalties from eleven books now combining to provide us with at least a *modest* living, I saw this as an opportunity to explore other book ideas I'd long kept tucked away on the back burner. Perhaps typically, the one that appealed to me most was the one most likely to present difficulties in finding a publisher, since historical fiction didn't fit the lists of either of the two companies I'd been working with, nor was it a genre my agent Bette specialised in.

Nevertheless, I had always been intrigued by what is regarded as perhaps the most momentous event in the history of Mallorca, the youthful King James 1 of Aragon's Christian 'Reconquest' of the island from its Moorish (Muslim) rulers in 1229; so I decided to research the facts and maybe fictionalise the highlights into a short novella of a hundred or so pages. I thought I'd weave the yarn round the king's unlikely confidante, a young Mallorcan Christian of humble station, and balance his exposure to the horror and brutality of war against an unexpected encounter with two Muslim women – one older than himself, the other younger – revealing heart-rending aspects of his past and sowing the seeds of a forbidden romantic relationship punishable by death. I would also make a point of including Mallorcan locations still familiar to present-day visitors. This, I felt, would keep me creatively occupied during breaks in ongoing promotional work for the next few months.

Three years later, I had been so captivated by the documented details of the saga that I had adapted them into an 'epic' novel, which I named *Song of the Eight Winds* after an ancient Moorish chant sung by Mallorcan fishermen to this day. Running to a total of 150,000 words, it was almost double the length of most of my existing books! And, yes, you guessed right – publisher after publisher turned it down, the general opinion being that historical fiction was such a specialised subject that it would be difficult to successfully introduce the work of an author whose name had already become synonymous with other genres.

There I was – typecast, slotted into pigeonholes I'd never recognised myself, and diametrically opposed to what I'd always considered to be the very essence of the creative process: spontaneity and improvisation. For it's a fact that you can take a jazzman out of jazz, but you can't take the jazz out of a jazzman. In any event, I wasn't prepared to spend years knocking my head against publishers' doors again (at seventy-one, I reckoned there was no time for that now anyway), so it seemed fate had pushed me towards another watershed, and this one promised to have an even greater bearing on my continued involvement in the book business than the last…

*

While active as a record producer back in the '70s, I'd had occasion to set up a small music-publishing facility for the primary purpose of protecting the copyright of certain compositions I was involved with. My eventual departure from the music scene had rendered the 'company' redundant, but it now occurred to me that it might be worth exploring the possibility of resurrecting it and adapting it to suit my current situation. After all, more and more authors, both established and aspiring, were independently publishing their own books these days, so surely the process couldn't be beyond the wit of even a confessed 'techno dummy' like me. A quick word with son Charlie to check that I could count on having the benefit of his computer skills, and we were on our way.

One of the first requirements was to convert the book's working manuscript into formats suitable for the creation of both print and ebook editions, and this called for the assistance of experts. Conversely, creating a design for the cover wasn't a problem, since Charlie himself worked as a computer graphics artist. The need to comply with the more mundane stipulations of procuring a bar code and an ISBN (statutory identification number), plus registering the book's details on a dedicated worldwide database was just a matter of getting stuck in and patiently taking one thing at a time.

At the risk of over-simplifying matters (and I stress that this was never intended to be regarded as a 'How-to' book), the final procedure involves uploading the master files onto a specialist internet platform (e.g. Amazon's Kindle Direct Publishing, or KDP for short), where they will be printed, sold and shipped on demand, without any need for the author/publisher to invest in expensive print runs and associated warehousing. In fact, depending on how much of the 'prep' work you can do yourself, the only cost involved can be as little as a few pounds for the eventual proof copy of the paperback.

By such means *Song of the Eight Winds* was finally 'on the market', and in a fraction of the time it would have taken most conventional publishers to do the job. However, two vitally important aspects we couldn't match were those concerning publicity and distribution. Any conventional publishers worth their salt will have the clout that 'indies' lack when seeking coverage of a book's release in the media, and also when getting it into 'bricks-and-mortar' bookshops on a nationwide basis.

For all that, I'd found the process to have been as enjoyable as it had been enlightening, and I could hardly have been more satisfied with the outcome, limited though initial sales were likely to be. The biggest surprise was that, in marked contrast to the negative attitude of some publishers towards my attempt to 'invade' the sacrosanct territory of historical fiction, book critics turned out to be refreshingly positive...

> *"History comes to life through Kerr's skill as a storyteller."* ('Historical Novels Review' Magazine)

"Fantastico! Beautifully written, amazing research, a joy to read." (Amazon UK)

"An action-packed yarn, entertaining and not just dry history." (East Lothian Courier)

"Researched in meticulous detail. Extremely well written in an easy style, with many exciting sub plots." (Books4Spain.com)

"An intelligent swashbuckler – clarifies the historical relationship between Muslim and Christian polities almost without taking a side." (Amazon USA)

Despite such encouraging comments and as much as I was tempted to tackle a sequel to *Song of the Eight Winds*, the harsh reality of the situation was that I couldn't afford to spend another three years researching and writing one. Our 'housekeeping' nest egg, not to mention Ellie's 'pocket money' savings, had already been dipped into with increasing frequency of late, so it was essential that I find a way of making amends – and soon. Ironically, both Chestervale Publishers and Pillion Press had just offered suggestions that might well have provided solutions, but with the best will in the world, I found myself unable to fall in with either.

In Chestervale's case, the idea was to latch onto a currently 'on-trend' type of travelogue built round what they referred to as an 'X-factor' or 'hook'. This could be along the lines of replicating Robert Louis

Stevenson's celebrated trek through the Cévennes accompanied by a cement mixer instead of a donkey, or journeying to some remote land on a skateboard to take part in their annual tiddlywinks championships. I've deliberately made these examples too far-fetched to be taken seriously, but they do illustrate how I felt about gimmicky themes that bore no relationship to the type of family-based memoir that had become my stock-in-trade. Square pegs and round holes.

Pillion's position, meanwhile, was that they were now in the process of rationalising their business by linking authors to genres that best suited the lists on which they planned to concentrate. Pigeonholes. And the one they'd selected for me? Crime writing. My trilogy of humour-laced *Bob Burns Investigates* mysteries could be expanded, they felt, into a series, with each case following the already-established pattern of beginning in Scotland before moving on to all sorts of 'glamorous' foreign locations.

They may well have been right, and it went against the grain for me to turn down their well-intentioned offer. But I believed deep down that, at least for the present, I'd said all I had to say in a genre I wasn't naturally drawn to, and would probably never have become involved with had it not been for agent Libby throwing me in at the deep end twenty years previously to help me learn to 'swim' as a writer.

It was inevitable, then, that I was obliged to part with the two companies I had to thank for giving me my first breaks as a published author. Happily, I did so on the best of terms, for although the paths travelled hadn't been without some puddles, we had all managed to keep our feet dry enough to avoid catching a cold. Now, though, I had to find a way to continue earning a reasonable income, and I'd have to do it by paddling my own canoe, while avoiding the entrance to that infamous creek I alluded to earlier.

* * * * *

Chapter Twenty-Four
'CARRY ON SCRIBBLING!'

*

The most appealing aspect of publishing your own books is that, depending on how prudently you go about it, you can keep the lion's share of revenue from sales, *plus* retain all primary rights and make your own decisions as to whom and on what terms you assign the 'subsidiaries'. I had learned the hard way about such intricacies, so there was no need to continue paying an agent to liaise on my behalf with a company that seemed unlikely to publish my work from now on anyway. Bette Tanner was a woman of the world, so understood the situation and accepted it without demur.

The slate had been wiped clean, and vital knowledge acquired while publishing *Song of the Eight Winds* taken on board. But I knew the freedom of 'doing my own thing' would be offset by the need to find ways of compensating for not having the marketing muscle of a traditional publisher for support.

I had been toying with the idea of using social media as a free platform on which to spread news about my books for the past couple of years, although I admit to not being particularly taken by what many regarded as a revolutionary development in mass communications. I still preferred to engage with people on a one-to-one basis by exchanging 'real' letters or, in the interests of modernity *and* economy, by email. Son Charlie didn't hesitate to put me right:

'It's the year 2012, Don P, and as they say in Spain, carrier pigeons are strictly for the birds – unless you're gonna eat them!'

I got the message, and promised to emerge from the Dark Ages by giving Facebook and Twitter a try soon. I also roped Charlie in to spruce up the www.peterkerr.co.uk website he'd helped put together following the publication of *Snowball Oranges* twelve years earlier. It would now contain everything anyone needed to know about my books, including foreign language editions, forthcoming events, online retail connections, and even links to free sample chapters. But all of this would only have passing value if I didn't keep refreshing the stock on my new cyber stall. And this meant writing another book.

I believed that a further benefit of being an 'indie' would be freedom from any obligation to work within the confines of one genre, as stipulated by both Chestervale and Pillion. At the same time, it could be argued that, having endured so many knockbacks over the years, I should have been grateful for securing a foothold in even one pigeonhole, never mind two. And I was, but with reservations. For while it makes sense for shops to separate books into individual categories on their shelves, and while publishers, particularly smaller ones, can benefit from specialising in one particular niche, such prerequisites can stifle the creative process of any author with an aversion to being permanently pegged. And this, with 'improvisation' and 'spontaneity' the bywords, provided a natural progression towards my decision to write an account of my experiences as a jazz musician.

Having said that, it hadn't escaped me that I would have risked jumping from the frying pan into the fire by writing a book so focused on jazz that I would actually have been creating a more cramped pigeonhole for myself than either of those I was leaving. But seeds of a broader approach had already been sown in my mind.

Ever since making brief mention in *Thistle Soup* of my involvement as a young bandleader in the 'Trad Jazz Boom' of the early '60s, people who remembered those days had asked how our livelihoods had been impacted by the sea change in popular music brought about by the sudden surge in popularity of 'beat groups' that had previously been playing interval spots at our gigs in venues like Liverpool's Cavern Club. But other, predominantly younger people were more interested in what everyday life had been like for my generation in the postwar years leading up to that. Putting those two factors together I had a ready-made template for what evolved into *Don't Call Me Clyde!* which, as would become apparent as the narrative progressed, also included hitherto untold revelations about the turbulent rise and demise of Scotland's premier jazz band, the legendary Clyde Valley Stompers.

The formula worked: a crossover had been established between nostalgia and intrigue, an odd combination of themes which nevertheless won the approval of critics and book-buyers alike: *"Laced with all the wit and eye for the telling detail one might expect from this author. As intensely readable as it is enjoyable, whatever your taste in music."* (London Jazz News). And this provided all the encouragement I needed to have yet another go at genre-jumping.

One big *dis*advantage of not being signed to a publisher is, of course, the absence of an advance on royalties to subsidise the time spent writing your next book. So, although I no longer had the pressure of a deadline to meet, in terms of making a living there was actually even less time to lose than before. And to compound matters, my diary had never been more crowded with book promoting-dates, still predominantly generated by interest in the *Snowball Oranges* series, admittedly, but providing invaluable opportunities to draw attention to my more recent titles nonetheless.

On that very note, I had been invited to Warsaw the previous year by Agata Radkievicz, a local literary agent who had secured the publishing deal that led to the recently-released Polish-language edition of *Snowball Oranges* (otherwise *Pomarańcze w śniegu*). The purpose of the visit was to help publicise the book during a two-day programme of engagements incorporating ten press, four radio and two TV interviews, all conducted in English and, in the case of the live TV slots, simultaneously translated 'off-camera' into Polish for the viewers. The whole operation was a textbook example of organisation and communication, particularly since I couldn't even ask the time of day in my hosts' own language!

Whatever Polish words they'd put in my mouth must have been good ones, though, for shortly afterwards I received an invite to appear on: *'A wide-ranging bill of international authors in Poland's prestigious new literary showcase, the Big Book Festival of 2013'.* It's director Anna Król heralded it as: *'The first of its kind in Eastern Europe and one of only a few in the world – a mass event free for all comers, spread throughout dozens of different city locations, and simultaneously taking place online and in reality'.* I would be participating in: *'A discussion involving a writer, a monk and a philosopher. Three wise men on the road'.*

But it wasn't to be just any old monk and philosopher I'd be pitting my particular brand of 'wisdom' against. On the one hand there would be: *'A gregarious Black Friar who serves as a university chaplain specialising in theology of liturgy and Christian meditation, but also well-known for being a restless spirit, a likeable provocateur and harmless "scandalist" who likes to ruffle feathers and confront his listeners with difficult dilemmas'.* And on the other hand I'd have: *'A professor who heads the Faculty of Religious Research at the Polish Academy of Science's Institute of Philosophy and Sociology, himself an acclaimed author of several scholarly volumes and an essayist credited with hundreds of associated elaborations'.*

On reading those CVs, my instinctive reaction was to politely decline the invitation. For why on earth would anyone think of chucking an intellectual lightweight like me into the ring with a pair of heavyweights like that, especially when a perception of divine doctrines more profound than the lyrics of *Jesus Bids Us Shine* was called for? In this respect, I most assuredly did not qualify as one of the three wise men – 'on the road' or anywhere else.

However, I had met Anna Król in Warsaw the previous year when, in her capacity as head of the requisite PR company, she had been responsible for organising my timed-to-the-minute schedule of media interviews, and I'd noted an impish sense of humour lurking beneath her outward air of cool, unflappable efficiency. This moved me to suspect that the proposed debate with the two theologians was not intended to be as pious as her outline had suggested. But as ever, there would be only one way to find out, though on this occasion with the complication of having to cope with proceedings being conducted in Polish!

When the time came, my contribution would have amounted to nothing more than the occasional grunt and a gormless grin had it not been for the skill of the young lady who provided running translations from Polish to English for me and vice versa for the audience seated in the auditorium of the Festival Centre in downtown Warsaw.

The main premise to be explored was *'Is Travelling*

the Road to Happiness?' and the associated issues to be debated ranged from *'Literary footsteps – from sexism to hedonism'*, which the professor dominated with due dignity and a liberal dose of learned mystique; through *'How to get happy growing oranges'*, a subject my co-panellists were happy to leave on my plate; to *'Chicks, drugs and rock'n'roll'*, a topic with which the good friar denied personal acquaintance, but about which he was nevertheless only too willing to advance his theories – gleaned purely from hearsay, of course.

As Anna Król had astutely anticipated, the session developed into a fairly free-and-easy hour of banter, with members of the audience contributing pertinent questions and the occasional critical comment too. It had been a deliberately offbeat variation of a well-tried concept, and it had worked out well. But it didn't end there. Live-wire literary agent Agata Radkiewicz was waiting for me at close of play, all set to whisk me off to take part in two more 'experimental' events.

First, we took a taxi to a leafy square near the city centre, where a 'pop-up' meet-the-author venue had been created by placing a semi-circle of a few chairs opposite a park bench. On a picnic table at one end of the bench a colleague of Agata's was arranging a little display of *Pomarańcze w śniegu* for the edification of any inquisitive passers-by. And, sure enough, first one strolling citizen, then another and another dallied at the table, their small huddle gradually growing in the way that small huddles of inquisitive passers-by invariably do. Agata and her friend duly engaged them in conversation, and as the books and I were being pointed at in regular sequence, it was pretty obvious what was being talked about. Before long, a few people actually took a seat holding a copy of the book to flick through, while Agata ushered others along to my end of the bench and acted as interpreter in a chinwag about life in sunny Mallorca; and even about not-so-sunny Scotland, where some had relatives descended from Polish servicemen exiled there after the Second World War.

This festival was proving to be more than just another business-boosting showcase. After our little huddle had finally dispersed, Agata took time to fill me in on the thinking behind it...

When the Big Book Festival's advance publicity stated that it would be '*A mass event, free for all comers, spread throughout dozens of city locations*', that was precisely what was meant. So, this little ad hoc sideshow of mine was only one of many popping up all over the Polish capital at random times of the day. No admission charges were involved, since the sole aim of the exercise was to introduce the pleasures of reading to people who might not normally give it a thought. But from a purely commercial perspective, such an ostensibly altruistic approach could also be regarded as a unique opportunity to kick-start the sort of word-of-mouth chain reaction that is the pot of gold at the end of every author's rainbow.

Point taken, and carried forward to the next groundbreaking stopping point on Agata's route map, which turned out to be a university lecture theatre equipped with a big screen and all the technical gubbins required to host a video-linked confab between authors of various stamps in several different countries. What took place was completely off-the-cuff, but, fortunately for me, conducted in English and chaired by a veteran Polish broadcaster who knew his stuff and ensured that order prevailed. While politically contentious subjects were tactfully avoided, differing viewpoints on a few topical issues did combine to provide the audience with an hour of putting faces, voices and individual credos to the names on book covers. It was another example of the Festival's imaginative approach to reaching out to as wide a cross section of the book-reading public as possible.

I learned a lot from from taking part for just one day, while also developing the highest regard for the Polish people I'd met and the pride they took in their 'work', undertaken with conviction, generosity and, in the area of linguistics particularly, an admirable degree of patience!

* * *

Back in Scotland, in marked contrast to the team-spirited atmosphere that had prevailed in Poland, I was now faced with the reality of ploughing a lone publishing furrow, but looking forward to the challenge nonetheless. The first task would be to write that aforementioned book, and the quicker the better. Borrowing from another farming analogy, each cut of grass yields less hay, so sitting back to rely on a diminishing income from my existing books was not an option. Yet it had never been more important to dispel thoughts of immediate gain and to concentrate instead on playing a longer game, but with *enjoying* it the first rule. As good old President Calvin 'Press On!' Coolidge might have said, *'There is nothing in the world that succeeds better in speeding the lone ploughman's plough than having a good laugh'*. Something along those lines anyway.

With this in mind, I delved into my 'Projects Pending' file and retrieved one of the two feature-length film scripts I'd written as an on-spec exercise many years earlier. *The *Other* Monarch of the Glen* is an offbeat comedy caper set in the Scottish Highlands, and I was still familiar enough with the storyline to know that I'd have fun converting it into a novel. Also, that same familiarity would make it possible to complete writing the book in much less time than usual. Two birds with one stone. Perfect. Or so I thought.

I hadn't realised just how much work would be involved in using the written word to convey description of actions, reactions, places and characters that had been left for the camera to capture in the screenplay, and often with only the sketchiest of dialogue as backup too. This turned out to be a confrontation with several more rungs on the learning ladder, and many slipped steps had to be re-negotiated on the climb. It was a worthwhile exercise, though, and in the two years it took to complete I'd also managed to get through a packed programme of live events still being booked in the wake of the *Snowball Oranges* series.

I had never been busier, yet the passage of time, which now seemed to gain speed by the year, had eased us into a style of living that somehow accommodated a fair balance between work and that elusive quality of family life that had become our avowed intention when Archie and Jocky entered our lives. As Ellie had predicted, our two wee Border Terriers provided an inescapable stimulus for me to get off my backside at the computer and go for regular, fitness-promoting 'walkies'. The dogs were also great company for Ellie whenever I was away, as well as being a permanent source of good cheer for us both.

While the finished typescript of *The *Other* Monarch of the Glen* was being proof-read before conversion to the digital formats required for producing physical and electronic editions, son Charlie had been busy designing a cover featuring a tongue-in-cheek 'forgery' of Landseer's iconic painting of *The Monarch of the Glen,* in which the artist's majestic Highland stag had morphed into a grotesquely-grinning hairy 'coo'. By the time these various components had been assembled, another year had flown past, during which I had cannily hedged my bets by sending a synopsis of the book to a handful of publishers I *thought* might be interested in taking it on. They weren't, but at least I'd tried.

After all that, Christmas of 2017 was upon us before *The *Other* Monarch of the Glen* was ready for release. So much, then, for hopes of a quick and easy addition to our nascent publishing 'catalogue'. Still, we'd finally made it, but with any potential reward for our efforts now largely dependent on the reaction of reviewers…

"Pure fun – a pacey, racy Highland fling." (The Cryer Magazine)

"A book that keeps you turning pages enthusiastically, with more than a few laughs along the way." (Undiscovered Scotland Magazine)

"A high-spirited and crazy caper with many mad adventures and tangled plots." (The Majorca Daily Bulletin)

"A pleasingly bonkers read that sets a trap and makes you want to find out what happens next." (London Jazz News)

The use of 'pleasingly bonkers' in that last review could have been taken at best as a backhanded compliment, if not an actual kick in the literary pants, but in the context of this particular book I couldn't have hoped for a more favourable endorsement. Those two words encapsulated the mood of the book, and with luck would chime with an appropriate readership. I had reason to be grateful – *and* optimistic. The downside of this, though, was that the type of humour indicated would risk alienating potential readers whose funny bones weren't tickled by anything too wacky. The ubiquitous 'subjective' word again. But this is the price you pay for having an itch to be independent, and it brings with it a necessity to find ways of winning back lost readers *and* to attracting new ones. With no publishers' publicity and marketing people to call upon for assistance, the only tools I had at my disposal were two fingers – the ones I used for typing. So, with time being even more of the essence than ever, I plumped for the same way of keeping the pot boiling as last time: I'd re-write my other 'on-spec' screenplay as a novel, making full use of recently-learned lessons to help the process along...

*

A vaulted chamber beneath the ruins of a castle known as *Goblin Hall* (locally *Goblin Ha'*) near the pretty village of Gifford in East Lothian had provided me with the inspiration to write the eponymous film script all of eighteen years earlier. Legend has it that the castle was erected in ancient times by a wizardly nobleman using gangs of satanic dwarfs as labourers, and it was on this foundation that I built a fantasy adventure aimed at a family audience.

The story followed the trials and tribulations of two young children lured into the subterranean lair of Zorn, a brilliant though evil sorcerer who is using them as bait to ensnare his arch rival of many centuries, a lovable but dippy old wizard called Mungo. Although Mungo has lost most of the magical skills that once set him above all other exponents of the mystic arts, he alone has any chance of rescuing the children from Zorn's clutches. And so the adventure unfolds, involving scary encounters with prehistoric monsters, the inevitable battles between armies of good and bad goblins, and even the life-saving, though comic, interventions of a flying piglet called Wilbur, who speaks American slang.

At the time, I had already amassed enough rejection letters for my other writing efforts to wallpaper the living room, so it didn't come as any great surprise that no movie-makers made an offer for dramatisation rights to the script. But this made it all the more satisfying to finally bring my *Goblin Hall* story 'out of the vault'. Remodelling the screenplay as a book was bound to present me with many problems similar to those I'd encountered when performing the same task for *The *Other* Monarch of the Glen*, and I believed this would make the job easier second time around. However, while the content of *Monarch* had been prominently humorous, the main theme of *Goblin* was a combination of suspense, nightmarish situations and hair-raising encounters, which had to be tempered for younger readers while also being sufficiently gripping to engage their elders. In addition, I had included interludes of tension-relieving comedy which I also hoped would register with both age groups. Enter Wilbur the jive-talking flying piglet, who would have stolen the show if I hadn't clipped his wings, which wasn't easy when the little tearaway was giving me so much fun. You may recall that I mentioned before how easy it is to allow fictional characters to hijack your narrative. This was a case in point and illustrates the other aspect of the story that posed fresh problems when working on the adaptation: in addition to elements in its original format that I'd entrusted to the eye of the camera, there were also lengthy and often complex sequences which would require the use of computer-generated animation to bring to life.

As the only previous attempt I'd made at writing for children had been the lyrics of songs I composed for the Krankies' *Fan-dabi-dozi* album almost forty years earlier, there had been many more rungs on the learning ladder to scale and more slipped steps to re-trace. Much as I enjoyed the challenge, it took considerably longer than anticipated to complete, and it was April 2020 before the book – my fifteenth in twenty years – was finally published. In many ways, writing it had forced me out of the nearest I had to a 'comfort zone' with even more of a jolt than when tackling historical fiction, so I was on tenterhooks while waiting to find out if the venture had been successful, at least in respect of being noticed by the intended audience. Happily, my anxieties were soon quelled…

"Both children and adults will be captivated by this exciting story. A thrilling escapist adventure."
(East Lothian Life Magazine)

"A magical fantasy adventure for all the family."
*(*Edinburgh Life Magazine)

The primary circulation area of those two periodicals covers the region of Scotland in which Goblin Ha' Castle is located, so, together with a half-page feature in the local *East Lothian Courier,* their reviews helped news of the book's release reaching the right target. As had been proven way back when *Snowball Oranges* was first published, there's much to be said for developing demand by generating interest on your 'home turf' first. But those magazines were also read worldwide by émigré Scots, so perhaps this fantasy novel, while never expected to be more than a one-off experiment, might actually help spread awareness of my other books too. A long shot, perhaps, but well worth the effort all the same.

It was about this time that I received a call from Marina Jessup, from whom I hadn't heard since the expiry several years previously of her film/TV option agreement on *Snowball Oranges*. She had doggedly pitched a pilot script to TV networks as a potential series, but without any takers. Ironically, the reason usually given was that *A Year In Provence* – which had been so successful as a book that publishers had been put off others in a similar vein (including mine) – hadn't emulated that success as a TV series, resulting in networks being put off other projects in a similar vein (including mine). But undaunted, Marina had now formed a joint production company with major film studios in Spain, and intended to use the strength of this connection to resume the adaptation and development of my Mallorcan stories for television. Thus, with patience the obligatory name of the game and hope springing eternal, I happily signed up to a new agreement. Fingers crossed – yet again!

Meanwhile, the publication of *Goblin Hall* coincided with the global spread of the deadly Covid-19 virus, and the resultant 'lockdown' regulations in the UK put paid indefinitely to any promotional activities that involved travelling. But resourceful organisers of book festivals and the like soon found ways of compensating by setting up 'virtual' author appearances via online conference hook-ups. Although I would miss taking part in live events, I can't deny that I was also looking forward to having a break from 'hitting the road' for a while. I was now pushing eighty-two, and the pleasure I still got from personal contact with readers was beginning to have the shine taken off it by what had become the grind of making the journeys involved.

However, I certainly had no intention of retiring. For me, writing wasn't just a means of earning a bob or two to top up my old-age pension, it had become a way of life that I really enjoyed, and I couldn't imagine waking up to a new day without the buzz of some spontaneous scribbling to look forward to. Besides, now that I was going to be at home a bit more, shutting myself up with my computer in the 'playpen' would prevent me from getting under Ellie's feet too often – even if I *occasionally* spent as much time snoozing as actually playing with words!

But indulging in secret snoozes wouldn't earn me any pension-boosting 'bawbees', so I duly set my mental alarm clock to '*Inspiration*', and that very night I had a dream in which I was able to have conversations with dogs by tuning into the mysterious telepathy I'd long believed our canine pals use to communicate – in addition to sniffing each other's backsides, that is. Anyhow, in the cold light of day, what I thought I'd do was put myself inside the mind of Jen, a Border Collie who had been part of our family during the years we farmed at Cuddy Neuk back in the '70s and early '80s. As anyone acquainted with Border Collies will appreciate, it is a very presumptuous person indeed who attempts to adopt the persona of a creature utterly convinced it is superior in every respect to any human it may encounter – particularly with regard to those deluded enough to think they actually *own* it. I grasped the nettle anyway and put my mind to seeing, and writing about, life through Jen's eyes.

Although belonging to a breed universally renowned for its insatiable appetite for work, Jen had a distinct aversion to anything even remotely associated with the notion. She was a free spirit, with living life to the full and having fun in the process her first concern. And if that tended to detract from other more 'useful' qualities with which she was assumed to be endowed, then so be it. Still, she was the most faithful (in her own unwavering Collie way), affectionate (in her own undemonstrative Scottish way) and intelligent (in her own slightly 'loopy' way) companion you could hope to have, and I regarded it a privilege to help record her story.

JEN, a Border Collie's Tale (An old farm dog looks back on her life) was published in 2021, with reaction to it summed up by the following from American literary critic Alice L. Powers…

> *"Devotees of Peter Kerr's other books will find a departure here. The familiar humour is here, but also pathos and an appreciation for the brevity and joy in life, whether human or canine."*

And that, in some ways at least, could also serve as a summary of this memoir of my own. The older you get, time does seem to pass with ever-increasing haste, making you all the more grateful for every day that fate grants you. Looking back now over a lifetime of eighty-four years, I suppose my attitude has been similar to Jen's regarding living life to the full, although I've been blessed (or cursed!) with a work ethic that would elicit a firm, and probably sweary, rebuke from Jen. But for Ellie and me, it has been the satisfaction derived from working for ourselves and the relative freedom accompanying it that has been the main reward, rather than any material or financial gain.

From setting my heart on following in my farming grandfather's footsteps as a child to becoming a deskbound grower of sentences and paragraphs has meant a total change of outlook, given that it was actually to escape the confines of office work that prompted me to 'go independent' all of sixty-five years ago. And there's no denying there have been moments along the way when I've been reminded of the downside of having relinquished financial security in doing so. But those moments have only ever been fleeting and have never spawned a modicum of regret. You make your bed to lie on, and put up as best you can with whatever lumps the mattress eventually develops. For instance, Ellie and I have not had a holiday in the twenty-five years since my first book was published, but we have never felt the need for one, for where better to be beavering away together than in a uniquely beautiful corner of Scotland like East Lothian? We count ourselves lucky.

As mentioned earlier, I never presumed while writing this memoir to advise any aspiring authors on how to realise their dream, nor was the book intended to either inspire or deter anyone from trying. Instead, I'll end by paraphrasing a tag line borrowed from an old 1950s TV series…

"There are eight million stories on the rocky road to authordom. This has been one of them."

Here's to happy reading and, if you're so inclined, to happy scribbling too. Cheers!

*

THE END

* * * * *

If you enjoyed this book, you may also like the following titles by Peter Kerr:

'SNOWBALL ORANGES'
- One Mallorcan Winter -

First in the bestselling series of five books charting the Kerr family's often hilarious adventures after leaving Scotland to grow oranges for a living on the Spanish island of Mallorca.

"This should do for Spain what A Year in Provence did for France. Graphic descriptions of mouthwatering local delicacies and breathtaking scenery." (Sunday Post Magazine)

"Engagingly written, bringing the sights, sounds and smells of its locale vividly to life." (The Scotsman)

"This charming, cheerful book will appeal to anyone looking for a different take on Spain and Mallorca" (Library Journal, USA)

(Paperback ISBN: 978-1399946612)

(Kindle E-book ASIN: B0BVGRNPKP)

The other four titles in the series are *One Mallorcan Summer* (previously published as Mañana, Mañana): *Viva Mallorca!: A Basketful of Snowflakes: From Paella to Porridge.*

'THISTLE SOUP'
- *An Autobiographical Prequel to Snowball Oranges* -

East Lothian is 'The Garden of Scotland' and the setting for this delightfully idiosyncratic story of country life, from the time of the Second World War onwards. This book will appeal, not only to those who are interested in the Scotland of today, but also to people who recall, or have been told about, rural ways that are gone for ever.

"The story of his boyhood, a family and its farms. Amusing, interesting, moving and true to-life." (The Scotsman)

"Beautifully written, gently humorous, a real gem of a book." (Amazon UK)

(Paperback ISBN: 978-0957306226)
(Kindle E-book ASIN: B00AG7DGJ4)

www.peter-kerr.co.uk

'JEN'
- A Border Collie's Tale -

Narrated by Jen herself: an old farm dog looks back on her life in this spin-off from Thistle Soup, Peter's heart-warming memoir of country times past. Often hilarious, occasionally sad, here are the down-to-earth farmyard philosophies of a slightly sweary, doggedly self-assured, yet ultimately vulnerable old four-legged friend.

"An appreciation for the brevity and joy in life."
(Alice L. Powers – Literary Critic)

"A splendid narrative with a fascinating point-of-view approach." (Southside Broadcasting)

"Superbly written, insightful and straight from the collie's mouth, a story that will make you feel you're having a joyous break from the complexity of the current human world."
(Amazon UK)

(Paperback ISBN: 978-1527298385)
(Kindle E-book ASIN: B098R7DXPX)

'DON'T CALL ME CLYDE!'
- Jazz Journey of a Sixties Stomper -
(An Autobiographical 'Companion' to Thistle Soup)

The Clyde Valley Stompers became, in the 1950s, Scotland's premier jazz band and first-ever super group. In 1961, at just twenty years of age, Peter 'Pete' Kerr inherited leadership of 'The Clydes' after they'd move their base from Glasgow to London. Despite many set-backs, the band stormed the charts the following year with their version of *Peter and the Wolf*, and were launched into the glitzy world of mainstream popular music. But, as Peter would discover to his cost, it was also a world tainted by greed. This is a story that will enlighten and surprise in equal measure.

"Laced with all the wit and eye for the telling detail one expects from this best-selling author". (London Jazz News)

"Entertaining and intriguing, even if you're not into jazz." (Toun Cryer Magazine)

"The story of a young man realising his dream of playing jazz for a living." (The Glasgow Herald)

(Paperback ISBN: 978-0957658622)

(Kindle E-book ASIN: B01GA55JCM)

'FIDDLER ON THE MAKE'
- The Cuddyford Chronicles -

When the sleepy Scottish village of Cuddyford is colonised by well-heeled retirees and big-city commuters, Jigger McCloud, a jack-the-lad local farmer with a talent for playing the fiddle and an eye for the ladies, isn't slow to make a quick buck at their expense. Comic shenanigans, quirky characters and sinister ploys abound in this not-everyday story of country folk.

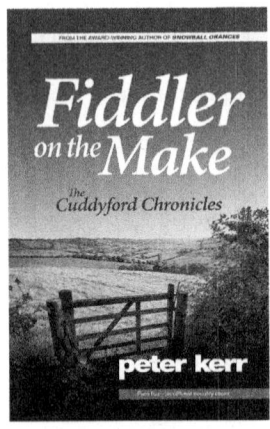

"A hoot – pure fun – an observation on the absurd."
(Welsh Books Council)

"A delicious, delightful and devilishly funny gem of a novel."
(Stornoway Gazette)

(Paperback ISBN: 978-0957658615)

(Kindle E-Book ASIN: B00CQJZ6GQ)

Full details are on Peter Kerr's website:
www.peter-kerr.co.uk

'THE MALLORCA CONNECTION'
- *Bob Burns Investigates* -

The first in a trilogy of tongue-in-cheek Bob Burns mysteries. The droll Scots sleuth features in a quirky whodunnit that begins in Scotland and ends in Mallorca, where intrigue and mayhem mingle with the crowds at a fishermen's fiesta. A rare combination of suspense and comedy.

"A really gripping page-turner that's peppered with laughs." (Amazon UK)

"Well off the wall ... escapist and liberally laced with humour." (Edinburgh Evening News)

(Paperback ISBN: 978-0957306240)

(Kindle E-Book ASIN: B00AU2GF16)

Other titles in the series are *The Sporran Connection* and *The Cruise Connection.*

Full details of these and all Peter Kerr's other books are on his website:

www.peter-kerr.co.uk

'SONG OF THE EIGHT WINDS'
- *RECONQUISTA* -
- *An Epic Tale of Medieval Spain* -

It's 1229, the year of the Christian 'Reconquest' of Mallorca from the Moors, a Muslim people of Afro-Arabic origin who have ruled Spain in cultural splendour for five hundred years. A substantial and compelling novel inspired by one of the most momentous and lastingly-celebrated events in the history of this enchanting Spanish island.

"History comes to life through Kerr's skill as a storyteller."
('Historical Novel Review')

"Fantastico! Beautifully written, amazing research, a joy to read." (Amazon UK)

"A magnificent adventure, an heroic tale, a sweeping epic."
(Dumfries & Galloway Standard)

(Paperback ISBN: 978-0957306219)

(Kindle E-Book ASIN: B008ELVJT8)

Full details are on Peter Kerr's website:

www.peter-kerr.co.uk

'THE GANNET HAS LANDED'

In this humour-tinged romantic adventure, a young Scottish veterinary student applies for a gap-year job as a guide in Africa, where he also hopes to find time to study the wildlife. Instead, he finds himself in Mallorca, thrust in at the deep end of the madcap package tour business – a hapless fish out of water, for whom the nearest thing to wildlife appears to be the hordes of rowdy holidaymakers pouring off the gannets (charter planes) from the UK. Problems are bound to arise, as does the bewitching influence of Mallorca and a beautiful young Mallorquina called Catalina.

"A gentle, amusing romance, with enough travel elements to make the discerning reader consider discovering the real Mallorca." (Dumfries & Galloway Standard)

"A great tale. Kerr's dry wit is a delight." (Welsh Books Council)

"Makes fiction seem like real life. Vivid word pictures – humour-laced and escapist." (essentialwriters.com)

(Paperback ISBN: 978-0957658660)

(Kindle E-Book ASIN: B00BZRE9GS)

www.peter-kerr.co.uk

'THE *OTHER* MONARCH OF THE GLEN'
- *A Quirky Caledonian Caper* -

An opportunity to acquire a fortune arises when the flat-broke and feckless laird of Strathsporran Castle uncovers a valuable work of art – but only if its existence remains secret. Skulduggery and amorous anomalies abound as the laird becomes embroiled in an audacious scam with two unlikely shooting guests. But who's conning whom? And what other secrets will the grouse moors of Strathsporran reveal?
Pure fun – a pacey, racy Highland fling.

"An entertaining, laugh-out-loud tale ... a high-spirited and crazy caper" (Majorca Daily Bulletin)

"A pleasantly bonkers yarn of the sort Tom Sharpe used to spin." (London Jazz News)

(Paperback ISBN: 978-0957658684)

(Kindle E-Book ASIN: B0781QRXMV)

Full details are on Peter Kerr's website:
www.peter-kerr.co.uk

'GOBLIN HALL'
- A Fantasy Adventure -

A humour-spiced family fantasy named after a haunted chamber that lies beneath the ruins of Yester Castle near Gifford in East Lothian. Two young children are lured into the subterranean world of Zorn, an evil sorcerer who is using them as bait to ensnare his arch enemy Mungo, a lovable but dippy old wizard friend of the children. Goblins and monsters abound as the kids journey through the underworld to a good-versus-evil showdown in Zorn's lair. But not everything may be as it seems!

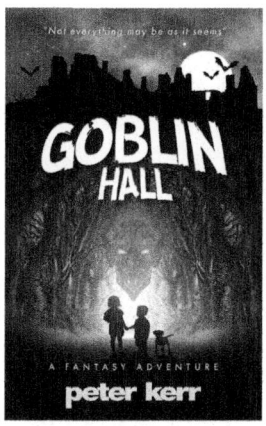

"Both children and adults will be captivated by this exciting story."
(East Lothian Life Magazine)

"A magical fantasy adventure for all the family."
(Edinburgh Life Magazine)

(Paperback ISBN: 978-0957658691)

(Kindle E-Book ASIN: B0871LGJCV)

Full details are on Peter Kerr's website:
www.peter-kerr.co.uk

Full details of these and all Peter Kerr's other books are on his website:

www.peter-kerr.co.uk

Printed in Great Britain
by Amazon